Postcolonial Feminist Interpretation OF THE Bible

MUSA W. DUBE

Chalice Press.
St. Louis, Missouri

Biblical quotations, unless otherwise noted, are from the *New Revised Standard Version Bible*, copyright 1989, Division of Christian Education of the National Council of Churches of Christ in the United States of America. Used by permission. All rights reserved.

Cover design: Lynne Condellone
Interior design: Elizabeth Wright
Art direction: Michael Domínguez

This book is printed on acid-free, recycled paper.

Visit Chalice Press on the World Wide Web at
www.chalicepress.com

10 9 8 7 6 5 4 3 2 1   00 01 02 03

Library of Congress Cataloging–in–Publication Data

Dube Shomanah, Musa W., 1964-.
    Postcolonial feminist interpretation of the Bible / Musa W. Dube
        p.   cm.
    Includes bibliographical references and index.
    ISBN 0-8272-2963-1
    1. Bible—Feminist criticism—Africa, Sub-Saharan. 2. Postcolonialism—
Africa, Sub-Saharan.   I. Title.
    BS521.4.D83   2000   00–008998
    220.6'082—dc21

Printed in the United States of America

Postcolonial
Feminist
Interpretation
OF THE Bible

This book is dedicated to my son
Aluta L. Dube
for all the joy that he brings

Contents

Preface

Many friends, colleagues, and institutions contributed toward the conceptualization and compilation of this book. My first thank-you goes to the University of Botswana, which granted me a study leave and also sponsored my fieldwork research. A very, very special thank-you goes to Prof. Fernando F. Segovia, who gave me a reading course in postcolonial theories and guided this study. Thank you, Fernando, for believing in my capacity. Your encouragement and faith in my work was your greatest gift to me—one that I will always treasure. I also wish to thank my then-professors in Vanderbilt University, Mary Ann Tolbert, Daniel Patte, Douglas Knight, Victor Anderson, and Myriam Chancy, who have immensely contributed to the conception and completion of this work by giving their various skills.

While I was on study leave, and living in a foreign country, many friends and colleagues contributed toward this work in their many ways of giving. Scarritt Bennett Center provided hospitality and community spirit to me and my son, Aluta L. Dube. Nicole Wilkinson, Ladelle C. Dilli, and Julie Noltie not only provided many friendly hugs but also shared with me the burden of writing in the language of the colonizer, by reading and editing my work. Leticia Guardiola-Saenz, Jerome Morris, Mary Muse, Pio Apelu, Avis Littleton, Sue Johnson, Inelle Bagwell, John Collett, Martha Williams, Norma Fletcher, Dot and Bill Graves, Angela and Carter Savage, and the Multicultural Fellowship in Belmont Methodist Church were not only friends but also family.

During a significant part of my study leave my sisters and mother, Margret Tafa, Mmasepatela Florence Setume, Magdeline Dube, Beatrice Dube, and Agnes Tafa, took turns parenting my son. It was through your solidarity that I was afforded "a room of my own" to research and write this book. I am forever indebted for your support. You have demonstrated that sisterhood is power.

Finally, my greatest thanks to Jon L. Berquist for agreeing to make my work available to the public.

This book belongs to all of you.

PART I

Defining the Problem

Modern imperialism was so global and all-encompassing that
virtually nothing escaped it; besides, as I have said, the
nineteenth-century contest over empire is still continuing today.
Whether or not to look at the connections between cultural texts
and imperialism is therefore to take a position in fact taken—
either to study the connection in order to criticize it and think of
alternatives for it, or not to study it in order to let it stand...[1]

Edward Said

---

[1]Edward Said, *Culture and Imperialism* (New York: Alfred A. Knopf, 1993), 68.

1

The Postcolonial Condition
and the Bible

Oral Stories, Debates, and Colonial Heroes

During the decades of the armed struggle for liberation in sub-Saharan Africa, an anonymous short story, orally narrated and passed on by word of mouth, became popular. The story held that "when the white man came to our country he had the Bible and we had the land. The white man said to us, 'let us pray.' After the prayer, the white man had the land and we had the Bible."[1] The story summarizes the sub-Saharan African experience of colonization. It explains how colonization was connected to the coming of the white man, how it was connected to his use of the Bible, and how the black African possession of the Bible is connected to the white man's taking of African people's lands. Admittedly, the story holds that the Bible is now a sub-Saharan African book, but it is an inheritance that will always be linked to and remembered for its role in facilitating European imperialism.

Those of us who grew up professing the Christian faith in the age of the armed struggle for liberation, from World War II to South African independence in 1994, were never left to occupy our places comfortably. Debating societies in high schools and colleges passed one motion after another and constantly summoned us to the debating floors. We were called

---

[1]Because of its oral circulation, the story tends to appear among different authors with slight differences, but with basically the same plot. The above version is taken from Takatso Mofokeng, "Black Christians, the Bible and Liberation," *Journal of Black Theology* 2 (1988): 34.

upon to explain the ethics of our religion: to justify its practice, its practitioners, and its institutions. Debating societies demanded to know why the biblical text and its Western readers were instruments of imperialism and how we, as black Africans, justify our faith in a religion that has betrayed us—a religion of the enemy, so to speak. In these questions and motions lies the foundation of my quest; that is, given the role of the Bible in facilitating imperialism, how should we read the Bible as postcolonial subjects?[2]

Difficult as these motions were, historical records gave us no support. To start with, at the Berlin conference of 1884, where the European imperial powers met to divide the map of Africa amongst themselves and to draw a constitution on how to do it, the role of missionaries, among other agents of imperialism, was recognized and given its rightful place. The constitution read, "Christian missionaries, scientists, and explorers, with their followers, property and collections, shall likewise be objects of especial protections."[3] This protection implies several things. First, missionaries as Bible readers, whose perspectives of justice were presumably informed by this text, were not ethically opposed to the imperial project of their countries. Second, this protection could imply that missionaries were useful in promoting the imperialism of their countries. In other words, missionaries and other imperialist agents were all informed and influenced by the same culture, which includes the biblical faith. The latter point leads to the third implication: that any attempt to distance missionaries from the rest is at best superficial. In fact, Andrew Walls's analysis suggests that there was little or no dividing line between missionaries and their colonizing counterparts. He notes that

> the missionary pioneer was spoken of in the vocabulary of the imperial pioneer. With some notable exceptions, British missions became overwhelmingly concentrated in areas that were, or were to become, part of the British Empire. Sometimes missionary occupation preceded annexation or political penetration and sometimes it followed; sometimes, as in Uganda, Nyasaland, and Bechuanaland, it was intimately associated with the establishment of British rule; sometimes, as in eastern Nigeria, it was obviously associated with the reconciliation of annexed peoples to a new way of life under the British crown. Occasionally, as in the Upper Niger, it took place against the representatives of secular power.[4]

On the whole, Walls notes that "missionary opinion, like most British opinion in the high imperial age, for the most part took the empire for

---

[2]The term *postcolonial* as used here describes the panorama of modern imperialism, beginning with the process of colonization, the struggle for political independence, and the emergence of the neocolonial globalization era.

[3]Louis L. Snyder, ed., *The Imperialism Reader: Documents and Readings on Modern Expansion* (New York: Van Nostrand, 1962), 211.

[4]Andrew F. Walls, "British Missions," in *Missionary Ideologies in the Imperialist Era: 1880–1920,* ed. Torben Christensen and William R. Hutchinson (Aarhus: Aros, 1982).

granted, and the question of abdication was never seriously raised."[5] According to Walls, "many of the writers on missions saw a sort of manifest destiny for Britain as the principal Christian influence in the world."[6] This harmonious relationship of missionaries and the imperial agendas of their compatriots is indeed evident in the mission reflections of Josiah Strong, a Congregationalist minister. Strong proudly noted that the Anglo-Saxon has a "genius for colonizing," for "he excels all others in pushing his way into new countries."[7] For Strong, the Anglo-Saxon was not only "divinely commissioned to be, in a peculiar sense, his brother's keeper," but as such was indeed his indisputable destiny.[8] Strong states:

> Is there room for reasonable doubt that this race…is destined to dispossess many weaker races, assimilate others, mold the remainder, until, in a very true and important sense it has Anglo-Saxoned mankind? Already the English language, saturated with Christian ideas, gathering up into itself the best thought of all ages is the great agent of Christian civilization throughout the world; at this moment affecting the destinies and molding the character of half the human race.[9]

Seemingly, Strong's ethics are not in conflict with dispossession of weaker races, their assimilation, and their being "Anglo-Saxoned." He tries to show that the English language and the culture of the Anglo-Saxons are "saturated with Christian ideas," hence its eligibility as a "great agent of Christian civilization." In the latter claim one finds that the attempt to make a distinction between the missionary and other imperial powers is superficial given that they were both from the same culture. As Strong asserts that the English language is saturated with Christian ideas, it follows that English thinking, its ethics, and its perception of reality are heavily informed by biblical ideas. Similarly, if biblical ideas "divinely commissioned them" to be their "brother's keeper" or to have a "genius for colonizing," we cannot divorce the biblical text from informing and inspiring their imperialist violence.

To speak of a divinely commissioned genius in colonizing is to speak of David Livingstone.[10] Livingstone, a doctor, botanist, explorer, ethnographer, and mapmaker, is a shining example of a missionary who openly championed colonial domination of sub-Saharan Africa. Declaring that

---

[5]Ibid., 159.

[6]Ibid., 165.

[7]See Louis L. Snyder, "Josiah Strong on the Anglo Saxon Destiny, 1885," in *The Imperialism Reader,* 122–23.

[8]Ibid., 122.

[9]Ibid., 123.

[10]See Timothy Holmes, *Journey to Livingstone: An Exploration of an Imperial Myth* (Edinburgh: Canongate Press, 1993), xv, where in a secret letter addressed to an influential colonial figure he writes, "My objectives, I may state, have something more than meets the eye. They are not merely exploratory, for I go with the intention of benefitting both the African and my own countryman…I tell to none but such as you in whom I have confidence."

"civilization–Christianity and commerce–should ever be inseparable," Livingstone appealed to his compatriots to colonize Africa: "I beg to direct your attention to Africa...I go back to try to make an open path for commerce and Christianity; do carry out the work which I have begun."[11] To persuade his people, Livingstone capitalized on rampant human trade in the interior of Africa.[12]

Not only was such an appeal and promise made, it was done. Livingstone braved the continent of Africa, moving from one ethnic group to another, from one river to another, from coast to coast, and from one forest to another. He kept a detailed description of the vegetation, terrain, customs, people, diseases, trade; he drew maps; he explored the navigable rivers; and he reported the findings to his targeted parties back home.[13] His efforts were meant to invite and stimulate the interests of traders, geographic societies, and missionary societies, that is, various colonial agents who might occupy and civilize Africa. And in this he was indeed successful, opening Africa for Western commerce, civilization, and Christianity.

If at the debating societies, the Berlin conference, the mission writings, and the legacy of David Livingstone were an overwhelming historical attestation of the connection of biblical texts, their readers, and their institutions to imperial domination of Africa, we also grew up with the South African apartheid regime. Apartheid, a violent and exploitative ideology of racial discrimination, was propounded by Bible readers and supported by their institutions, based on the biblical texts. But apartheid only followed the dispossession of South African people of their lands and property by white settlers, who claimed to be a "chosen race" with the right to take the land, to settle on it, and to displace the natives in the best way possible, which, in this case, became apartheid. Therefore, on those debating floors we never won an argument, for historical attestation was simply against us. The question of why the biblical text, its readers, and its institutions are instruments of imperialism has remained unanswered, yet is still urgently posed. The anonymous short story quoted at the beginning of this chapter is a story that captured this history succinctly, and unavoidably invoked reflections and questions. The short story also articulates the deep sense of betrayal for those of us who have endured the exploitation and

---

[11]Norman E. Thomas, ed., *Classic Texts in Mission and World Christianity* (Maryknoll, N. Y.: Orbis Books, 1995), 68.

[12]See ibid., 67–68, for Livingstone's double standards in the commitment to stop slavery. He states that he is leaving southern Africa and going into the interior for many reasons, "amongst which were considerations arising out of the slave system carried on by Dutch Boers." In short, Livingstone does not want to face and fight the enslavement of black people by white people in southern Africa. He prefers to stop slavery practiced by Arabic people and African kings in the interior of Africa.

[13]See David Livingstone, *Narrative on an Expedition to the Zambezi and Its Tributaries, and of the Discovery of the Lakes Shirwa and Nyassa, with Map and Illustrations* (New York: Harper & Brothers, 1866). See also Livingstone's *Missionary Travels and Researches in South Africa: Illustrated* (Philadelphia: J. W. Bradley, 1858).

the humiliation of Western imperialism but still dared to call ourselves Christians. The story is an experience that compels us to search for answers for ourselves as well as to hold a critical conversation with Westerners.

Therefore, the motions of debating societies remain a genuine quest for understanding: They pose the question of the ethics and politics of the Bible, the question of Western imperialism and the Bible, and the question of how we should read the Bible given this history of its role, its readers, and its institutions. This is the problem of the Bible and postcolonial demands and challenges.

The centrality of the Bible in facilitating Western imperialism remains evident to African people and provides the cause for much reflection. It has not only occupied African oral stories and debates; it still occupies most African critical writers of literature, philosophy, theology, and biblical studies, as the following discussion highlights.

African Writers, the Bible, and Imperialism

Literary Writers

Inevitably, the issue of imperial domination has informed and occupied much of African literature, and with it, the concept of the European novel as an imperialistic instrument. As Barbara Harlow points out, "the writers and critics writing within the context of organized resistance movements comprehend the role of culture and cultural resistance as part of the larger struggle for liberation."[14] Among the many African writers who have concerned themselves with imperial domination and resistance, I will briefly discuss the views of Ngugi wa Thiongo.[15]

In his books *Decolonizing the Mind* and *Moving the Center: The Struggle for Cultural Freedoms*, Ngugi is primarily concerned with the use of English literature and language in the colonization of sub-Saharan Africa. He argues that the modern marketing of the so-called humanist tradition of literature to universal standards undermined the fact that, like every piece of literature, it was bound to its context and culture. So through this allegedly universal humanistic tradition, "African children who encountered literature in colonial schools and universities were thus experiencing the world as defined and reflected in the European experience of history...Europe was the center of the world."[16] This employment of imperialist literature was an integral part of colonization, alienating the subjugated from their own languages, religions, environments, and cultures.

---

[14]See Barbara Harlow, *Resistance Literature* (New York: Methuen, 1987), 10.

[15]See also Appiah A. Kwame, *In My Father's House: Africa in the Philosophy of Culture* (New York: Oxford University Press, 1992); and Chinua Achebe, *Hopes and Impediments: Selected Essays* (New York: Doubleday, 1989).

[16]Ngugi wa Thiongo, *Decolonizing the Mind: The Politics of Language in African Literature* (London: James Curry, 1986), 93.

In addition, Ngugi shows the role of the Bible to be equally central when he notes that both "William Shakespeare and Jesus had brought light to the darkest Africa" and recalls that his colonial-era teacher used to say that "Jesus and Shakespeare used very simple English."[17] Not surprisingly, these statements closely reflect Josiah Strong's claim that the English language is "saturated with Christian ideas"; that is, we see perspectives from the colonizer and the colonized writers that make no distinction between English culture and Christianity. On the grounds of these experiences, Ngugi unhesitantly holds that in the imperial subjugation of Africa "the weapon of language is added to that of the Bible and the sword."[18] For Ngugi, it is evident that the "English, French, and Portuguese came to the Third World to announce the Bible and the Sword."[19]

Philosophical Writers

V. Y. Mudimbe examines the construction of the image of Africa, its motives, and its sources.[20] He begins with the central event that has marked and engineered the invention of Africa, namely, European colonialism. According to Mudimbe, colonialism or colonization, which "means organization, arrangement," has meant the tendency "to organize and transform non-European areas into fundamentally European constructs."[21]

Mudimbe's explication of how such constructs are achieved brings the Bible, its Western readers, and its institutions into the mosaic of what he terms the "colonizing structures." Colonizing structures include the procedures and policies that promote "the domination of space, the reformation of natives' minds, and the integration of local economic histories into Western perspective."[22] This triple project involved many actors such as explorers, soldiers, traders, anthropologists, missionaries, scientists, and map-makers—positions that were sometimes held by one individual, as in the case of David Livingstone. All these actors collected, constructed,[23] and distributed a discourse of African Otherness. On the basis of their constructions, policies were drawn to justify the imperial subjugation of Africa.

---

[17]Ibid., 91.

[18]Ngugi wa Thiongo, *Moving the Center: The Struggle for Cultural Freedoms* (London: James Curry, 1993), 31.

[19]Ibid.

[20]V. Y. Mudimbe, *The Invention of Africa: Gnosis, Philosophy and the Order of Knowledge* (Indianapolis: Indiana University Press, 1988), 1.

[21]Ibid., 1.

[22]Ibid., 2–4.

[23]See Musa W. Dube, "Consuming the Colonial Cultural Bomb: Translating *Badimo* into Demons in the Setswana Bible (Matt. 8:28–34; 15:22; 10:8)," *Journal for the Study of the New Testament* 73 (1999): 33–59, in which an analysis of colonial missionary translations indicates that they equated *Badimo*, the sacred mediators of Botswana, to demons. The translation suggested that Botswana venerated evil powers prior to the arrival of Christianity.

In the colonial subjugation of Africa, Mudimbe gives the missionary the center stage. He finds that "of all these bearers of the African burden," the missionary was also, paradoxically, the best symbol of the colonial enterprise…He devoted himself sincerely to the ideals of colonialism: the expansion of Civilization, the dissemination of Christianity and the advance of Progress."[24] To substantiate this assertion, Mudimbe quotes the following words of missionary Pringle:[25]

> Let us enter upon a new and nobler career of conquest. Let us subdue Savage Africa by justice, by kindness, by the talisman of Christian truth. Let us thus go forth, in the name and under the blessing of God, gradually to extend the moral influence…the territorial boundary also of our colony, until it shall become an empire.[26]

Pringle's overt commitment to the use of the "talisman of Christian truth" to "subdue Savage Africa" and to "extend the territorial boundaries" for their countries makes it apparent that a missionary "with equal enthusiasm…served as an agent of a political empire, a representative of a civilization, and an envoy of God."[27] Accordingly, Mudimbe holds that there was "no essential contradiction between these roles" for "all of them implied the same purpose: conversion of African minds and space."[28]

Judging by the words of Livingstone, Strong, and Pringle, there was indeed no contradiction between missionary roles and colonizing ones. The critical question, however, is: How is their thought related to the biblical text and what are the implications of this relationship for a postcolonial biblical reader? For example, do Pringle's words "let us go forth in the name and under the blessings of God," Strong's phrase that the Anglo-Saxon is "divinely commissioned…to be his brother's keeper," and Livingstone's efforts "to make an open path for commerce and Christianity" have a biblical base? If we can establish a biblical text that calls on its readers to "go forth" under divine commission, then first the intimate relationship of the missionary with the "colonizing structures" must be sought in the ideology of the biblical text. Second, the question of how we should read the Bible in the postcolonial era becomes vital, both to the former colonizer and the formerly colonized.

Alluding to these questions, Mudimbe is quick to point out that his books are not primarily about the history of African anthropology or the colonial conversion of Africa, but about "a master charter" or "a tradition"

---

[24]Mudimbe, *The Invention of Africa*, 47.
[25]Mudimbe does not give Pringle's first name.
[26]See Mudimbe, *The Invention of Africa*, 47, quoted from D. Hammond and A. Jablow, *The Myth of Africa* (New York: The Library of Social Science, 1977), 44.
[27]Ibid., 47.
[28]Ibid.

whose popular interpretation marks everyday practices of the Western community and witnesses to their historical becoming.[29] According to Mudimbe, "the Torah is such a charter in the Jewish tradition. The New Testament served a similar mission in the Christian West."[30] In short, the Western colonialist construction of the African subject and the participation of Western Bible readers and their institutions in colonizing structures reflect an interpretation of their master charter, the New Testament.

In his recent book *The Idea of Africa,* Mudimbe probes further into the traditions of the West and the various constructions of Africa in Western history as well as the motives behind it. He examines texts from Greco-Roman times to the last five centuries. What becomes evident is that the Greco-Roman texts have always constructed people of different areas as "barbarians" and "savages."

However, he notes that in the last five centuries the science of savages took a sharply pronounced turn. Explorers, adventurers, traders, soldiers, anthropologists, missionaries, colonialists, and travelers of different persuasions collected and constructed consistent images of savagery. These constructions invited and validated European imperialism. That is, their constructions authorized "the mission of the stronger race to help their inferior brethren to grow up."[31] Given the rhetorical function of these constructions, Mudimbe notes that "from a Christian point of view, to oppose the process of colonization or that of slavery could only be morally wrong."[32] Consequently, Christianizing, colonizing, civilizing, as well as enslaving become part of the mission to save.

In fact, this self-validating project is evident in the above quotations of Strong, Livingstone, and Pringle. Strong speaks of "weaker races," Livingstone decries rampant slave trade, while Pringle speaks of "Savage Africa." Their constructions are paralleled by an invitation to redeem or to civilize. For instance, Strong recommends dispossession, assimilation, the molding of weaker races into Anglo-Saxons; Livingstone calls for Western Christianity, commerce, and civilization; Pringle, on the other hand, recommends the entrance into the nobler career of conquest, the subjugation of Savage Africa, the extension of territorial boundaries by applying various strategies, among them the talisman of Christian truth.

The centrality of Christian texts in facilitating Western imperialism is also the main focus of Ali A. Mazrui's magnificent book *Cultural Forces in World Politics.* Mazrui's main thesis is not only "to demonstrate that both ideology and technology are rooted in culture" but also "to demonstrate

    [29]See V. Y. Mudimbe, *The Idea of Africa* (Indianapolis: Indiana University Press, 1994), xiii.
    [30]Ibid.
    [31]Ibid., 37.
    [32]Ibid.

that at the international level the class struggle of the world is often culturally rather than economically defined."[33] He notes:

> God, gold and glory! Captured in a slogan, these are in fact the
> three basic imperatives in the history of cultural diffusion. Why
> do men burst forth from their boundaries in search of new hori-
> zons? They are inspired either by a search for religious fulfillment
> (the God standard) or by a yearning for economic realization (the
> gold standard) or by that passion for renown (the quest for glory).[34]

Between the three standards, Mazrui asks, "Which particular force–
God, gold or glory–is supreme in the drive for cultural diffusion?"[35] His
answer to this question focuses on the Judeo-Christian-Islamic ideology of
monotheism and their tendencies "to divide the human race between believers and unbelievers, between the virtuous and the sinful, between the
good and evil, between us and them."[36] Mazrui holds that both the monotheistic and dualistic constructions were among the earliest forces that sanctioned men and women to burst their boundaries to convert the sinful, the
unbelievers, and the evil because there was a desire "to convert every human being to their faith."[37]

Among the monotheistic and dualistic religions, Mazrui singles out
Christianity, followed by Islam, for its exceptional global impact. That being
the case, he probes further into the relationship of the God and gold standards in the history of Christian countries. Mazrui traces the merger of
these two standards to the conversion of Emperor Constantine I in the
fourth century as the point when "Christianity became an imperial religion rather than a religion of the underdog."[38] As he sees it, this merger
meant that

> the God standard had taken over an Empire and shared the
> temporal splendor which went with it. European Christianity
> became less a grassroots movement and more an imperial system.
> Notwithstanding, the idea that the world was one derived from a
> merger between the Greco-Roman and the Judeo-Christian
> legacies.[39]

This merger, maintains Mazrui, moved cultural dominance from the Semites
to the Anglo-Saxons. From this point on, just as Jesus had

---

[33]Ali A. Mazrui, *Cultural Forces in World Politics* (London: James Curry, 1990), 1, 14.
[34]See ibid., 29.
[35]Ibid.
[36]Ibid., 13.
[37]See ibid., 30. See also Rene Maunier, *The Sociology of Colonies: An Introduction to the Study of Race Contact,* vol. 1 (London: Routledge, 1949), 154–92, who also grounds the earliest motivations of colonial imperialism in religion.
[38]Mazrui, *Cultural Forces,* 36.
[39]Ibid., 33.

advised his followers to give to Caesar what was Caesar's and unto God what was God's[,] Jesus's recognition of Caesar as sovereign on earth was part of the background to modern European conceptions of sovereignty. Man was King on earth, and God was king in heaven.[40]

In regard to the merger of the Christian God and gold standards and its impact on Africa, Mazrui notes that

> Europe on the whole was prepared to offer its religion, languages and culture to Africans–but only in exchange for land, mines, labor, energy and other economic riches of Africa. Jomo Kenyatta in the old colonial Kenya was more profound than he may have realized when he observed: "when the white man came to Africa he had the Bible and we had the land. And now? We have the Bible and he has the land."[41]

Mazrui's interpretation of this oral story is that Western imperialism in Africa was "a classic case of offering culture in exchange for material goods– as Europe was exporting arts and ideas and importing economic riches."[42]

Biblical and Theological Writers

Inevitably, the connection of Western imperialism and the biblical text and its readers has also occupied African theological and biblical writers.[43] Among many of these, I shall briefly look at Kwesi Dickson's *Uncompleted Mission: Christianity and Exclusivism* and Canaan Banana's recent article "The Case for a New Bible."[44]

Kwesi Dickson begins by identifying the main purpose of the church as the mission to the world. But then he notes that "the church through its movement from continent to continent, country to country, and people to people, has seemed particularly exclusivist."[45] He defines exclusivism as a "*tabula rasa* doctrine which maintains that the culture of those being evangelized cannot be looked upon in any way as a basis upon which to build," that is, "for Christianity to establish roots among people, their culture…must give way altogether."[46]

Dickson finds this exclusive perspective contradictory to the goals of the mission (evangelizing). He thus examines the roots of the Christian

---

[40]Ibid., 36.

[41]Ibid., 6.

[42]Ibid.

[43]It is almost a standard format for African theological writers to begin by discussing the arrival of missionaries with imperial forces. See Emmanuel Martey, *African Theology: Inculturation and Liberation* (Maryknoll, N.Y.: Orbis Books, 1993), 36–57.

[44]See also Itumeleng Mosala, *Biblical Hermeneutics and Black Theology in South Africa* (Grand Rapids, Mich.: Eerdmans, 1989), whose book was born in the struggle against a particular form of imperialism, that is, in apartheid South Africa.

[45]Kwesi Dickson, *Uncompleted Mission: Christianity and Exclusivism* (Maryknoll, N.Y.: Orbis Books, 1991), 3.

[46]Ibid., 124.

mission's exclusivism—beginning from the Hebrew Bible and the New Testament, through the Reformation doctrines, to the modern Western missionaries. Dickson seeks to establish not only the roots and maintenance of exclusivism but also how it informed the thinking and approach of Western Christian missions in the African continent.

In his examination of the Hebrew Bible's attitude toward people of different cultures, Dickson finds both inclusive (Gen. 12:3; Zech. 14:16; Isa. 2:2–4; Mal. 1:5–14) and exclusive attitudes (Deut. 7:14; 8:19–20; 18:9–14; 23:4; Isa. 44:6; Neh. 7:5; Ezra 9:12). Despite this tension, Dickson notes that the exclusivist perspective predominantly prevailed. Accordingly, Dickson maintains that the Hebrew Bible exclusivism was carried over to the New Testament. He focuses on Paul, the major exponent of the Gentile mission, and finds Paul's letter to the Galatians hesitant to live up to its gospel of freedom. For example, in Galatians 4:8–11 "Paul adopts an attitude toward the traditional religion of the people of Galatia…which is uncompromisingly contemptuous,"[47] for he categorically describes the Galatian divine figures as "beings that by nature are not gods" (v. 8). Dickson therefore holds that the roots of exclusivism were maintained in the New Testament when the "early church was unable to face…the issue of continuity between the Jewish and Christian traditions and other people's traditions."[48]

Similarly, the Reformation, with its doctrines of *Sola Scriptura* and a Pauline influence, and the modern Western missionaries of the eighteenth and nineteenth centuries were building on Christian scriptures that were already exclusivist. Dickson insists that

> the New Testament evidence is clear. What became a feature of Africa in the modern period—shepherding converts into closely-knit Christian communities away from what were seen as dangerous influences—was already a feature of the church outreach in Paul's time…[49]

However, Dickson holds that in the modern missions these exclusivist tendencies took another turn when Christianity was identified with Western culture. For example, Ernst Troeltsch "identified Christianity with Western Culture, to the extent that he did not consider it possible for a non-Westerner to understand the Christian faith."[50] As Dickson sees it, the perspective of Troeltsch, which was also prevalent among missionaries of the time, logically "maintained that non-Western inquirers would have to leave their cultures behind in order to appreciate the Christian faith."[51] Consequently, there were many missionaries who, according to Dickson,

---

[47]Ibid., 68.
[48]Ibid., 59.
[49]Ibid., 69.
[50]Ibid., 83.
[51]Ibid.

then "showed a commitment to the eradication of African culture."[52] In short, the "mission understood as a Westernization process" in the eighteenth and nineteenth centuries was inseparable from European cultural imperialism.[53]

Likewise, Canaan Banana in his article "The Case for a New Bible" calls for editing, revising, and adding to the Bible with the noble aim of "embracing the rich plurality of human experience in response to God."[54] He summarizes the aim of his article in the following words:

> The challenge I am posing for Christians and all who ascribe to the present Bible is that we must expand the frontiers of archeological research and excavation to encompass the entire universe. Religious shrines and traditions of the peoples of Asia, Africa, Europe, the Caribbean and Latin America must surely be important sources of God's revelation. Nothing can be lost by studying how these peoples perceived and worshipped God in their own individual circumstances with the view of drawing from their rich heritage to broaden our understanding of God's activity in human history.[55]

Banana recognizes that the Bible is an important book of the church and that it includes liberating messages; nevertheless, he holds that "no matter how we emphasize the liberating and correcting strands within today's Bible, there remains the sense in which, unless one embraces the Christian concept of God, one is not fully a person of God."[56] Banana is making a case, similar to that of Dickson, against the cultural imperialism of Western Christianity.

However, Banana's call for an inclusive Bible is based not only on its religious exclusivism but also on the concerns of gender, race, apartheid, and colonialism, which, as he points out, have been propounded from the biblical text. He contends that there must be editing, revising, and adding to the Bible, because the history of the Christian church is a catalog of exploitation in the name of Christ. Among the long list of what he calls a sordid history of the Bible, he tabulates the "exploitation of the people of the 'new world' to the colonization of Africa in the great mission thrusts of Western civilization."[57] Banana adamantly calls for an inclusive Bible that takes the diversity of God's creation seriously, for, as he maintains, "the history is long…of the use of the Bible as a justification for exploitation; the self-serving adoption of one group as 'superior' to another."[58] Instead

---

[52]Ibid., 85.
[53]Ibid., 124.
[54]Canaan Banana, "The Case for a New Bible," in *"Re-Writing" the Bible: The Real Issues,* ed. J. L. Cox, I. Mukonyora, and F. J. Verstraelen (Gweru: Mambo Books, 1993), 30.
[55]Ibid., 21.
[56]Ibid., 29.
[57]Ibid., 21–22.
[58]Ibid., 19.

of maintaining the exaltation of one group above the rest, which authorizes the oppression of the rest who stand outside this circle, Banana recommends that the extension of the Bible must begin with the assumption that all creation is holy.

Thus far, in my definition of the problem, I have spoken of missionaries as Bible readers and their historical acts as performances that reflect the ethics of their texts and institutions. I have also spoken of the Christian religion, which designates the religious practice whose main acts are informed by biblical texts. Such designations seek to connect the acts of biblical readers and Christian institutions to their text, as the above reviewed African oral stories and scholars' arguments demonstrate. However, the purpose of such a connection is to let the acts of the readers illuminate the meaning and implications of the text for us as well as to direct us to a new ethical approach in the postcolonial era. What are the implications of the connection of biblical texts to Western/modern imperialism for postcolonial biblical interpretation? How should we read the Bible as postcolonial subjects?

Toward Postcolonial Biblical Interpretations

In sum, when it comes to the connection of cultural texts, in this case the Bible, its readers, and its institutions, to Western imperialism, there is no call for special pleading. The evidence is overwhelming. The challenge, however, is how to grasp the serious implications of this historical attestation; that is, what ethical responsibility does it lay on contemporary Western and non-Western biblical scholars? Second, how can postcolonial subjects read the Bible without perpetuating what Banana recognizes as a self-serving paradigm of constructing one group as superior to another?

But first it must be asked, What is the postcolonial condition and who are its subjects? The word *postcolonial* has been coined to describe the modern history of imperialism, beginning with the process of colonialism, through the struggles for political independence, the attainment of independence, and to the contemporary neocolonialist realities.[59] This definition emphasizes the connection and continuity between the past and the present, between the colonizer and the colonized. *Postcolonial subjects,* on the other hand, describes both the former colonizers and the formerly colonized, what today falls under such broad categories as First World and Two-Thirds World,[60] developed and underdeveloped, Western and non-Western. Homi Bhabha adds an important aspect to the definition by insisting that *postmodernity, postcoloniality,* and *postfeminism* are "terms that insistently gesture to the beyond...They transform the present."[61] That is,

---

[59]See Bill Ashcroft, Gareth Griffiths, and Helen Tiffin, eds., *The Empire Writes Back: Theory and Practice in Post-colonial Literatures* (New York: Routledge, 1989), 2.

[60]The term *Two-Thirds World* is used here, instead of the commonly used *Third World,* to emphasize that the latter is actually the majority in the world.

[61]Homi Bhabha, *The Location of Culture* (New York: Routledge, 1994), 4.

postcolonial is not about dwelling on the crimes of the past and their continuation, but about seeking transformation for liberation. The term *postcolonial subjects* describes a people whose perception of each other and of economic, political, and cultural relationships cannot be separated from the global impact and constructions of Western/modern imperialism, which still remain potent in forms of neocolonialism, military arrogance, and globalization.

If the postcolonial era is a world that is cognizant of the global impact of Western or modern imperialism, which, as Said points out, "was so all-encompassing that virtually nothing escaped,"[62] how should we read cultural texts that were instrumental to its establishment? For the postcolonial subjects of African origin the connection of biblical texts to Western imperialism has had several implications for reading the biblical text. To elaborate on these, I will focus on various interconnected points depicted by the oral story, that is, issues of the land, race, power, readers, international connection, contemporaray history and liberation, and gender.

Land

First, as the story of the arrival of a white man and his exchange of the Bible for black African lands indicates, geography is central to postcolonial biblical hermeneutics. That is, the issues of Western geographical possession and expansion and non-Western dispossession are inseparably tied to the biblical text. The story proceeds as follows: First, the land was occupied by black Africans. Second, the white men came in and took it. Third, in its place black Africans were given the Bible. The story does not give any further details beyond the announcement of the prayer. But by implicating the Bible in the taking of black African lands, biblical texts are marked as powerful rhetorical instruments of imperialism. For unless the biblical values authorized coming into foreign lands and geographically dispossessing foreign people, such an expansionist program would have been ethically inconceivable for its Western readers.

Race

The assertion that "when the white man came to our country he had the Bible and we had the land" implicates race relations in postcolonial hermeneutics. The story insists that the imperial power of the white race has been legitimized through the biblical texts, and the victimization of the black race through the same text. Inevitably, the assertion challenges Western readers to be aware of their history of hegemonic power and to scrutinize their current interpretations to avoid repetition of the victimizing of non-Western races.

---

[62]Said, *Culture and Imperialism,* 86.

Power

Closely tied to the centrality of race and geography in postcolonial biblical hermeneutics is the issue of power distribution over the global landscape. Power is unequally distributed both geographically and racially through the use of cultural texts. For instance, black Africans initially owned the land, a material good, but they lost the geographical control to the white race, who in addition to their own lands, expanded to other areas. While this was a story that captured the colonial times and inspired fighting for independence, biblical readers can no longer ignore the unequal distribution of power along the postcolonial landscape and how it was effected through the biblical text, among many other things. Therefore, a postcolonial reader is challenged to ask why this was effected through the Bible; why biblical texts endorsed unequal power distribution along geographical and racial differences; why, in the wake of political independence, power has remained unequally distributed; and how to read for empowering the disempowered areas and races or creating a better system.

Readers

Postcolonial history has some specific implications on the impact and values of the Bible. As the African critical writers analyzed above show, biblical texts have authorized Christian believers to enter and take the lands of non-Christian believers, either under the ideology of converting them, as Mazrui and Mudimbe hold, or under the self-serving paradigm of claims of chosenness or superiority, as Canaan Banana and Dickson argue. These scholars perceive some continuity in what the text claims and what its Western believers perform. To single out the ideology of chosenness, they trace its origin to the Hebrew Bible and find its adoption in the New Testament, in the Reformation, and in the acts of Western Christian colonizers as attested to by histories of apartheid in South Africa and elsewhere. In short, the text may have its own historical world and environment, but the text also travels in the world and participates in history, continuing to write its story far beyond its original context and readers. The text continues to live and to inscribe its authority through its Western readers and their institutions that uphold it. In addition, the text has maintained a recognizable impact through its various readers and their different institutions, regardless of whether this was the intention of the author or not.

Insofar as the centrality of geography and the ideology that authorize the entering and taking of the lands of foreign people is traced to the Exodus-Canaan mythological story, the postcolonial historical experience strongly suggests that at the heart of biblical belief is an imperialist ideology. If imperialism means "to think about distant places, to colonize them, to depopulate them," then at the core of ancient Israel's foundational story is an imperialist ideology, which operates under the claims of chosenness.[63] This means that while Israelites were repeatedly victims of imperialism, and while they resisted and awaited their own freedom, their yearnings also embodied the right to geographically expand to lands that might be occupied. This is seen even in some of the messianic figures evoked in apocalyptic literature. Likewise, New Testament texts, written under the domination of the Roman Empire, resisted the imperial oppression in their own ways but also articulated the right to propagate their own version of imperialism. Consequently, from Constantine's conversion, Christianity became "unique in its imperial sponsorship" because its texts have always harbored an ideology of geographical expansion to foreign lands.[64]

International Connection

The above exposition of the problem has strongly shown that, historically, the Western interpretation of the Bible has had a direct impact on African realities, ranging from culture to politics to economics. This history, unfortunately, cannot be willed away or ignored without maintaining its imperialistic tendencies. Moreover, it continues to have adverse effects in Africa and elsewhere. The apparent international nature of biblical impact calls for a global ethical commitment in the postcolonial world of Bible readers. Here the issues of particularity and universality stand in sharp tension and beg for attention. While universal interpretations have fostered imperial domination, withdrawal to particularist interpretations is not necessarily the answer. The paradigm of universal interpretation has had a long historical establishment, and it is supported by firmly established Western institutions such that to simply withdraw to particularist interpretation is to leave the oppressive universal paradigm in place. Furthermore, the current imperialism of the multinational media and the financial institutions, which distribute Western material and cultural goods more effectively than ever before in history, makes it almost unethical for biblical interpreters to ignore the increasing reality of universality. Therefore, there is a need to struggle with the issues of both particularity and universality: to assess the power relations that foster the one-way traffic of universality and to think of liberating ways of interdependence.[65] In short,

---

[63]Ibid., 78. See also Robert Allen Warrior, "A Native American Perspective: Canaanites, Cowboys and Indians," in *Voices from the Margin: Interpreting the Bible in the Third World,* ed. R. S. Sugirtharajah (Maryknoll, N.Y.: Orbis Books, 1991), 280–87.

[64]Wayne Meeks, *The First Urban Christians: The Social World of the Apostle Paul* (New Haven, Conn.: Yale University Press, 1983), 1.

[65]See Said, *Culture and Imperialism,* 262–336, on the idea of interdependence rather than independence. He holds that no country, people, or nation is really independent of others, but that rather we are all dependent on one another. He holds that the very act of colonizing attests that even metropolitan centers need the Two-Thirds World for survival.

Western readers can no longer pretend that their reading of the Bible has no effect on those outside their immediate cultures, continents, or countries.

The apparent international history of the biblical texts compels postcolonial readers to ask if their reading continues to inscribe, to authorize, and to activate those readings that validated the domination, subjugation, and conquering of the non-Western/non-Christian world. It calls on biblical readers to search and to articulate a reading that shows why the past interpretations authorized the imperial colonization of the non-Christian Other and to seek liberating ways of reading for interdependence. This implies that the readings of these two groups, the West and the non-West, must take cognizance of each other's presence and the ethical obligations that imperial history has placed on both sides. Failure to examine this historical connection and its implications is, as Said says, to take a position that has already been taken, which is to maintain the imperialistic paradigm of the West.

Contemporary History and Liberation

The arrival of the Bible in the hands of the white man and the taking of land is a phenomenon intimately tied to the last few centuries. Consequently, the meaning of the biblical text is pursued primarily for the contemporary concerns of our world. Black African writers focus on how the meaning of biblical texts has shaped and continues to shape international relations of the postcolonial world. The above review, for instance, shows that they focus on such biblical values as monotheism, dualism, chosenness, and evangelization of the world, and how they have shaped the current economic, political, and cultural issues of the North and South. Even more importantly, the fact that the arrival of the Bible in Africa was tied to the white man's taking of the black African's land binds biblical interpretation to the current struggles for liberation. It is well known that South African victory against apartheid marked the end of political struggle for independence in the African continent. However, the association of various schools and cultural texts, in this case the Bible, with imperial subjugation, which converted black African spaces and minds into white European constructs, highlights the complexity of the struggle for independence. Basically, colonial subjugation was not just a simple geographical control of black African lands by white people. It was a complex network of the molding of black African minds and spaces according to and for the material benefit of the West, as both Mazrui and Mudimbe point out. It follows, then, that political independence of Africa—and that of most Two-Thirds World countries—was not attained by simply winning the geographical rule of their countries, as is quite evident by now. Political independence was just one step toward liberating ways of interdependence. To read the Bible as postcolonial subjects, therefore, is to participate in the long, uncompleted struggle for liberation of these countries and to seek liberating ways of interdependence.

Likewise, the connection of the biblical texts with Western imperialism has meant that the postcolonial Bible cannot be discussed in isolation from other disciplines. This is attested to by its centrality with people whose discipline is not religion, as evidenced by Ngugi, Mudimbe, and Mazrui. Perhaps this approach is best traced to David Livingstone, the legendary missionary who labored to open up Africa for what he regarded as the inseparable kind: Christianity, commerce, and civilization. Livingstone tied the Christian texts to the spheres of politics, economics, and culture from the very introduction of the biblical texts into sub-Saharan Africa. It is against this background that Mazrui interprets the oral story of the arrival of the Bible in sub-Saharan Africa as summarizing "a classic case of offering culture in exchange for material goods."[66] These factors, therefore, tie the biblical text to various international realities of life such as economics, politics, and social affairs. In view of this historical background, to divorce biblical interpretation from current international relations, or to discuss it primarily as an ancient text, becomes another Western ideological stance that hides its direct impact on the postcolonial world and maintains its imperial domination of Two-Thirds World countries.

Gender

There is also an issue of gender, which is visible by its absence. The story of imperialism speaks of white males versus "we" the Africans. In both cases women are either subsumed or absent. This absence in many ways captures gender relationships and oppression in imperialism; that is, both women and men of certain nations participate together in oppressing women and men of distant countries. This fact has complicated global feminist struggles, for even among the marginalized women, there are oppressors and oppressed. Women in the colonized spaces not only suffer the yoke of colonial oppression but also endure the burden of two patriarchal systems imposed on them. Women in colonizing countries, on the other hand, become indicators of imperial civilization, enjoying some privileges but certainly oppressed for their female gender.

In sum, Africans' admission that they now have the Bible implies that this text is no longer just a Western book. It is also a postcolonial book, laden with the postcolonial burdens and challenges. The postcolonial landscape is drawn with the colors of Western imperialism, depicting inclusive histories of unequal geographies, unequal races, unequal distribution of power, denial of difference, and silencing of women. Simultaneously, the postcolonial landscape is flashed with the riotous colors of resisting African voices and others of the Two-Thirds World, who assert the dignity of

---

[66]Mazrui, *Cultural Forces*, 6.

their lands, cultures, races, and differences, and challenge Westerners to ethical distribution of power over the globe. Nonetheless, the postcolonial landscape is still marked by many collaborative servants who continue to assert, consciously or unconsciously, the dominance of the West and the cultural suppression and exploitation of non-Western cultures and economies. Western feminisms have also served in this capacity.

2

The Postcolonial Condition
and Feminisms

Chapter 1 defined the problem of postcolonial Bible interpretation by highlighting the need for a reading of the Bible in which imperialistic strategies are confronted, exposed, and arrested by postcolonial subjects. My goal, however, is to take both imperialism and patriarchy seriously. This second chapter, dedicated to defining the problem, therefore seeks to show why we need postcolonial *feminist* interpretations of the Bible. Accordingly, the chapter focuses on how Western feminist discourses have inscribed themselves within the Western imperialist parameters in order to point the way forward toward postcolonial readings of the Bible.

Many contemporary Western biblical scholars, male and female, acknowledge that the Bible is an influential book of the West. For example, Elisabeth Schüssler Fiorenza notes that "biblical texts affect the perceptions, values, and imagination not only of Christians, but of Western cultures and societies."[1] Similarly, the opening statement of *The Postmodern Bible* states: "We begin with a truism: the Bible has exerted more cultural influence in the West than any other single document."[2] Later, in their chapter on ideological criticism, the authors point out that "in Western culture the stories most influential in shaping and producing ideology are found in the Bible."[3] What I find lacking in these acknowledgments,

---

[1]Elisabeth Schüssler Fiorenza, *But She Said: Feminist Practices of Biblical Interpretations* (Boston: Beacon Press, 1992), 47.

[2]The Bible and Culture Collective, *The Postmodern Bible* (New Haven, Conn.: Yale University Press, 1995), 1.

[3]Ibid., 276.

however, is an attempt to take seriously the implications that should accompany such acknowledgments. Unfortunately, this gap includes feminist biblical scholars, and it is a problem that needs to be addressed in order to promote and establish strategic coalitions among women of different backgrounds and situations, across borders, and beyond narrow identity politics.[4] To highlight the need for postcolonial feminist biblical hermeneutics, I will begin by reviewing some of Chandra Mohanty's and Laura Donaldson's criticisms of Western feminisms before I turn to biblical feminists.

Mohanty's critique focuses on the use of the category of "woman" in Western feminist discourse as a universally homogeneous entity. A woman is supposedly oppressed by the man wherever she is, and patriarchy is constructed as universal and absolute. On the contrary, Mohanty argues that such theoretical constructions maintain the superiority of Western women over against non-Western women. Mohanty maintains that the homogenizing of women not only imposes the Euro-centric feminist categories of analysis and denies diversity but also constructs the Two-Thirds World women as helpless victims, burdened by several layers of oppression, who must now be redeemed by their Western counterparts. Such a monolithic portrayal, as Mohanty notes, "limits theoretical analysis as well as reinforces Western cultural imperialism."[5]

To substantiate how homogenizing categories of analysis remain in the mainstream of colonial discourse, Mohanty assesses Maria Ross Cutrufelli's book *Women of Africa: The Roots of Oppression.* Cutrufelli unhesitantly says, "My analysis will start by stating that all African women are politically and economically dependent," and proceeds to say, "Either overtly or covertly, prostitution is still the main if not the only source of work for African women."[6] This statement is, of course, outrageous and a massive character assassination for African people as a whole, but it shows the effects of homogenizing across cultures. More importantly, the significance of Cutrufelli's homogenizing portrayal lies in what it reflects. First, her writing is firmly informed and remains totally inscribed within the parameters of imperial rhetoric of subjugation—one that is captured by what Pringle adjectivized as "Savage Africa." Thus, Cutrufelli participates in the old and persistent imperialist science of savagery, which epitomizes Africa as a paragon of evil. Only within such a Western context and tradition does her statement become possible and acceptable.

---

[4]Mary Ann Tolbert, "The Politics and Poetics of Location," in *Reading from This Place: Social Location and Biblical Interpretation in the United States,* vol. 1, ed. Fernando F. Segovia and Mary Ann Tolbert (Minneapolis: Fortress Press, 1995), 313–14.

[5]Chandra Mohanty, "Under Western Eyes," in *Colonial Discourse and Postcolonial Theory: A Reader,* ed. Patrick Williams and Laura Chrisman (New York: Columbia University Press, 1994), 214.

[6]Quoted in Mohanty, "Under Western Eyes," from Maria Ross Cutrufelli, *Women of Africa: The Roots of Oppression* (London: Zed Books, 1983), 3.

As in the words of Josiah Strong, David Livingstone, and Pringle quoted in chapter 1, in Cutrufelli's statement we see a reproduction of the ideological foundations of imperialist rhetoric. In both cases it serves to justify the invasion and destruction of different cultures in order to save them from their own shortcomings. This approach maintains the West as the center of all cultural good, one with a supposedly redemptive impulse, but one that always proceeds by placing all other cultures at the periphery. It works by a process of selection and suppression that portrays the Other negatively while continuously uplifting its own superiority. The approach constructed both the colonizer and the colonized, and it was so thorough in its method that it permeated even the liberationist feminist discourse.

That this imperial rhetoric permeated Western feminist writers becomes evident in Mary Daly's monumental work *Gyn/Ecology*. Daly portrayed all African women as victims of genital mutilation. It is true that this practice exists in some parts of East, West, and North Africa, but a homogenizing construction of all African women was, indeed, consistent with the science of savagery. Daly's homogeneous portrait did not go unchallenged. Audre Lorde critiqued it primarily for its selection and suppression, that is, presenting a homogeneous picture of victims and suppressing all liberating themes of African women.[7] Daly did not respond to Lorde's letter of protest—the refusal to respond was in itself consistent with the imperial tendency to hold no dialogue with or listen to Two-Thirds World races.[8] In this fashion, Daly's homogenizing discourse, like that of many other Western feminist writers, remains within the parameters of the larger imperial discourse of domination.

Laura Donaldson, on the other hand, focuses on how Western feminist reading practices maintain the imperial rhetorical strategies of subjugation. The maintenance is characterized by omission in interpretation of texts. Donaldson analyzes nineteenth-and twentieth-century novels and the movies produced from these books, and finds that critics have systematically bracketed imperial textual constructions of subjugation. She finds readers and film producers using "anti-sexist rhetoric to displace questions of colonialism, racism, and their concomitant violence."[9] This bracketing is accomplished through concentrating on white women characters without questioning either the authority and rule of white travelers and explorers in foreign lands or the portrait of non-Western characters in English novels, films, and paintings. Thus, feminist readings have also bracketed the challenge of exposing and critiquing imperialist ideologies in cultural texts, hence participating in their maintenance.

---

[7]See Audre Lorde, *Sister Outsider: Essays and Speeches* (Freedom, Calif.: Crossing Press, 1984), 66–71.

[8]See also Mazrui, who calls the tendency of North America to distribute its ideas and goods to the utmost corners of the Third World while refusing to listen to non-Westerners "a dialogue of the deaf," *Cultural Forces,* 116–29.

[9]Laura Donaldson, *Decolonizing Feminisms: Race, Gender, & Empire-Building* (Chapel Hill: University of North Carolina Press, 1992), 62.

In sum, the problem that is described by Mohanty and Donaldson demonstrates the failure to recognize the connection of imperial domination with cultural texts. Mohanty shows this to be a problem of writing without assessing and avoiding imperial textual paradigms. Donaldson, on the other hand, shows that it is a problem of reading imperialist texts without exposing their colonizing literary strategies.

The failure of Western feminists to recognize and to subvert imperialist cultural strategies of subjugation means that their advocacy for women's liberation has firmly retained the right of the West to dominate and exploit non-Western nations. This necessitates a move toward postcolonial feminist interpretation, since most Two-Thirds World women are alienated from participating fully in the articulation of women's liberation precisely because they recognize their counterparts to be jealously guarding their imperialist traditions. This position has complicated the relationship of international women's movements, hindering the formation of strategic coalitions that go beyond narrow identity politics. However, much will be won by adopting postcolonial feminist practices and strategies that are not complacent about the imperialistic agendas, a factor that is pertinent to biblical feminisms.

Colonized or Colonizing Biblical Feminisms

The problem of reproducing imperial strategies of subjugation is also evident among Western feminist biblical practitioners. To highlight this problem, Schüssler Fiorenza's monumental reconstructionist efforts toward putting women back into history will be discussed, as well as some voices of Two-Thirds World and non-Christian feminists. An assessment of some aspects of Schüssler Fiorenza's latest works, which define feminist biblical practice as a rhetorical-hermeneutics informed by the logic of radical democracy/equality, rather than the logic of Western identity, will also be carried out. Last, African Independent Churches' (henceforth AICs) women readers will be introduced for their paradigm of resisting both imperialism and patriarchy.

The particular focus on Schüssler Fiorenza's works is prompted by three reasons: First, her interests are relevant to my focus on missionary stories of travel and their ideology; second, her work is certainly among the most thorough and influential in biblical feminism; third, Schüssler Fiorenza has consistently defined her feminist hermeneutics as theological, a factor that makes it somehow easier to relate to Two-Thirds World women, who tend to be religious.

Two interrelated aspects of Schüssler Fiorenza's arguments will be addressed: her earliest efforts to put women back into history, and her recent efforts in feminist biblical interpretation as a rhetorical practice. Each of these points will be discussed in conjunction with her idea of the *ekklesia* of women. My aim is to show that these efforts, for all their liberational intentions, promises, and major contributions, have inscribed themselves within the imperial rhetoric of subjugation. More importantly, my aim is to highlight that the challenges and demands of the postcolonial era must be confronted, for unless the pervasiveness and persistence of imperial rhetoric in reality and texts, through ancient and current times and over different people and places, is recognized, studied, and called into question, its reinscription will be inevitable, even among well-meaning feminists. And, worse, it will continue to hinder the building of meaningful coalitions that go beyond narrow identity politics among international feminists.

Restoring Women to History

Schüssler Fiorenza's aim in reconstructing early Christian origins is not only to put women back into history but also to "restore the history of Christian beginnings to women."[10] Unlike post-Christian feminists who have deserted Christian traditions, declaring them irredeemably patriarchal, Schüssler Fiorenza holds that "Western women are not able to discard completely and forget our personal, cultural, or religious Christian history."[11] She insists on a reconstructive project that will place women at the center of early Christian history, "because it is precisely the power of oppression that deprives people of their history."[12] In other words, for Western women to surrender their heritage is to surrender their power. Schüssler Fiorenza undertakes this major project because the patriarchal authors of biblical texts, compilers, readers, and translators of the past and present, as well as the church and academy have authorized the marginalization of women in the society in general. Also, these texts are not just ancient books, but scriptures that continue to affect women and men. Therefore, Schüssler Fiorenza seeks to develop a feminist heuristic model that will enable her to reclaim Christian history as women's history and to place them at the center of the early church's missionary movement, not as subordinates but as equal partners.

In doing this, she uses a feminist historiography that works around the present biblical canon with patriarchal occlusion of women and its androcentric practitioners, in order to reconstruct a canon of the discipleship of equals, which places women and men at the center of early Christian beginnings. This allows her to show that many women of various economic and social standings, such as Prisca, Lydia, Junia, and Phoebe, were active missionaries in the early church who traveled to spread the gospel and who used their property to house the churches, in spite of the androcentric interpretations and translations that have excluded women's presence and contributions.

---

[10]Elisabeth Schüssler Fiorenza, *In Memory of Her: A Feminist Theological Reconstruction of Christian Origins* (New York: Crossroad, 1983), xx.

[11]Ibid., xix.

[12]Ibid.

Clearly, Schüssler Fiorenza's reconstructive efforts are ethically motivated and committed to the empowerment of Western women. Nevertheless, her reconstructive efforts, with all their ethical commitments and rhetorical influence on biblical studies in general, have bracketed imperial prescriptions and constructions of the biblical texts; hence, they have maintained the violence of imperial oppression against non-Western and non-Christian biblical feminists. The bracketing of imperialism takes two interrelated forms: downplaying the imperial setting of the early Christian origins and demonstrating no effort to expose its ideology and its impact.

In her reconstruction of early Christian origins, Schüssler Fiorenza downplays the imperial setting by constantly referring to the Roman Empire as "the Roman world," "the Greco-Roman world," and Rome as a "political center" and not an imperial center. She speaks of "the dominant patriarchal ethos of the Greco-Roman world," of the "existing social order" and the "Hellenistic-Roman" world as patriarchal, without explicitly pointing out that it was also an imperial world, and that imperialism is a system of oppression that demands attention in any liberational endeavor.[13] Thus, her reconstruction presents the final occlusion of women in early church history as "the struggle between the emerging Christian movement and its alternative vision, on the one hand, and the dominant patriarchal ethos of the Greco-Roman world on the other," that is, "a shift in cultural horizons."[14] This presentation sets up the patriarchal oppression by Gentile and Jewish men of women as the main oppression of women in the Roman world. The Roman imperial oppression of the Jewish people, both women and men, as well as of other colonized peoples, is sidestepped.

Under this occlusion of the imperial oppression, the Jesus movement is then presented as an independent movement that critiques the patriarchal Judaic structures or the existing social order of the Roman world in general. As a result, the oppression of imperial Rome, a central factor in the collaboration of the elites of Israel and the subsequent tightening of cultural boundaries that further marginalized women in Judaism, does not arise. The very rise of the Jesus movement and various other groups such as the Pharisees, Zealots, Essenes, or Qumran communities, who sought to offer alternative visions given the imperial occupation and the imposition of its culture, its economy, and its political leadership, become hidden in Schüssler Fiorenza's reconstruction. Likewise, that the lowest class of any colonized people always bears the brunt of imperial subjugation is not related to the fact that the Jesus movement consisted of poor peasants, who had to pay taxes and live with little or no land and hence became very critical of the collaborating elites of their nation.[15] These factors disappear

---

[13]Ibid., xxiii, 67, 73, 77, 82, 99, 100, 103, 160, 164, 175, 176.
[14]Ibid., 92, 82.
[15]See Richard A. Horsley, *Sociology and the Jesus Movement* (New York: Crossroad, 1989), 67–144.

in Schüssler Fiorenza's reconstruction. In the process, her critique blames the victims of imperialism, equates them with the imperialist oppressor, and hides their exploitation.

Second, Schüssler Fiorenza brackets and maintains imperial violence by not exposing its ideology or addressing its impact in history. Because Schüssler Fiorenza does not recognize imperialism as a distinct form of exploitation that denies women and men of foreign lands their political, cultural, and economic autonomy by imposing its systems of power for its own benefit, her reconstruction is not in a position to recognize and to subvert the ideological strategies of imperialism. For instance, asking about the ideology of imperialism would problematize the transformation of the Jesus movement from a movement of exploited rural peasants in a colonized territory to a movement of urban dwellers, with a fair number of self-sufficient professionals or artisans, in the Roman imperial cities; from being a resistance movement within the colonized Jews to a missionary-oriented religion of the Gentiles in the empire. Neither are the implications of adopting imperial structural forms of the time such as the household and the client-patronage system, regardless of women's leadership, seriously problematized.[16] Likewise, the ideology behind the compatibility of Christian missionaries and imperialism in history, that is, why and how they have been compatible through various times and places, is not questioned. Consequently, in her efforts to place women at the center of early Christian origins, Schüssler Fiorenza inscribes her reconstruction within the oppressive discourse of imperialism.

The maintenance of imperial strategies of subjugation becomes evident when Schüssler Fiorenza reconstructs the theological self-understanding of early Christian missionaries. She celebrates the "proclamation of the *universal* lordship of Christ-Sophia addressed to the Hellenistic world," and she unproblematically holds that "Jesus Christ the Sophia of God...appears on earth and is now exalted as the Lord of *all cosmos,*" and that "the pre-Pauline "temple tradition" understands the Christian community as temple in order *to distinguish it from the unbelieving world*" (emphasis mine).[17] According to Schüssler Fiorenza,

> this movement stresses that women and men are the children of God, the Holy people, the temple community among whom the Spirit dwells. The boundaries here are not drawn between women and men, Jewish and gentile Christians, but between believers and unbelievers. Faith in Christ Jesus and not religion, race, or sex, draws the line between the holy community and the domain of Belial, the temple of God and idol worship.[18]

---

[16]See Wayne Meeks, *The Moral World of the First Christians* (Philadelphia: Westminster Press, 1986), 32–38.

[17]Schüssler Fiorenza, *In Memory of Her,* 190, 193.

[18]Ibid., 196.

This reconstruction is liberating and inclusive because it allows women and men to be equal participants of the holy community temple and to travel, proclaiming the universal Sophia of God. Ironically, dualism and hierarchy, as ideological constructions that are recognized for denying gender difference and equality, are not further questioned when they pertain to different cultures. On the contrary, Schüssler Fiorenza gladly embraces the dualism of "the holy community and the domain of Belial," "the temple of God and idol worship," and "believers and non-believers" without recognizing these binary oppositions as prescriptive constructions whose main aim is to deny cultural differences between men and women of diverse races, religions, and nations and that have been at the core of Western imperial self-validation.

Similarly, the implications of demolished boundaries or space—the temple, which is now replaced by a mobile community of holy Christians traveling under the authority of Jesus, the Sophia of God, the "Lord of all cosmos"—is not problematized. Its mobility, however, disavows specific geographical and cultural boundaries in order to claim the whole world—an ideology that finally authorizes imperialism. In sum, Schüssler Fiorenza's reconstruction is an option for Christian women, but it embraces dualism, universalism, and hierarchical constructions that validate and characterize imperialist strategies of subjugation on non-Christian/non-Western cultures. Her reading makes a good example of the use of what Donaldson has termed "anti-sexist rhetoric to displace questions of colonialism." But because it entertains imperial strategies of subjugation, its option for women becomes seriously compromised to the point where it is simply spelled out as reclaiming a heritage to empower white, Western Christian women to compete with white, Western Christian men in dominating the world. And for my concerns, this alienates Two-Thirds World and non-Christian women from participating fully in the feminist biblical discourse.

Schüssler Fiorenza's reconstruction to privilege gender oppression over imperialism is not unique to her. Many other Western liberationists always seem inclusive, but when it comes to application, their theories restrict full liberation to Western white people, as attested by such outstanding liberationists as Abraham Lincoln, Karl Marx, Elizabeth Cady Stanton, Mary Daly, and so on. Schüssler Fiorenza is also faithful to this paradigm. By so doing, she subscribes to the right of the West and its Christian traditions to impose and dominate women (and men) of Africa, Asia, and Latin America; the natives of settler colonies of North America, Australia, and Canada; and Jews, who have experienced the violence of the Christian imperialist ideology. It is an ideology that proceeds by devaluing different cultures with constructions such as "idol worship," or "domain of Belial," or "unbelievers." This mention of the Other women brings me to the second point in Schüssler Fiorenza's reconstructive efforts, namely, *the ekklesia* of women.

Inscribing Authority on Women

Schüssler Fiorenza defines the *ekklesia* of women as the hermeneutical center of feminist biblical interpretation. Its goal is "to assert women's religious power and liberation from all patriarchal alienation, marginalization, and oppression."[19] As a theoretical articulation, the *ekklesia* of women holds out hope to all feminists struggling for liberation. Therefore, I bring it up here precisely to highlight how the collaboration of Schüssler Fiorenza's liberational discourse undercuts its liberational intentions and alienates Two-Thirds World and non-Christian women—to the extent that the *ekklesia* of women is almost equivalent to the *ekklesia* of white, middle-class Christian feminists.

Schüssler Fiorenza holds that "the locus of divine revelation and grace is therefore not the Bible or the tradition of a patriarchal church, but the *ekklesia* of women and the lives of women who live the option for our women selves."[20] The strength of this theoretical articulation is that authority is transferred from oppressive biblical texts to the various voices of biblical and theological feminists naming and subverting oppression as they have encountered it. Moreover, the *ekklesia* of women seems to fully embrace equality, solidarity, and inclusivity, as Schüssler Fiorenza asserts that "patriarchy cannot be toppled except when the women who form the bottom of the pyramid, triply oppressed women, become liberated. All women's oppression and liberation is bound with that of the colonized and economically most exploited women."[21] In short, authority is supposedly in the voices of various feminists struggling to articulate liberation from the oppressive biblical texts: that is, in all women from the Two-Thirds World and the One-Third World; from non-Christian and Christian traditions. This is where theory and practice fall apart. That is, while a casual look at Two-Thirds World and non-Christian feminists' writings suggests that the devaluing of their religious traditions through Western imperial Christianity is a central concern, Schüssler Fiorenza's reconstruction of the theological understanding of early Christians, on the other hand, subscribes to the dismissal of non-Christian traditions. The following brief look at women of the Two-Thirds World and non-Christian biblical feminists will highlight the point.

Voices of Other Women

Mercy Oduyoye and Elizabeth Amoah in their article "The Christ for African Women" assertively say, "Most Christians refer to Scripture meaning the Hebrew Bible and its supplement, the New Testament, but we would

---

[19]Elisabeth Schüssler Fiorenza, "The Will to Choose or to Reject: Continuing Our Critical Work," in *Feminist Interpretation of the Bible,* ed. Letty Russell (Philadelphia: Westminster Press, 1985), 126.

[20]Ibid., 127.

[21]Ibid.

like to start with a reference to the "unwritten scriptures" of the Fante of Ghana."[22] They insist that "all communities have their stories of persons whose individual acts have had lasting effects on the destiny and ethos of the whole group."[23] The reasons for reaffirming their religions, alongside their biblical faith, is made much more explicit by Rosemary Edet and Bette Ekeya in their article "Church Women of Africa: A Theological Community." They observe that among African people there is "alienation because evangelization has not been that of cultural exchange but of cultural domination or assimilation," resulting in "a loss of cultural and material identity."[24] They conclude by asserting that "African women theologians have the task of reclaiming the theological heritage stored in the participation of African women in traditional religions."[25]

Similarly, Kwok Pui-lan, a Chinese woman, holds that in the nineteenth century "the Bible was a 'signifier' of a basic deficiency in the 'heathen' culture. This is a Western construction superimposed on other cultures to show that Western culture is the norm and it is superior."[26] Hammering on this concern, Kwok Pui-lan emphatically says, "Other religious feminists such as Jewish, Muslim, Buddhist, and Goddess worshippers…would be watching carefully what Christian feminists have to say on the uniqueness of the Christian faith."[27] She leaves no doubt about why they are watching, but asserts,

> For a very long period of history, the institutionalized Christian Church has adopted a vehemently exclusivist position in talking about truth, revelation, the Bible, and Christ. When missionaries arrived in Asia, Africa, and Latin America, trying to convert people, they condemned our ancestors, trashed our gods and goddesses and severed us from our indigenous cultures. Many missionaries, both male and female, accused indigenous traditions of being oppressive to women without the slightest recognition of the sexist ideology of Christianity.[28]

---

[22]Elizabeth Amoah and Mercy Oduyoye, "The Christ for African Women," in *With Passion and Compassion: Third World Women Doing Theology,* ed. Virginia Fabella and Mercy Amba Oduyoye (Maryknoll, N.Y.: Orbis Books, 1990), 35.

[23]Ibid., 36.

[24]Rosemary Edet and Bette Ekeya, "Church Women of Africa," in *With Passion and Compassion: Third World Women Doing Theology,* 3.

[25]Ibid., 9.

[26]Kwok Pui-lan, "Discovering the Bible in the Non-Biblical World," in *Voices from the Margin: Interpreting the Bible in the Third World,* ed. R. S. Sugirtharajah (Maryknoll, N.Y.: Orbis Books, 1991), 301.

[27]Kwok Pui-lan, "Doing Theology from Third World Women's Perspective," in *Feminist Theology from the Third World: A Reader,* ed. Ursula King (Maryknoll, N.Y.: Orbis Books, 1994), 63.

[28]Ibid., 68.

Carol Devens-Green, a Native American, also points out that in the nineteenth century,

> young Americans, inspired by the Great Commission "Go into the World and preach the gospel to the whole creation" (Mark 16:15), flocked to mission boards. They yearned to bring the light of the Gospels to the "heathens" who, they assumed, would gratefully accept both the Word and the culture that accompanied it. Believing that Christianity and "civilization" were synonymous, they were convinced that native ways must be abandoned to achieve salvation.[29]

In a similar note, Amy-Jill Levine, a Jewish woman, begins her commentary on "The Sibylline Oracles" by asserting that "I engage texts in pursuit of a feminist and Jewish agenda...my work seeks to counter in particular those who would view Judaism as monolithic, as having ended in Golgotha, or as a singularly repressive foil to a more sexually egalitarian reading of Christian origins."[30]

One gathers similar currents from a Hispanic author, Ada Maria Isasi-Diaz, in her article, "*La Palabra de Dios en Nostras*–The Word of God in Us," where she presents the *mujerista* biblical hermeneutics. In doing this, Isasi-Diaz advocates a "non-biblical Christianity" because, as she says, "it has been a good vehicle for the inclusion of Amerindian and African beliefs and practices in our *mestizo*, an inclusion at the heart of popular religiosity."[31]

These quotations highlight several points. First, the Christian imperialist stance of devaluing other religious cultures is not peripheral to the liberational quest of non-Christian and non-Western Christian feminists. Second, any feminist endeavor that seeks to recognize inclusivity, solidarity, and equality in the hermeneutical center should question why Christianity has been unique in imperial sponsorship. Third, it is evident that a central part of their resistance involves the reaffirmation of their various religious traditions, denigrated by Western Christian practitioners and texts. Fourth, cultural domination is connected to material loss, economic loss. Finally, the quotations underscore my point that there is a major problem necessitating a postcolonial feminist biblical practice, one that recognizes that the world is already inscribed within the parameters of imperial domination, collaboration, and resistance, and that the Bible is intrinsically involved in all these. Therefore, as biblical feminists, we can only ignore the

---

[29]Carol Devens-Green, "Native American Women, Missionaries, and Scriptures," in *Searching the Scriptures, A Feminist Introduction,* vol. 1, ed. Elisabeth Schüssler Fiorenza (New York: Crossroad, 1993), 131.

[30]Amy-Jill Levine, "The Sibylline Oracles," in *Searching the Scriptures: A Feminist Commentary,* vol. 2, ed. Elisabeth Schüssler Fiorenza (New York: Crossroad, 1995), 99.

[31]Ada Maria Isasi-Diaz, "*La Palabra de Dios en Nostras*–The Word of God in Us," in *Searching the Scriptures,* vol. 1, 90.

challenges and demands of postcolonialism in our practice at the risk of reinscribing imperial violence and hindering the creation of meaningful coalitions among women of various cultural backgrounds.

The above review, however, reflects Schüssler Fiorenza's earliest works. At this stage, I turn to some of her recent works to assess briefly how her feminist discourse of liberation avoids or writes into imperialist strategies of the West. I will look at her effort to construct feminist biblical interpretation as a rhetorical practice, that is, situating "biblical scholarship in such a way that its public character and political responsibility become integral parts of our literary readings and historical reconstructions of the biblical world."[32] I will assess whether her own practice is faithful to its theoretical articulation in the *ekklesia* of women, which is now described as a hermeneutical space informed by a radical logic of democracy/equality rather than the logic of Western identity. In particular, I will comment on three aspects: patriarchy as *kyriarchal;* reading the Canaanite/Syro-Phoenician from a historical-rhetorical perspective; and the project *Searching the Scriptures,* volume 2.

The Rhetorical Space of Radical Democracy

In her book *But She Said,* Schüssler Fiorenza underscores an extended struggle with international systems of oppression and exploitation as she works out a rhetorical feminist practice of biblical interpretation. One of her major questions is, "How can feminist biblical hermeneutics situate its readings of the Bible in such a way that they do not reinscribe the patriarchal discourse of subordination and obedience."[33] As she says, her concerns are informed by Two-Thirds World and socialist feminists, who have continually called into question the white middle-class feminist discourse for subscribing to cultural imperialism and privileging gender oppression over other forms of oppression. This project leads her to seek a much more profound understanding of patriarchy as "a pyramid of interlocking dominations."[34] Schüssler Fiorenza proposes the *ekklesia* of women as a feminist hermeneutical space informed by the logic of radical democracy rather than the Western logic of identity.

To begin with patriarchy, Schüssler Fiorenza, who has always had a wider understanding of this term, seeks to move feminist biblical interpretation from an understanding of patriarchy as a sex-gender system to an understanding of patriarchy as a pyramid of multiplicative oppression. In the latter understanding, patriarchy is not merely a rule of the father but a *kyriarchal* system, the rule of the master/Lord, whereby "elite propertied men have power over those subordinate to and dependent on them."[35]

[32]Schüssler Fiorenza, *But She Said,* 45.
[33]Ibid., 5.
[34]Ibid., 6.
[35]Ibid., 117.

This patriarchal system, according to Schüssler Fiorenza, was characteristic of Greek democracy and informed the contemporary Western understanding of democracy. The *kyriarchal* democratic system was stratified according to class, gender, and race. Beginning from the bottom, it consisted of slaves, freed persons, tenants and clients, freeborn children and kin, lady of the house, professional workers, and, at the highest peak, free, propertied Greek men. The latter formed the *ekklesia* and represented civilization and culture. Below the bottom of the pyramid, there were foreign societies, regarded as uncultured barbarians, living in an uncivilized wilderness.

Schüssler Fiorenza, however, holds that the Greek patriarchal democracy was not interested in a universal political order. Therefore, Western history was also informed by the Roman imperial/colonialist monarchical pyramid of the patriarchal household. The latter supposedly adds the universal perspective to the Greek system and transforms it into an imperialist democracy. According to Schüssler Fiorenza, the modern Western democracy is modeled after

> classical patriarchal discourse [that] was inscribed in Christian Scriptures, re-articulated in Christian theology, and reproduced in modern political science. This discourse emerges in varied ways: it manifests itself in the Enlightenment philosophers' construction of the "Man of Reason," it surfaces in Euro-American racist discourses on the "White Lady," and in the Western colonialist depiction of "inferior races" and "uncivilized savages." Indeed, like the "White Lady," Christian religion was considered to be a civilizing force among the savages.[36]

With this understanding of patriarchy as a *kyriarchal* pyramid of interlocking systems of domination, Schüssler Fiorenza names Eurocentricism as "universal kyriocentric," that is, the rule of white fathers and "white elite women of Christian religion" insofar as "they have served as civilizing conduits of patriarchal knowledge, values, religion, and culture."[37] Instead of reinscribing this Western logic of hierarchical democracy, Schüssler Fiorenza suggests that a rhetorical feminist biblical interpretation must articulate "an oppositional democratic imagination." She proposes the *ekklesia* of women as a feminist rhetorical space marked by a shift from the "Western logic of identity" to the "logic of radical equality."

Basically, this is an admirable theoretical articulation that seeks to get to the roots of the Western *kyriarchal* system. As the above quotation shows, Schüssler Fiorenza's argument resonates with Mudimbe and Mazrui, but it does not adopt ideological criticisms and suggestions advanced by Dickson

---

[36]Ibid., 122.
[37]Ibid., 123.

and Banana. Besides, there are a number of problems with this definition of patriarchy/*kyriarchy* as imperialism.

First, I find the attempt to define patriarchy as imperialism potentially co-optive, because even colonized people have their various forms of hier-archical and stratified patriarchal systems, but they are not equivalent to imperialism. The collapsing of patriarchy and imperialism does not help to keep Western women clearly aware of a different form of oppression in which they participate. It complicates the conversation between non-Western and Western women by mystifying imperialism. The attempt to shy away from the word *imperialism* is, in fact, consistent with Western structures that have avoided this terminology in order to maintain its dominance.[38] Consequently, a question needs to be asked and clearly explicated as to what differentiates patriarchy from imperialism and what transforms a patriarchy into imperialism. For instance, Schüssler Fiorenza holds that Greek democracy was not interested in a universal political or-der, yet, as we know, prior to the Roman Empire, Alexander the Great (332–323 B.C.E.) led his armies to establish an empire unparalled in Greek history.[39]

Second, the description of *kyriarchy* as imperialism is useful but has its limitations. It is useful because it allows one to comprehend why it is a distinctively Western thing to construct different people negatively, as at-tested by the discourses of Orientalism and Savage Africa. This is in fact the universalized Western ethic; perhaps, in recent times, one can speak of Western patriarchy as synonymous with imperialism. At the same time, it is limited for a number of reasons. First, the terminology is just another way of mystifying imperialism. Second, while a *kyriarchal* system occurs when "elite propertied men have power over those subordinate to and dependent upon them," imperialism is more than that.[40] Imperialism in-cludes ruling other propertied men and women, who in fact do not need to depend on their subjugators. It involves constructing the subjugated in such a way that they finally believe they need to depend on their rulers, as well as creating structures that will finally keep them dependent. Also, unlike *kyriarchy,* imperialism involves both propertied and poor classes, men and women of certain nations acting together to dominate distant nations and races by imposing their systems of power. In fact, poor women and men of colonizing nations assume massive power once they enter colo-nized spaces.

Third, the idea of the *ekklesia* of women is problematic because it is an attempt to occupy the highest class of Western/white male *kyriarchal* democracy. This ideal dangerously befriends imperialist tendencies, for it

---

[38]See Mary Louise Pratt, *Imperial Eyes: Travel Writing and Transculturation* (New York: Routledge, 1992), 2.

[39]John Stambaugh and David L. Balch, *The New Testament in Its Social Environment* (Phila-delphia: Westminster Press, 1986), 13–14.

[40]Schüssler Fiorenza, *But She Said,* 117, 123.

also invites women from different cultures to yearn for and attempt to occupy the place of a white male, a position usually unreachable but set up for the subjugated to keep imitating the empire. Schüssler Fiorenza's ideal can, however, be redeemed by faithfulness to its terms, that is, the logic of radical democracy/equality. As I understand it, the logic of radical democracy, at a national level, should be a practice that no longer wants to include and construct people as unequal subjects along race, gender, religion, and class categories. At an international level, it should be a practice committed to deliberate efforts not to construct foreigners and their cultures negatively nor to impose one's cultural, economic, and political standards, but to affirm differences and to seek liberating interdependency. Anything short of this theoretical commitment to the logic of radical democracy will cause the *ekklesia* of women to emerge cloaked in the white male discourse of imperial domination.

Despite these criticisms, I do believe that Schüssler Fiorenza's theoretical articulations of *kyriarchy* and *ekklesia* of women do go a long way toward counteracting imperialism, if followed. The question is, therefore, does Schüssler Fiorenza honor her theoretical goals in her rhetorical-hermeneutical practice? Does she abide by the logic of radical democracy/equality, or does she slide into the logic of Western identity? A brief assessment of her historical-rhetorical reading of the Syro-Phoenician/Canaanite woman and *Searching the Scriptures,* volume 2, will address these questions.

Schüssler Fiorenza rereads the story of the Syro-Phoenician/Canaanite woman from a feminist historical-rhetorical perspective. Since this is a mission story, a narrative that validates universalism, one expects Schüssler Fiorenza to be cautious not to reproduce the *kyriarchal* relationships. Indeed, one expects her reading to be strictly obedient to the logic of radical democracy. Therefore, how it constructs foreign people, how it conceives power relations between women and men, between classes and races, and between nations and religions should be subject to a critical feminist-rhetorical analysis—an analysis underlining "its public character and political responsibility." Schüssler Fiorenza, however, quickly activates the reading of *In Memory of Her.* She wants to make the Syro-Phoenician woman "visible again as one of the apostolic foremothers of the Gentile Christians," for "by moving her into the center of the debate about mission to the Gentiles, the historical centrality of Paul in this debate becomes relativized."[41] Evidently, the debate does not dwell on how the mission is conceived and how the power relations it advocates may duplicate *kyriarchal* domination. Schüssler Fiorenza is not primarily suspicious that the characterization of this foreign woman as a helpless dog, begging for crumbs from the master's table, evokes a *kyriarchal* ideology of subordination. Her argument, however, is still a credible rhetorical approach to the androcentric interpreters

---

[41]Ibid., 97.

in the Western academy and the church. Unfortunately, when the argument is perceived in this way, the reading becomes a debate between white Western Christian women and white Western Christian men seeking to share in the power of dominating the whole world. Schüssler Fiorenza's reading thus falls short of the logic of radical democracy in the *ekklesia* of women and remains inscribed within the imperial ideology of domination of non-Western and non-Christian worlds. Consequently, it alienates the Other women, who have been constructed as helpless dogs, heathens, and savages in order to validate their subjugation.

With regard to *Searching the Scriptures,* volume 2, it is a feminist "commentary that seeks to transgress canonical boundaries in order...to undo the exclusionary *kyriarchal* tendencies of the ruling canon."[42] It seeks "to bring to the fore and make audible again the subjugated voices and suppressed traditions that left traces in ancient writings."[43] It is notable that, unlike *In Memory of Her,* in her recent works, Schüssler Fiorenza speaks of the Roman Empire, names its needs, scrutinizes its ideology, and suggests that its systems of power were central factors in the selection and suppression of differences in the formation of biblical canon. She holds that the current biblical "canon reflects an androcentric selection process and that it has functioned to incalculate a *kyriarchal* imperial order."[44] Schüssler Fiorenza holds that by "recognizing these harmful effects of the early Christian struggles over canonization as a means to the *kyriarchal* co-optation of the *ekklesia,* feminist biblical scholarship cannot remain within the limits drawn by the established canon."[45]

All this is well put and powerful, but does it obey the logic of radical democracy in its practical application? To begin with, to transgress the boundaries by dealing with Christian-Jewish extracanonical texts is a comfortable way of rocking the boat, given that male biblical scholars have always dealt with these texts. The approach is especially comfortable when compared with Canaan Banana's case for a new Bible, one that considers all world perceptions of the divine as worthy of affirmation and study. *Searching the Scriptures,* volume 2's transgression of boundaries, therefore, does not go far enough. It does not stand up to the stretch of the imperial suppression of differences at a global scale. It does not take seriously that the Bible is a Western book and the West is an imperial center. Yet this is still a radical logic of equality insofar as Christian and Jewish Western feminists are concerned. Insofar as the majority of the Two-Thirds World is concerned, the project is one of

> inviting feminist scholars in religion from around the world to
> bring their expertise and perspectives to this celebration...to

---

[42]Schüssler Fiorenza, "Transgressing the Boundaries," in *Searching the Scriptures,* vol. 2, 5.
[43]Ibid., 4.
[44]Ibid., 8.
[45]Ibid.

internationalize the ongoing common feminist struggles and ecumenical-interreligious conversations regarding the cultural heritage of ancient Christian and Jewish writings.[46]

In short, the logic of radical democracy invites international women to the *ekklesia* as long as they speak the language of the "civilized" and the "cultured" and not necessarily to bring traditions that were devalued by Western *kyriarchal* logic and to seek out liberating ways of coexistence—a move that would truly destabilize the exclusionary and subversive center. The irony lies in that while this project recognizes that the Roman imperial church suppressed and marginalized voices that must be resurrected, this practice is only applied to the Christian and Jewish cultural texts. The approach ignores the fact that modern Western empires, their Christian churches, and their texts have suppressed the religious texts of the Two-Thirds World and natives of the Americas, Australia, and Canada. The approach also ignores the writers from these places who constantly make it known and affirm their suppressed texts. This, to me, is what amounts to "a dialogue of the deaf": the power of the First World to close its ears to the voices of the Two-Thirds World while it disseminates its ideas and material goods to them.[47] The point, however, is that the lack of dialogue makes it questionable whether the authority lies in the feminist voices of women or in patriarchal and imperialistic Western texts. If authority is still in feminist voices, there is a need to qualify these voices. As it stands, they can hardly be identified with the Two-Thirds World feminist voices.

The demands and challenges of the postcolonial era, however, do not allow for this approach anymore. The implication of the postcolonial era is that the Christian Bible no longer coexists with Jewish texts alone, as I believe it never did even in ancient times, but with many other texts of the world. The Bible no longer belongs to Western Christians alone; rather, Two-Thirds World people, including the natives of North America, Canada, and Australia, have had the Bible ever since the days when their lands were taken during a prayer. We therefore need a model of reading that takes seriously the presence of both imperialism and patriarchy, and seeks for liberating interdependence between genders, races, nations, economies, cultures, political structures, and so on. A brief introduction to the AICs women readers paves the way to such reading practices.

Semoya Readers: African Independent Churches Women

African Independent Churches (AICs)[48] denote a group of churches that began as a protest movement against the white-male-only leadership

---

[46]Ibid., 3.

[47]Mazrui, *Cultural Forces,* 116–27.

[48]An earlier version of what appears as pages 40–43 has been published as Musa W. Dube, "Readings of *Semoya*: Batswana Women's Interpretations of Matt. 15:21–28," *Semeia* 73 (1996): 111–29.

in the missionary-founded churches of the nineteenth century.[49] African Christians walked out of the Western-founded churches and began their own, where they could serve God with all their gifts and freedom. As Mosala correctly explains, the name "African Independent Churches connotes a specifically religious vision of the wider African struggle for liberation from colonialism, capitalism, racism, and cultural chauvinism."[50] Their protest was, therefore, not only closely tied to the beginning of political liberation movements against colonial rule, it was in itself a resistance to Western cultural imperialism. Colonial preachers

> appeared determined to instill in their converts...Western values and distaste especially for traditional religious values and culture, which were considered inferior and primitive. African converts were expected to adopt a new identity based on the Western-Christian order. Africans as a whole were not convinced about the inferiority of their religious and cultural values.[51]

This continued assertion of African religious worldviews in the face of structured derogation was in itself an act of political resistance against cultural imperialism.

Therefore, the rise of AICs marked the earliest groups of African Christians who freely sought to yoke the wisdom of biblical and African religions in the service of life and diversity. In keeping with the language of song, drama, dance, symbols, and ritual, such a creative integration was hardly characterized by an academic interpretation of scripture or a systematic theological debate according to Western theological orthodoxy. Instead, the discourse of cultural interdependence unfolded itself informed, guided, and justified by perceptions of what enhances and restores life in God's creation. It is this approach that has made the AIC the biggest church on the African continent in terms of its membership, its distribution, and its growth rate. Its membership represents not only those who have a high appreciation of both African and biblical religious perspectives, but primarily those who will not let cultural imperialism stand in the way of listening for and hearing the Spirit in order to serve God's creation.

Various studies of AICs show that pneumatology is central to the approach of these churches.[52] *Moya,* "the Spirit," is an ever-present agent of God among all the believers. Women and men receive the Spirit, which

---

[49]See John B. Ngubane, "Theological Roots of the African Independent Churches and Their Challenge to Black Theology," in *The Unquestionable Right to Be Free: Black Theology from South Africa,* ed. Itumeleng Mosala and Buti Tlhagale (Maryknoll, N. Y.: Orbis Books, 1986), 71–90, for the rise of AICs.

[50]See Itumeleng Mosala, "Race, Class, and Gender as Hermeneutical Factors in the African Independent Churches' Appropriation of the Bible," *Semeia* 73 (1996): 44.

[51]Ngubane, "Theological Roots of the AICs," 75.

[52]See Inus Daneel, *Quest for Belonging* (Gweru:Mambo Press, 1987), 259–63; G. C. Oosthuizen, *Post-Christianity in Africa: A Theological and Anthropological Study* (London: C. Hurst, 1968), 119–42.

empowers them to prophesy, heal the sick, assist those searching for jobs, restore family relations, ensure a good harvest and good rains, ensure good reproduction of livestock, and dispel the ever-intruding forces of evil from people's lives. Healing, as a manifestation of the presence of the Spirit, is an act of restoring life as a whole. The centrality of the *Moya* as an agent of restoration through healing has earned these churches the name *Dikereke tsa Semoya,* "Churches of the Spirit," while the healing manifestation of the Spirit has also earned them the name of *Dikereke tsa Phodiso,* "Churches of Healing."

Interestingly, women have always played a central role in these churches as founders, bishops, archbishops, prophets, faith healers, preachers, and ministers.[53] In fact, the rise of AICs and their spirit of protest and integration of religious cultures is traced to a woman, Kimpa Vita, a Congolese Catholic Christian who was renamed Donna Beatrice at baptism. Kimpa Vita proclaimed that the Spirit of Saint Anthony had taken possession of her. Empowered by the Spirit, Kimpa Vita's preaching became "a powerful protest against the Catholic Church" and the colonial government.[54] She wanted all crosses, crucifixes, and images of Christ in the Catholic Church to be destroyed because, as she said, they were just as good as the old fetishes. She proclaimed that God would restore the subjugated kingdom of Kongo. Of significance, however, was Kimpa Vita's articulation of a culturally integrated Christianity. She held that Christ came into the world as an African in Sao Salvador and that he had black apostles. Inus Daneel places this proclamation within its proper anti-imperialist context by observing that "her proclamation gave expression to a deep yearning: the yearning for a Christ who would identify with the despised African," for "how could the White Christ of the Portuguese images, the Christ of the exploiters—how could he ever help the suffering African, pining for liberty?"[55]

With this radically subversive proclamation for both the colonial church and government, Kimpa Vita was recognized as a dangerous thinker. She was thus condemned to death and was burned at the stake in 1706. The centrality of women in AICs, however, could not be ended with the martyrdom of Kimpa Vita. A line of other women ever since has heard and responded to the word of the Spirit to serve as church founders, leaders, prophets, and faith healers.[56] Outstanding among these are Ma Nku,

---

[53]See Bengt Sundkler, *Zulu Zion and Some Swazi Zionists* (Oxford: Oxford University Press, 1976). Sundkler holds that while there are a number of AIC churches that are very patriarchal, on a larger scale they have given "women a central and honored position...because in the last resort these terms were regarded as those of ultimate authority, the Spirit," 79–93.

[54]See Daneel, *Quest,* 46, for a brief discussion of the rise and proclamation of Kimpa Vita.

[55]Ibid.

[56]See Mazrui, "Gender, Religion and War," In *Cultural Forces,* 182–84, on the discussion of a number of outstanding African women, such as Alice Lakwena of Uganda, Hawo Osman Tako of Somalia, and Alice Lenshina of Zambia, and how they employed religious power to assume political positions in their societies.

Grace Tshabalala, Alice Lenshina, and Mai Chaza, who became founders and leaders of some massive AIC movements in the first half of this century in Southern Africa and elsewhere.[57] Moreover, the women of Botswana with whom I have worked (see chapter 9, below), being leaders and founders, show that this tradition of women responding to the word of the Spirit is still alive.

Most AIC women leaders attribute their leadership to a revelation, a vision—which normally recurs, instructing one to preach, heal, and prophesy—or to the experience of divine healing after a long illness.[58] The Spirit that reveals and gives one a vocation and power operates with a significant independence from the written word. This point was underlined by Bishop Virginia Lucas when asked, "Why are you a female church leader when the Bible seems to suggest otherwise?" She responded, "I have been asked this question several times before. I always tell people that when God spoke to me through the Spirit, *God never opened the Bible to me.* Instead, God's Spirit told me to begin a church and heal God's people, which is what I am doing"[59] (emphasis mine).

It is against this historical background—political protest of racial and religious discrimination, a search for cultural liberation through integrating biblical views with African religious views, and an experience of God's Spirit empowering both women and men of various races to serve creation— that the interpretative practices of Botswanan AIC women should be understood. Their approach should be seen not only as a mode of political resistance but also a demonstrated will to cultivate a space for liberating interdependence against false and oppressive boundaries, which are too often maintained at the expense of nurturing the reality of diversity and interdependence in God's creation. Their approach resists both patriarchy and imperialism.

Arresting Patriarchy and Imperialism

Chapters 1 and 2 have shown how the West, the Bible, and imperialism are interconnected in order to underline the serious challenges and demands of the postcolonial era in biblical studies and in feminist biblical practices. I therefore propose that feminist biblical readers must also become decolonizing readers: those who demonstrate awareness of imperialism's pervasive exploitative forces and its literary strategies of domination, who demonstrate a conscious adoption of feminist

---

[57]See Daneel, *Quest,* 46–59. Sundkler, in *Zulu Zion,* acknowledges the centrality of women in AICs, but brackets the subject by noting that it is an "exciting task awaiting the new generation of African women scholars," 79–93.

[58]Daneel, *Quest,* 157–60. Even among the women with whom I have spoken, this experience was always given as the reason for their spiritual positions.

[59]Bishop Virginia Lucas is a founding member of the Glory Healing Church in Mogoditshane, Gaborone. Her quoted words are an inclusive translation from the Setswana language.

decolonizing strategies, and who demonstrate a genuine search for liberating ways of interdependence between nations, races, ethnicities, classes, genders, and sexual and religious orientations. This will demand taking both patriarchy and imperialism seriously in our feminist biblical practice.

To confront imperialism as a postcolonial feminist, one must, first, recognize that patriarchal oppression overlaps with but is not identical to imperialism; second, recognize its methods and strategies of subjugation in cultural texts and reality; third, identify the patterns of resistance it evokes from the subjugated; fourth, recognize the use of the female gender in colonial discourse as well as explicate how postcolonialism exposes some women to double or triple oppression. To this end, Part 2 highlights the institution of the empire and its literary-rhetorical methods in ancient and contemporary texts. The primary purpose of Part 2 is, therefore, to highlight the literary-rhetorical methods that characterize the power struggle between the colonizer and the colonized. Its goal is to cultivate postcolonial strategies of reading the Bible that resist and decolonize both patriarchy and imperial oppression and to seek to articulate the liberation of women and men of different races and nations.

PART II

Empire and Method

*Imperialism is not a slogan. It is real, it is palpable in content
and form and its methods and effects...Imperialism is total: it
has economic, political, military, cultural and psychological
consequences for the people of the world today.*[1]

Ngugi wa Thiongo

*This is the conception of Empire:...to know no bounds. Did not
Babylonian sovereign Hammurabi give himself the title of "King
of the Four Corners of the World?*[2]

Rene Maunier

---

[1]Ngugi, *Decolonizing the Mind,* 2.
[2]Maunier, *Sociology of Colonies,* vol. 1, 19.

3

Introducing Postcolonial Theories

The term *empire* describes an ancient and persistent relationship of dominance and suppression between different nations, countries, races, and continents. Imperialism is the process of building an empire through the imposition of political, economic, and social institutions of one nation over a foreign one.[1] In the past it tended to lead to colonialism, that is, the geographical occupation and control of one nation by another. Geographical control within the history and imagination of the empire is, therefore, a central subject in the studies of imperialism.

Studies of imperialism show that from ancient to contemporary times three main factors have repeatedly motivated and justified imperialism: God, glory, and gold.[2] Different terms are used to describe the same factors. Some identify them as power, moral responsibility, and economic interests;[3] others speak of spiritual, material, and power motivations.[4] In addition to the justifications of imperialism, how the imperial powers impose their control on foreign lands and how the dominated respond have recently become subjects of intense study under the umbrella name of postcolonial studies and methods. There is a particular focus on how cultural texts are central means in both the imposition of and resistance to imperialism.[5]

---

[1]For these definitions see Mudimbe, *Invention of Africa*, 1–2, and Said, *Culture and Imperialism*, 7–9.

[2]See Mazrui, *Cultural Forces*, 29.

[3]See Phillip Darby, *Three Faces of Imperialism: British and American Approaches to Asia and Africa 1870–1970* (New Haven, Conn.:Yale University Press, 1987).

[4]See Maunier, *Sociology of Colonies*, vol. 1, 154–260.

[5]For an in-depth study on the area, see Harlow, *Resistance Literature;* David Quint, *Epic and Empire* (Princeton, N.J.:Princeton University Press, 1993); and Said, *Culture and Imperialism.*

Evidently, postcoloniality affects all the social institutions of the concerned nations and races. Nonetheless, the term *postcolonial* will be used here to refer to literary theories developed from studying literature and its participation in the institution of imperialism. As stated earlier, the term *postcolonial* does not denote that colonialism is over, since the latter did not simply consist of geographical and political domination but also included cultural and economic structures that persist to this day. Postcolonial, therefore, refers to an overall analysis of the methods and effects of imperialism as a continuing reality in global relations.

The term *postcolonial* in literary studies became common in the past decade, but it examines a phenomenon that is quite ancient.[6] In biblical literature, for example, the Exodus myth of the promised land and Israel's subjugation by the Babylonian, Persian, Syrian, Hellenistic, and Roman empires attest to imperialism as an ancient and persistent phenomenon. Biblical literature is often defined along the lines of preexilic, postexilic, and First and Second Temple, terms that recall Israel's major encounters with imperialist forces. This indicates that biblical literature was shaped by a constant struggle with imperial phenomena; that is, it was born from the relationships of endorsing, resisting, or living with imperial powers. Similarly, the Western classics *The Odyssey* and its counterimitation *The Aeneid* and the long genealogy of the epic genre in Western culture attest to the persistence of imperialism and how texts have been central means in its creation, maintenance, and destruction since ancient times.[7]

Recent centuries witnessed unparalleled imperial movements. The Spanish, Portuguese, German, French, British, Russian, and North American imperial powers affected almost the whole globe. Accordingly, these massive empires were accompanied by an unparalleled production of literary texts. The age of the novel, anthropology, natural history, mapmaking, ethnography, travel narratives, and biography remains unrivaled by prior historical periods of the world.

Yet postcolonial studies and methods are not just about a history, for imperialism persists. Under the facade of multinational corporations, universal media, and international monetary bodies, military and ideological muscle imperialism has proven its capacity to mutate and persist in ever new and remarkable forms—what is now termed globalization or neo-colonization. Similarly, globalization's interconnection with texts is attested by the age of the information superhighway, which is really a flow of

---

[6]See Frantz Fanon, *The Wretched of the Earth,* trans. Constance Farrington (Harmondsworth, England: Penguin, 1967) for one of the earliest systematic analyses of the modern ideology of colonization and its impact on the colonized.

[7]See David Quint, *Epic and Empire.* In this excellent study on the genealogy of the epic genre, Quint shows that Western imperial travelers of different kinds and times always wrote the story of their journeys and the lands they saw. But in actual fact they reproduced the base forms, images, encounters, characters, and structures of *The Odyssey* to describe every land.

information from the former colonial metropolitan centers to the whole world. The latest mutation attests to imperialism as a central reality in the making of global relations, affecting men and women, privileging some and oppressing others, and finding ways to repeatedly justify and maintain itself across the globe. Therefore, postcolonial studies and methods, as many of its Two-Thirds World proponents repeatedly say, seek not just to win a place in academic critical institutions that are complicit with the powers of oppression, but primarily to remain as an oppositional body of literature that seeks to understand and expose the making of global expansion and exploitation as well as to search for better ways of imagining and building just international relations.

Given that postcolonial literary studies are based on the historical phenomenon of imperialism that has persisted from ancient to current times, taking different forms and methods, practiced by different imperial races on culturally and geographically different subjects, postcolonial methods constitute of necessity a complex body of theories and methods.[8] To simplify it, perhaps two factors can be identified as central to postcoloniality: First, how literature is used by imperial powers to impose and justify their institutions, and how the colonized also employ literature to reject the empire and to assert their liberation. Second, the main subject of postcolonial literature is control over the land, particularly its resources. Under this broad umbrella, there are countless ways of examining the manifestations of imperialism, or what one may term the power struggles of the colonial giants and their resisting victims.

To begin with the literature of colonial powers, postcolonial studies examine some of the following aspects: how foreign literature is imposed on a colonized nation to convert it to the culture of imperial powers, that is, assimilation or colonization of the mind.[9] Methods may range from the imposition of a foreign but "neutral" body of literature (what was termed humanist) on different nations to the use of literature that openly derogates the subjugated, thus alienating the colonized from themselves and leading them to embrace the dominant powers.[10] Its methods may also involve the production of literature by the dominant powers for its colonizing people back in the so-called mother countries, justifying why their nation has inherent rights of superiority or divine sanction to impose its political, economic, and social institutions on other nations. Last, colonizing involves the reproduction of literature of different genres about the subjugated and

---

[8]See Snyder, *The Imperialism Reader,* 19–44; and Albert Szymanski, *The Logic of Imperialism* (New York: Praeger, 1981) for the various forms of imperialism over space and time.

[9]Ngugi, *Decolonizing the Mind,* 5. See also Achebe, "An Image of Africa: Racism in Conrad's *Heart of Darkness,*" in *Hopes and Impediments* (New York: Doubleday, 1988), 1–20. They both discuss the effects of so-called humanist and Western classics on African students.

[10]See Achebe, "An Image of Africa: Racism in Conrad's *Heart of Darkness,*" 1–20. See also Ngugi, *Moving the Center,* 12–24.

their lands: how their poverty, richness, barbarism, ungodliness, laziness, or kindness lays a duty or a divine right on the superior nations to impose themselves by force or coercion. All these bodies of literature from different times—such as *The Odyssey*, Exodus, *The Tempest*, and *Heart of Darkness*—come to inspire, sustain, and sanctify the institution of imperialism in histories that are disparately removed from their own original production. On these grounds, the term *imperializing literature* will also be used to designate literary rhetorical strategies that propound the ideologies of imperialism.

Decolonizing Literary Practices

From the victims of imperialism, there is no lack of literature born from the encounter with imperialist forces.[11] One finds literature of resistance that seeks to raise the consciousness of the subjugated in order to counteract the claims of the dominant forces. It assumes some of the following forms: the revival and emphasis of precolonial mythology and literature leading to pronounced nationalism, nativism, or stringent enforcement of cultural boundaries; the production of new literature addressing the colonized and the colonizer; and the rereading of imperialist literature. The literature of the colonized also arises from particular forms of imperial subjugation such as captivity after conquest (leading to slavery, exile, or diaspora),[12] immigration to imperial centers due to dispossession, poverty, unrest, and alienation from one's land through total loss of power in settler colonies or displacement.[13] Thus, the term *decolonizing* will also be used to denote literary strategies that resist imperialism.

Collaboration, Resistance, and Literature

Often the colonized are forced to collaborate with the colonizing powers at various stages of their suppression. They begin to advance the agendas of the oppressor and to proclaim their superiority by choice or by the mere fact of living under the ruling institutions of the colonizer. The collaboration of the colonized, whether by force, choice, or intimidation, often instigates internal fighting among the colonized. The elites and leaders, whose positions of power make them vulnerable to collaboration, are immediately recognized by lower classes, usually the hardest hit by the imperial exploitation, to be benefiting from the exploitative situation. This

---

[11]See Said, "Resistance and Opposition," in *Culture and Imperialism,* 191–262. In this section, Said shows how modern imperialism stimulated a literary response from the colonized.

[12]See Fernando F. Segovia, "Towards a Hermeneutics of the Diaspora: A Hermeneutics of Otherness and Engagement," in *Reading from This Place,* vol. 1, 57–73; and "Toward Intercultural Criticism: A Reading Strategy from the Diaspora," in *Reading from This Place,* vol. 2, 303–30, for an exposition of diaspora hermeneutics from a Hispanic and biblical/theological perspective.

[13]This includes literature of African Americans, Native Americans, Australian aborigines, refugees, and many other groups whose independence may be totally irrecoverable except by imagination.

recognition has two effects: It hides the face of the real enemy and leads the colonized either to fight against one another or to compete against one another for the favor of the colonizing power. New Testament literature and the presence of various competing interest groups such as the Essenes (Qumran), the Pharisees, followers of John the Baptist, the Jesus movement, the Zealots, and the Sadducees are excellent examples of how the presence of an external force can lead to intense division and competition.[14] The internal competitions are almost always to the advantage of the colonizing powers, who easily exploit the weak divided nation. These internal conflicts and competitions often give rise to pro-imperial literature from the colonized. On these grounds, postcolonial literary studies of nativity, hybridity, biculturalism, and the subversion of languages of imperial forces are theorized as forms of both collaboration and resistance. Hybridity becomes a form of resistance, for it dispenses with dualistic and hierarchical constructions of cultures, which are used to claim the superiority of colonizing cultures, and shows that cultures grow and are dependent on borrowing from each other.

Autoethnographic Literary Strategies

Collaboration also leads to what Mary Louise Pratt terms autoethnographic literary strategies.[15] That is, the literary response of the colonized is partly shaped by the textual forms of their imperial counterparts. Subsequently, the literature of both groups mirror one another. Autoethnographic patterns tend to be common, since even colonizing powers, at some point in their history, were victims of some imperial oppression. To write themselves as deserving powers, they imagine myths that validate their right to dominate and dispossess people of distant lands. David Quint best captures the foundation of autoethnographic literary patterns when he notes that "the losers who attract our sympathies today would be—had they only power—the victors of tomorrow."[16] Evidently, the prevailing model in postcolonial literature has maintained "that those who have been victimized losers in history somehow have the right to become victimizing winners, in turn."[17] The stories of Exodus, *The Aeneid*, and *Heart of Darkness* are excellent examples of former losers claiming power: Narratively speaking, Israelites were victims of Egyptian enslavement

---

[14]See Andrew J. Overman, *Matthew's Gospel and Formative Judaism: The Social World of the Matthean Community* (Minneapolis: Fortress Press, 1990); and Richard A. Horsley, *Jesus and the Spiral of Violence: Popular Jewish Resistance in Roman Palestine* (Minneapolis: Fortress Press, 1993), for studies that highlight that the presence of the imperial factor in first-century Palestine led to divisions, competitions, and conflict among the colonized groups and between the colonizer and the colonized.

[15]Pratt, *Imperial Eyes*, 6–7.

[16]Quint, *Epic and Empire*, 18.

[17]Ibid.

(historically, colonized by Babylon); Romans (Trojans) were historically victims of Greek imperial conquest; and the British were victims of the Roman Empire. Yet all claim a divine right or "duty" to travel and dispossess distant people.

Needless to say, autoethnographic literary constructions hardly offer alternative models of international justice. As the analysis in chapters 4 and 5 will show, imperializing texts of former victims are self-validating tracts that institute and sanctify the right of Israelites, Romans, and British to travel, to enter, and to dispossess nations that are distant and inhabited. In this way, the abundance of autoethnograhic literary constructions, among the colonized and the colonizer, also attest to the model of reversal in postcolonial literature. The colonized or formerly colonized, informed by the colonizer's intolerance for difference and unjustified claims of power, respond on the same terms.

Because the imitations or reversal models hardly offer liberative alternatives, the literature of both groups tends to be characterized by sharp dualisms, rigid cultural boundaries, vicious racisms, heightened nationalisms, and hierarchical structures that would license any power to victimize other nations. For example, both the Exodus[18] and *The Aeneid* narratives, written by those who were once subjugated, have offered excellent models for imperialism over the centuries and well beyond their original authors and readers.

In sum, postcolonial theories of literature examine the making and the subversion of imperialism, which in the past tended to lead to geographical colonialism. They examine how literature is an essential instrument in imperialism's power struggles. They analyze the literature of both the colonizer and the colonized: how it constructs or responds to the traveling, the entering, and the taking control of foreign lands by imperialistic nations. As recent anthologies indicate, postcoloniality analyzes the following aspects: the West as an imperialist center, nationalism, nativism, diaspora, hybridity, identity, language, education, history, media, intertextuality, place and displacement, production and consumption, universality and difference, representation and resistance, intellectuals and institutions, subalterns and resistance, and gender representation in imperial domination or subversion.[19] Postcoloniality, therefore, is a very complex phenomenon that involves texts from different times, places, and cultures and whose boundaries often blur. It propounds a myriad of methods and theories, all

---

[18]For further reading on the influence or use of the Exodus narrative in contemporary imperialism, see Thomas Buckingham, *Moses and Aaron* (New London: T. Green, 1729); and Edward E. Hale, *The Desert and the Promised Land* (Boston: C. C. P. Moody, 1863).

[19]See Patrick Williams and Laura Chrisman, eds., *Colonial Discourse and Postcolonial Theory: A Reader* (New York: Columbia University Press, 1994); and Bill Ashcroft, Gareth Griffiths, and Helen Tiffin, eds. *The Postcolonial Studies Reader* (New York: Routledge, 1995), for these various forms of postcolonial studies.

of which examine literature and its participation in the building, collaboration, or subversion of global imperial relationships.

Exodus and *Heart of Darkness*

The aim of Part 2 is to highlight the literary methods of imperialism's power struggles through the analysis of specific texts. Part 2 illustrates how the desires and revolts of the institution of imperialism are concretized in the production and reproduction of recognizable literary-rhetorical patterns. First, imperializing texts, or the literature of the colonizer, are analyzed. Texts under this category tend to claim power over foreign and inhabited lands. The literary-rhetorical methods they employ to justify traveling, entering, and taking control of distant and inhabited lands are highlighted. For the category of imperializing texts, two narratives, Exodus and *Heart of Darkness*, are extensively analyzed. Two others, *The Aeneid* and a poem, "The White Man's Burden," serve as a bridge from ancient to contemporary imperialism and highlight intertextuality in imperialist persistence. The former serves in the conclusion of Exodus, while the latter is employed in the introduction to the analysis of *Heart of Darkness*, providing a framework within which the European ideology of imperialism was acted out.

The two ancient texts are from Jewish and Western literature.[20] The biblical text is chosen not only because "the narrative text central to Western cultures' self-definition and understanding of the world is the Bible"[21] but also because "the displacing power in all texts finally derives from the displacing power of the Bible, whose centrality, potency, and dominating anteriority inform all Western literature."[22] The story of Exodus is chosen particularly because it is a base story, constantly recalled in the Hebrew Bible and New Testament. Therefore, to understand its ideology is imperative, precisely because it informs most of the so-called canonical texts. *The Aeneid*, too, is regarded as "the principal secular book of the Western World,"[23] while *Heart of Darkness* is regarded as "the classic colonial text" of modern imperialism.[24]

The reading of secular texts side by side with scriptures represents a deliberate methodological step. It is an interdisciplinary, intertextual, boundary-transgressing postcolonial feminist approach that guards against

---

[20]See Eric Auerbach, *Mimesis: The Representation of Reality in Western Literature* (Princeton, N.J.: Princeton University Press, 1946), 22–23, for a comparison of Hebrew Bible and Homeric epics. Auerbach holds that the styles of these two narratives "represent basic types" for a starting point in the examination of literary representation of reality in European culture.

[21]The Bible and Culture Collective, *The Postmodern Bible,* 277.

[22]Edward Said, *The World, the Text, and the Critic* (Cambridge, Mass.: Harvard University Press, 1983), 46.

[23]G. R. Wilson Knight, "Introduction," in Virgil, *The Aeneid,* trans. G. R. Wilson Knight (London: Penguin Books, 1956), 23.

[24]See Jonathan White, ed., *Recasting the World: Writing After Colonialism* (Baltimore: Johns Hopkins University Press, 1993), 20.

anti-Semitism.[25] It seeks to demystify the isolation of Christian texts from other cultural texts, an approach that tends to shield them from various critical investigations as well as to perpetuate some of the oppressive ideologies of the Bible. Also, biblical feminists' isolated focus on Jewish literature seems to hide the fact that patriarchy is prevalent in many other non-Jewish classical narratives. In the same way, imperialist ideologies are prevalent in both biblical and nonbiblical, Western and non-Western texts. In addition, the reading of secular and sacred texts together speaks to my own postcolonial experience. As Ngugi rightly notes that both "William Shakespeare and Jesus Christ had brought light to the darkest Africa,"[26] more than anywhere else, colonialism was accomplished through the Christian mission in Africa.[27] Imperialism was instituted through both the church and the English departments of schools.[28]

In fact, Rene Maunier traces the origins and development of imperialist ideology and shows that it encompasses literature of various institutions, races, genres, and times. To put the whole institution of imperialism within its wide parameters, to emphasize intertextuality in postcoloniality, I quote him at length:

> The doctrine of a chosen race or a missionary race is most certainly an ancient one. The Greeks formulated it; the Jews and Arabs proclaimed it. The Greeks stigmatized as "barbarians" all the peoples who did not speak Greek; they were the people who by decree of the gods might be enslaved. Isocrates proposed a union of the Greeks against all the barbarians. He was a colonialist before the word existed...Even Aristotle, most free-minded of men, considered it legitimate to conquer barbarians. The old Imperialism blossomed out under the Jews. With them it was destructive rather than constructive, for it was overwhelmingly a collective egoism. The idea of a Chosen Race triumphs in the Old Testament; the race of Israel by the rite of circumcision formed an indestructible blood-alliance with Jehovah; and therefore to it was promised the empire of the world. Genesis already says: "cursed be Canaan; a servant of servants shall he be unto his brethren..." It was the Arabs who put the seal on Old Imperialism and the

---

[25]See Susannah Heschel, "Anti-Judaism/Anti-Semitism," in *Dictionary of Feminist Theologies*, ed. Letty M. Russell and J. Shannon Clarkson (Louisville, Ky.: Westminster John Knox Press, 1996), 12–13, who holds that "the most problematic example of feminist anti-Judaism is blaming Judaism for militarism, violence, and genocide." Her elaboration indicates that part of anti-Semitic feminism emanates from reading and writing about the global impact of the Bible in isolation from other Western classical texts.

[26]Ngugi, *Decolonizing the Mind,* 91.

[27]See Vijay Mishra and Bob Hodge, "What is Post(-)colonialism," in *Colonial Discourse and Post-colonial Theory,* ed. Williams and Chrisman, 288.

[28]See Ngugi, *Decolonizing the Mind,* 9–18, 90–93.

Quran lays down the crudest rules for it. It is the idea of power for the sake of power, what the Arabs called *su'ubiyah'*, that is to say, domination in accordance with the will of God by his chosen People over all the people of Unbelievers...If Old Imperialism was not the invention of Europeans, the opposite is true of the New Imperialism, the modern imperialism of 19th and 20th centuries, whose proudest champion is surely Anglo-Saxon Imperialism. Creative, constructive rather than destructive, it is much more a means than an end. It finds its justification in right, no doubt, but also in duty and lastly in profit. If you must rule, it is because you ought, because you must—to benefit the whole world...To this end the chosen race devotes its efforts. The *"Imperial Task"* laid upon the chosen people is to give civilization to the whole world.[29]

Intertextually, the Exodus and *The Aeneid*, literary constructions about entering and taking possession of distant and inhabited lands, became some of the primary myths. They offered standard formats that informed a wide body of Western Christian literature, from the first to the twentieth century.[30] As Kwok Pui-lan correctly notes,

> The condemnation of cultures, religions, and peoples in Canaan can be seen as a forerunner of discrimination against all peoples who do not share the beliefs of Jews or Christians. The Canaanites were portrayed as worshipping idols, as promiscuous, and as having lower moral standards.[31]

To understand the ideology of the first canonical texts, whose influence was extended to global levels by imperializing powers, is, therefore, critical. Their privileged influence calls for an investigation into the role of genre, intertextuality, and imitation in the institution of writing, and how institutionalized practices have served to maintain and reproduce literary-rhetorical constructions that propound ideologies of imperialist orientation.[32]

This part of the book consists of five chapters. Chapter 3 has briefly introduced postcolonial theories of literature and justified the texts chosen for highlighting empire and method. Chapter 4 analyzes ancient imperializing texts, primarily the biblical story of Exodus and *The Aeneid*.

---

[29]Maunier, *Sociology of Colonies,* vol. 1, 32–33.

[30]See Quint, *Epic and Empire,* on the influence of its genre, and Northrop Frye, *The Great Code: The Bible and Literature* (New York: Harcourt Brace Jovanovich, 1982), on the influence of the Bible in general on Western literature.

[31]Kwok Pui-lan, "Racism and Ethnocentrism in Feminist Biblical Interpretation," 108, in Schüssler Fiorenza, *Searching the Scriptures,* vol. 1.

[32]See Elleke Boehmer, "Reading the Strange: An Empire of Imagination" and "The Travelling Metaphor," in *Colonial and Postcolonial Literature* (Oxford: Oxford University Press, 1995), 44–59, who discusses the use of intertextuality in the building of the empire, speaks of "dense textual referencing," "cross-connection between stories," "a hubbub of story-telling," "an interconnected intertextual milieu," and "transferability of empire's organizing metaphors."

Chapter 5 focuses on explicating the issues of empire and method in mod- ·
ern imperialism by analyzing *Heart of Darkness*. Chapter 6, on the other
hand, highlights the anti-imperial literary methods of decolonizing from
The Victims, a Botswana novel. It examines decolonizing literature, texts of
the colonized. Texts under this category are distinguished by the struggle
to regain power over their own lands and resources. They seek to decolonize
by adopting several anti-imperial literary strategies. Chapter 6 is introduced
with the poem "May Imperialism Perish Forever,"[33] followed by an analysis of *The Victims*. Its selection was based on the following: It comes from a
context that reflects my background; it engages biblical texts of Exodus,
Daniel, and John 4; it features women from one of the African Independent Churches; it treats historical events of Southern Africa; and it is
authored by a woman. The latter point is essential to my quest because
postcolonial male writers insisted on a "first things first" approach; that is,
imperial oppression is supposed to be given priority over patriarchal oppression.[34] Chapter 7 adds a fourth "G," gender, to imperialism's trio of
God, gold, and glory, and employs the insights of postcolonial theorists,
biblical feminists, and the African Independent Churches (AICs) women's
approach, discussed in chapter 2, to propose a postcolonial feminist biblical model: "Rahab's reading prism." The model is employed to read mission passages (Mt. 15:21–28; 28:18–20) and their various reading communities in Part 3. With this introduction to empire and method, we turn to
Exodus and *The Aeneid* to examine the ideologies of imperialism and its
literary strategies.

---

[33]Maina wa Kinyatti, ed., *Thunder from the Mountains: Poems and Songs from the Mau Mau*
(Trenton, N. J.: Africa World Press, 1990), 15.
[34]See Kirsten H. Peterson, "First Things First: Problems of a Feminist Approach to
African Literature," in *The Post-colonial Studies Reader,* ed. Ashcroft, Griffiths, and Tiffin,
251–54.

4

Method in Ancient
Imperializing Texts

The purpose of analyzing imperializing literature is to highlight how imperialism involves the reproduction of recognizable literary-rhetorical constructions that justify the traveling to and the taking control and possession of distant and inhabited lands. This chapter asks the following questions:

1. Does this text have a clear stance against the political imperialism of its time?

2. Does this text encourage travel to distant and inhabited lands, and if so, how does it justify itself?

3. How does this text construct difference: Is there dialogue and mutual interdependence, or condemnation and replacement of all that is foreign?

4. Does this text employ gender representations to construct relationships of subordination and domination?

The first three questions seek to illumine the literary-rhetorical methods of constructing what Mary Louise Pratt has termed "anti-conquest" and "contact zone" patterns in the literature of imperial settings.[1] "Anti-conquest" designates the literary strategies of representation by which the colonizers secure their innocence while asserting their right to travel to, enter, and possess resources and lands that belong to foreign nations, an

---

[1]Pratt, *Imperial Eyes,* 6–7.

aspect to be examined by question two. The "contact zone," on the other hand, is "the space of colonial encounters, the space in which peoples geographically and historically separated come into contact with each other to establish ongoing relations." The contact zone is vital to imperialism, for it is no exaggeration to say "colonialism is a contact of peoples."[2] The contact zone will be examined by question three.

At this stage, the imperializing texts (literature that propounds colonizing values) Exodus and Joshua 1–12, *The Aeneid*, "The White Man's Burden," and *Heart of Darkness* are examined.

Exodus: God, Method, and Empire-Building

Background

The story of the exodus, the emigration of Israelites from Egypt into Canaan, begins in the book of Genesis and stretches over to the books of Exodus, Leviticus, Numbers, Deuteronomy, and Joshua, thus underlining intertextuality and the reproduction of particular literary ideologies. The choice to focus on Exodus and Joshua 1–12, therefore, only serves to highlight the point of departure from one land, Egypt, mainly covered by Exodus, and the arrival in and possession of a foreign land, Canaan, vividly idealized and dramatized in Joshua. Both books are excellent examples for illustrating the literary-rhetorical constructions of the anti-conquest, contact zone, gender, and autoethnographic literary constructions in colonizing literature.

The historicity of Exodus and Joshua is highly debatable, since the departure and the occupation of Canaan are hardly verifiable in extrabiblical sources. Hebrew Bible research holds "that there is complete absence of any external written documents testifying to Israel's presence and subjugation in Egypt, to her immigration from that land, or to her conquest and her settlement there."[3] Of late the scholars' locus of opinion holds that "the book of Exodus reached its present form, final form, during the sixth century exile or soon thereafter."[4]

Nevertheless, whether the historicity of Exodus is established or not, in postcolonial studies myths of power that are not identical to historical facts, but whose rhetorical function is to empower its subjects to colonize or overcome colonialism, are common (examples include Darwinism, Western anthropological collections, negritude, and manifest destiny). The issues I seek to highlight from Exodus and Joshua 1–12 are, therefore, *not* necessarily about their historical factuality, but about their literary-rhetorical function in sanctioning or rejecting imperialist oppression. That is, my

---

[2]Maunier, *Sociology of Colonies,* vol. 1, 5.

[3]Nahum M. Sarna, "Exodus, Book of," in *The Anchor Bible Dictionary,* vol. 2, ed. David Noel Freedman (New York: Doubleday, 1992), 96–97.

[4]Walter Brueggemann, "Exodus," in *The New Interpreter's Bible: A Commentary* (Nashville: Abingdon Press, 1994), 680. Ironically, Exodus does not propose an alternative to their imperially imposed exile experience.

analysis focuses on the narrative world of the text, its ideology, and the history of the text in the world. The first question is, Does Exodus speak against the imperialism of its narrative world? The reading of the Exodus story is "on the surface," a literary reading.

Exodus and Egypt

Scholars identify the Egypt of the Exodus narrative world as an empire.[5] Slavery is a manifestation of imperialistic tendencies and often serves as a method of colonizing. This occurs when large numbers of people are intentionally and forcefully moved from their lands and resettled in different lands. The resettlement estranges the victims from their lands and serves as a strategy of weakening and controlling foreign lands through depopulation and displacement that invalidate all their social institutions.

The Exodus slave-master relations also revolve around matters of land control, economic matters. Narratively speaking, Israel's immigration into Egypt is bound up with the selling of Joseph into slavery, his remarkable rise to fame, and the subsequent voluntary immigration of his family after a reunion with the prosperous Joseph. The larger immigration is instigated by a search for economic means: They migrate during the years of severe drought in search for food. Pharaoh, who learns about the visit of Joseph's family, generously invites them to settle in the "best of the land of Egypt" and to "enjoy the fat of the land" (Gen. 45:17–20). Upon their acceptance, they are indeed granted a "holding in the land of Egypt, in the best part of the land, in the land of Rameses, as Pharaoh had instructed" (Gen. 47:11). Despite this seemingly happy settlement, the narrative privileges the implied reader to a much more complex plot than Pharaoh realizes.

The implied reader knows that Joseph, who meets and convenes with his brothers before Pharaoh's knowledge, assures them that his enslavement was God's plan: "Do not be distressed, or angry with yourselves, because you sold me here...God sent me before you to preserve for you a remnant on earth, and to keep alive for you many survivors" (45:5–7; see also Gen. 46:4; 15:7–14). Even as Pharaoh welcomes them and gives them the best of the land, the implied reader is aware of a much more complex plot. God says, "I myself will go with you to Egypt, and I will also bring you up again" (46:4). Thus, Jacob confides in Joseph, saying that "God Almighty appeared to me at Luz in the land of Canaan, and he blessed me, and said to me...I...will give this land to your offspring after you for a perpetual holding" (Gen. 48:3–4). The implied reader, who knows that the Israelites must finally leave the land of Egypt and go to Canaan, their God-given land, is acutely aware that Pharaoh's generous hospitality is beyond his knowledge or control. Pharaoh is just an actor in God's long-term plan for Israel. What remains unsaid is how they will leave. Generations later,

---

[5]See Drorah O'Donnel Setel, "Exodus," in *The Women's Bible Commentary,* ed. Carol A. Newsom and Sharon Ringe (Louisville: John Knox Press, 1992), 30.

their happy settlement turns into a sour master-slave relationship and provides the immediate reason for their great trek. The narrative of Exodus begins at this very point.

The book of Exodus attributes the enslavement of the Israelites to their threatening population growth, resulting in insecurities over land control (1:7–8). God sees their enslavement and their misery; God hears their cries and sends a servant, Moses, to say to Pharaoh, "Let my people go" (3:6–5:1). The dense repetition of the formula "Let my people go" in the first thirteen chapters of Exodus clearly underlines it as the main theme.

Rhetorically speaking, Exodus opens with God's mighty acts of liberation, God's response, God's strongest statement against slavery as a manifestation of imperialism. The narrative invites the implied reader to nod approvingly at God's acts of liberation. Nonetheless, Exodus makes no secret that the "victimized losers in history somehow have the right to become victimizing winners, in turn."[6] The resounding command to let God's people go is unhesitatingly twined with God's promise to give them the land of the Canaanites, the Hittites, the Amorites, the Perizzites, the Hivites, and the Jebusites—an inhabited land! How does the narrative hope to sustain the sympathies of the implied reader? Clearly, this is anti-conquest ideology at its best, a point to which I now turn in order to examine its literary manifestation.

Anti-conquest Ideology in Exodus

According to Pratt, anti-conquest ideology describes the literary strategies that allow colonizers to claim foreign lands while securing their innocence. In the nineteenth and twentieth centuries this ideology was expressed in the Anglo-Saxon moral claim of the "duty to the natives," which sugarcoated the violence of colonialism. To examine the anti-conquest literary constructions is, therefore, to look at the self-validating literary methods of imperialism woven into the imperializing narrative and how those methods anesthetize and sanctify the exploitative act to make it acceptable to the implied reader and the real readers of various times, who do not read against the narrative.[7]

Postcolonial studies show that the imperialist anti-conquest ideology is grounded on some of the following literary-rhetorical representations: first, a method authorizing traveling from one land to another; second, a method of constructing the image of the targeted land and its people; third, a method constructing the identity of the people who colonize distant lands; fourth, a method of employing female gender to articulate relations of subjugation

---

[6]Quint, *Epic and Empire,* 18.
[7]See Walter Brueggemann, *The Land* (Philadelphia: Fortress Press, 1977). His reading enters into the ideological claims of Exodus and flows with them rather than questioning the theological justice of claiming a land that is already inhabited by other nations.

and domination. These factors will now be examined in detail in the stated order from the story of Exodus.

Authorizing Travel: "Let my people go!"

One cannot overemphasize that Exodus is a text that commands and authorizes traveling from one land to another. Its very title, Exodus, means "going out." The first thirteen chapters focus on the struggle to go out of Egypt. Pharaoh is determined to keep his slaves, and God is equally committed to taking them out of Egypt. God wins. The Israelites begin their journey, but by the end of the book their journey is not over—they are still trekking to another land.

From the point of view of content, the theme of travel in Exodus is captured in God's unrelenting command to Pharaoh: "Let my people go." The command is emphasized through a method of verbatim repetition of this sentence (5:1, 14; 8:1, 20; 9:1, 13) as direct speech.[8] It is also emphasized through repeating the same command, with only slight verbal variation in reported speech and narration (8:20–21, 28–29, 32; 9:2, 7, 17, 28, 35; 10:4, 7, 20, 27; 11:1, 10; 13:3). Along with this dense command, the theme of traveling is further accentuated in the phrase "I will bring you up out of the misery of Egypt, to the land of the Canaanites" (Ex. 3:17; see related phrases in 3:8; 4:8; 7:4–5). The latter is also occasionally repeated with slight variations. The intense repetition of these phrases and sentences undoubtedly underlines that traveling is central to the book of Exodus. The major question, however, is how does Exodus justify the command to travel out of Egypt to Canaan, an inhabited land?

The immediate reason for their traveling out of Egypt to another land is God's response to their bondage and misery, but it is by no means the only or main reason. As shown above, Genesis frames the narrative within God's long-term plan for the Israelites, explaining their coming to Egypt and pointing to their ultimate traveling to and taking possession of Canaan. The book of Exodus picks up these themes and begins to actualize them. The literary methods employed to authorize the traveling to and taking possession of distant and inhabited land is grounded in the originator: God.

Anesthesia: God and Slavery

The anesthesia that sanitizes the anti-conquest in Exodus revolves around God. God is a major character in the narrative. God is the prime initiator, commander, and giver of land. God sees the misery of the people, hears their cry, and sends Moses to Pharaoh to say, "Let my people go." God's power even deliberately hardens the heart of Pharaoh into refusing to let the Israelites go, thus creating a space to unleash mighty acts and to

---

[8]See Robert Alter, *The Art of Biblical Narrative* (New York: Basic Books, 1981), for an excellent exposition on the Hebrew prose techniques of repetition, dialogue, characterization, and narration.

shake the heart of the Pharaoh into obedience (7:3–4, 14, 22; 10:1–2, 20, 27; 14:4). The deliberate hardening of Pharaoh's heart allows God's heroic acts of glory to be demonstrated. The overall effect of the characterization of God as the hero of Exodus is to sanctify and champion a perfect anti-conquest ideology. As the highest and most unquestionable authority to the implied reader, and to the many unresisting real readers of the past and present, God becomes a literary-rhetorical method of justifying Israel's travel from Egyptian slavery to a distant land.

The Egyptian slavery reminds God to unfold a long-standing plot to send the Israelites to a promised land. God is acting within the parameters of God's long-standing plan for the Israelites. Slavery is therefore a literary-rhetorical device. First, it serves to capture the sympathies of the implied reader from the beginning of the story. Second, it moves the plot of God's long-standing plan. God's intervention and liberation of Israel from slavery is certainly not God's statement against the institution itself. This is evident, first of all, in the law that God gives to them—it does not forgo slavery, it provides for it (21:1–11). Second, while they take possession of the promised land with God's declaring, "Today I have rolled away from you the disgrace of Egypt" (Josh. 5:9), Israelites enslave the whole race of Gibeonites who choose to make peace with them. The permanent status of "hewers of wood and drawers of water" (Josh. 9:16–27) is conferred on the Gibeonites.

Needless to say, traveling is only the means to an end in the colonizer's literature. Its real subject is the land and its resources. As will become evident, the literary methods used to represent a land to be colonized, like those used to justify traveling, also revolve around God, characterizing it as a God-promised land, a rich land, an inhabited land.

Colonizing the Land and People[9]

"I WILL BRING YOU...TO A LAND FLOWING WITH MILK AND HONEY"

Land is the main subject of the imperial anti-conquest literary strategies. Postcolonial methods show that most imperial narratives characterize their targeted lands and people either positively or negatively.[10] The land to be entered and taken is either embellished or tarnished. What are the literary methods employed in Exodus to legitimate traveling to, entering, and taking control of a distant land? How does Exodus characterize this land?

---

[9]I must point out that the construction of lands/place and people/race/nations, both of the colonizer and the colonized, is closely interconnected and not easily separable. Therefore, theoretical references given under the subtitles of all these factors, which I have endeavored to present separately, will be relevant to all others.

[10]J. M. Blaut, *The Colonizer's Model of the World: Geographical Diffusionism and Eurocentric History* (London: The Guilford Press, 1993), 3–26, describes the "spatial elitism" that accompanied modern imperialism and its origins. He shows how Eurocentrism regarded every other geographical place and people as lacking or deviant. He traces this thinking "from a very old conception of Christendom and the Roman imperial legacy," 18. See also Ashcroft, Griffiths, Tiffin, "Place," in *The Post-colonial Studies Reader,* 394–418.

To examine the first question, in Exodus the literary methods of constructing anti-conquest claims over a distant land are grounded on constructing a God-given promise. The targeted land is characterized as a God-promised land.[11] God, who promised their ancestors the land of Canaan and who promised to bring them out of Egypt, decides it is the opportune time. Thus, God says,

> I appeared to Abraham, Isaac, and Jacob as God Almighty...I also established my covenant with them, to give them the land of Canaan, the land in which they resided as aliens. I have also heard the groaning of the Israelites whom the Egyptians are holding as slaves, and I have remembered my covenant. Say therefore to the Israelites, "I will bring you into the land that I swore to give to Abraham, Isaac, and Jacob; I will give it to you for a possession. I am the LORD." (6:3–5)

That the Lord swore to give or promised the Israelites the land of the Canaanites is, therefore, not peripheral or separable from their redemption from slavery in the book of Exodus. It is a different face of the same plot. God's promise of a gift and the subsequent redemption from slavery become the narrative's literary-rhetorical strategy for justifying Israel's act of traveling to the land of the Canaanites and taking it for a possession. It is on these grounds that Cain Hope Felder holds that this yoking of freedom and slavery indicates "that the apparent Old Testament emphasis on freedom is little more than a sociopolitical or religious ideal, rather than a practical daily reality."[12]

Turning to the second question, how does the narrative characterize the promised land? Colonial narratives define the land and its inhabitants to validate its occupation.[13] In Exodus, the God-given land is characterized positively. It is described as "a good and broad land" (3:8, 17; 34:2). Its goodness is captured through its classic characterization: "a land flowing with milk and honey" (3:8). The characterization betrays economic interests, for to speak of "a land flowing with milk and honey" is to admit to material benefits and interests. In this way, God and slavery may be literary-rhetorical devices employed to sanctify traveling to and taking possession of a distant and inhabited land, but as postcolonial studies show, the economic factor, the gold factor so to speak, is never peripheral in colonizing literature. Therefore, the Exodus narrative uses the God, gold, and glory factors to claim the beautiful and beneficial land of their gaze.

---

[11]To emphasize the ideology of God's promise of land, the claim is invoked at the introduction of institutional celebrations such as the Passover (12:25) and the consecration of first-borns (13:4–5).

[12]See Cain Hope Felder, *Troubling the Biblical Waters: Race, Class, and Family* (Maryknoll, N. Y.: Orbis Books, 1989), 104.

[13]See J. M. Blaut, *The Colonizer's Model,* for imperialism's construction of geography and its aims.

Yet the book of Exodus also characterizes the targeted land as an inhabited land. The narrative is painfully honest that the promised land, the God-given land, is not empty! It repeatedly and methodically reiterates that God is giving the Israelites the land of "the Canaanites, the Hittites, the Amorites, the Perizzites, the Hivites, and the Jebusites" (3:8, 17; 6:4; 13:5; 23:23; 34:2). The formula is rarely changed—see, for example, 6:4, 13:11—but even in the latter two citations the land is still identified as inhabited. That the narrative insists on a God-given land but equally admits that the land is occupied by different nations or races brings two questions to the surface: First, what is the rhetorical function of this overt admission? Second, how are the occupants of the land characterized?

Clearly, the open admission that the promised land is inhabited underlines God as authorizer. As discussed above, the characterization of God as the initiator and hero in the narrative is a rhetorical device that sanctifies the acts of imperialism. The Exodus anti-conquest ideology maintains its innocence by appealing to the highest, unquestionable authority of God. If God gives the land, then, regardless of whether it is inhabited, the whole act is just.

In fact, the overt recognition of injustice is characteristic of many colonial narratives.[14] On the surface, it seems like a self-critical stance, but it is another side of the anti-conquest rhetoric. David Quint's study on epic writing and imperial journeys notes that imperial authors always admit the injustice of their imperialism, but this does not serve to stop them. His genealogical study of the epic shows how heroic epics of imperialism reproduce the character of a cursing native, originating from Odysseus' one-eyed, blinded Cyclops. In the curse, the injustice to the colonized is admitted and given a voice by the imperialist's narrative, only to be ignored.[15] The open acknowledgment of injustice serves a number of purposes: to underline the colonizer's capacity to judge and to know, to preclude criticism from the colonized, and to sanitize the conscience of the colonizing nation. Once injustice has been admitted, then the colonizer can proceed to claim the distant land, of course, by placing the people of the colonized lands under a particular light.

"THEY PROSTITUTE THEMSELVES TO THEIR GODS" (34:15)

How are the inhabitants of the land characterized? The characterization of the occupants of the targeted land brings up one of the central methods of anti-conquest strategies: the identity of the colonizer and the colonized.[16] Their identities are intertwined; they are constructed as acute

---

[14]This will be evident in my analysis of Joseph Conrad's *Heart of Darkness*, in Part 3.

[15]See Quint, *Epic and Empire*, 99–130.

[16]For further theoretical readings see Boehmer, "Colonized Others," in *Colonial and Postcolonial Literature*, 79–89; Mudimbe, "Discourse of Power and Knowledge of Otherness," in *The Invention of Africa*, 1–23; Maunier, "Part 1: An Introduction to the Study of Race Contact," in *Sociology of Colonies*, vol. 1, 3–129.

opposites of superior and inferior, Godly and ungodly, civilized and barbaric, manly and womanly, adult and childish, developed and under-developed, Christian and un-Christian, white and colored, and so on. The first of each pair always refers to the colonizers, endowing them with posi-tive traits that authorize them to dominate and dispossess people of the latter category, who are marked by their lack. This strategy is evident in the book of Exodus.

In its early chapters, Exodus identifies the inhabitants of the targeted land by the names of their races without saying anything explicitly nega-tive or positive about them for a while. Only their land is characterized positively, as a land of milk and honey. As the narrative progresses, how-ever, negative characterizations begin to emerge precisely when the iden-tity of the Israelites is being meticulously defined in the wilderness of Sinai, a point I shall address independently below. It is when the covenant with the nation of Israel is established that God warns them to have no other gods or make any idol (20:2–6, 23; 23:13). The seemingly general warning is then specifically connected to the native inhabitants of the promised land in 23:23–33 (a passage that puts together the identities of colonizer and colonized and the contact zone). It reads as follows:

> When my angel goes in front of you, and brings you to the Amorites, the Hittites, the Perizzites, the Canaanites, the Hivites, and the Jebusites, and I blot them out, you shall not bow down to their gods, or worship them, or follow their practices, but *you shall utterly destroy them and break their pillars in pieces...You shall make no covenant with them and their gods.* They shall not live in your land, or they will make you sin against me; for if you worship their gods, it will surely be a snare to you. (23:23–24, 32–33; emphasis mine)

The gods and practices of the inhabitants of the targeted land, or the culture that defines their character, is cast negatively. The natives' culture will cause God's people to "sin"; it will become a "snare" to them. Because Canaanites are the carriers of the culture of their lands, they must not be allowed to live in their own land! The original inhabitants must, therefore, be blotted out. This point is further repeated and underlined in 34:11–17, which reads:

> I will drive before you the Amorites, the Canaanites, the Hittites, the Hivites, and the Jebusites. Take care not to make a covenant with the inhabitants of the land to which you are going, or it will become a snare among you. You shall *tear down* their altars, *break* their pillars, and *cut down* their sacred poles (for you shall worship no other god, because the LORD, whose name is Jealous, is a jeal-ous God). You shall *not make a covenant with the inhabitants of the land,* for when they prostitute themselves to their gods and sacrifice

to their gods, someone among them will invite you, and you will eat of the sacrifice. And you will take wives from among their daughters for your sons, and their daughters who prostitute themselves to their gods will make your sons also prostitute themselves to their gods. You shall not make cast idols. (emphasis mine)

Issues of contact zone, gender, and the identities of the colonized and the colonizer are interwoven in this passage. The identity of the colonized is defined through contrasting it with the identity of the colonizer. The gods, prostitution, and sacrificial practices of the colonized are impure to the chosen people of God, the colonizer. The impurity threatens to pollute the colonizer; hence, the narrative recommends driving out, making no covenant, tearing down altars, breaking sacred pillars, cutting down sacred poles, and not marrying the native daughters. Because the traits of the colonized are so impure, the effective way to prevent pollution is not only to destroy their cultural symbols but also to "blot out" and "drive out" the people. God her/himself says, "I will cast out nations before you, and enlarge your borders; no one shall covet your land" (34:24). Basically, the narrative casts the people of the targeted land negatively in order to validate the annihilation of all the inhabitants. It is only when the superiority of the colonizing nation is firmly secured against that of the colonized that the anti-conquest ideology can posit that it is acceptable to dispossess, depopulate, resettle, enslave, or annihilate those who are supposedly less deserving. How then is the identity of the colonizer (Israel) in the narrative world of Exodus constructed?

"YOU SHALL BE MY TREASURED POSSESSION OUT OF ALL THE PEOPLES" (19:5)

The identity of the colonizer is critical.[17] Those who have the right to travel to, enter, possess, and control distant and inhabited lands must be shown to be exceptionally different and well-deserving above their victims.[18] Accordingly, for the Israelites to claim an inhabited land, their identity must clearly stand out; in this case, it is distinguished from every other nation. God says, "Indeed, the whole earth is mine, but you shall be for me a priestly kingdom and a holy nation" (19:5–6). The Israelites become a chosen race, a holy race. The construction of their identity begins early in the narrative, when God recalls the covenant with their ancestors (2:24–25; 6:3–4) and says, "I will take you as my people, and I will be your God" (6:7). God says Israel is "my firstborn son" (4:22). From there on, Moses speaks to Pharaoh, saying, "Let my people go." The possessive pronoun

---

[17]For further studies see Maunier, "Psychology of Expansion," in *Sociology of Colonies,* vol. 1, 135–51; Boehmer, "Wealth, Sweetness, Glory: Justifications for the Empire," in *Colonial and Postcolonial Literature,* 36–44.

[18]See Blaut, *Colonizer's Model,* 1–43, on the creation and function of Eurocentricism in modern imperialism.

"my" marks them out as a possession of God distinct from the Egyptians. Their unique identity is further underlined during the plagues, when God declares, "I will make a distinction between my people and your people" (8:23; see also 9:4; 11:6–7). As a reminder that God made a distinction between Israelites and Egyptians during the last plague, Moses is instructed to institute the celebration of the Passover (13:1–16).

In fact, the rest of the book (chapters 14–40) is dedicated to defining Israel as God's "treasured possession out of all the people" (19:5). The moment Israelites leave Egypt for the promised land, the plot is put on hold (13:17–14:4). During this period of forty years of wandering in the wilderness their identity as God's chosen people is stringently hewed through laws, covenant, purity rites, rituals, buildings, and God's mighty acts, as well as through conflict with God. God's chosen people, those qualified to enter the promised land, are only those born in the wilderness (Josh. 5:2–7). The stringent ways of constructing the identity of the Israelites as a holy and chosen race of God tellingly foreshadows the shape of the contact zone.

The Contact Zone

The contact zone is the meeting and clashing of two different cultures that were geographically and historically separated, and it is an unavoidable stage of colonialism. While different groups of people always travel and live with people of other cultures and lands, what distinguishes the colonizer's contact zone is its approach. Its method is distinguished by a desire to take control of a foreign land—culturally, economically, politically, and geographically. How does the Exodus narrative construct the contact zone? Does it adopt a method of dialogue and mutual interdependence, or condemnation and replacement of all that is foreign? Since the book of Exodus ends with the Israelites still trekking to their promised land, the narrative only projects how the contact zone should be established. Joshua 1–12, on the other hand, takes up the projected themes of Exodus and presents a highly dramatized contact zone. I shall highlight them according to the biblical order.

"MAKE NO COVENANT WITH THEM AND THEIR GODS" (23:32)

In Exodus, the earliest projection of the contact zone appears after the Israelites have crossed the Red Sea (15:14–15). The Israelites sing a song of triumph, telling the story of how the inhabitants of Philistia, Edom, Moab, "and the inhabitants of Canaan melted away," and of how terror and dread fell upon them after hearing about the mighty acts of God. The key word is "melt," which does not speak of dialogue, exchange, or preservation, but images dissolution of human bodies. A detailed projection of the contact zone is provided later, in the above quoted passages of 23:23–33;

34:11–17, 24; and also 17:14. In the first passage God says, "I will blot them out," that is, the inhabitants of the promised land. The second phrase that is used to describe the contact zone is "I will drive them out," repeated four times (vv. 28, 29, 30, 31). Last, God "will hand over" (v. 31) the native inhabitants to the Israelites. In the second passage the phrase "I will drive them out" is reused (vv. 2, 33). This contact zone, described with the words *melt, blot out, drive out, hand over,* is best summarized in the command, "You shall make no covenant with them and their Gods" (23:32), repeated twice in 34:12, 15.

It follows that Israel must avoid cultural contact with the natives of the land, their gods, and practices. Israel must "utterly demolish" and "break…in pieces" (23:24) the cultural symbols of the inhabitants of the promised land. This point is best summarized in 34:13: "You shall tear down their altars, break their pillars, cut down their sacred poles (for you shall worship no other god)." Cultural contact is described with verbs that wholly shout "destroy." What is said in Exodus, however, is just an instruction. In Joshua's narrative world these instructions are applied and brought to realization.

"EVERY PLACE…YOUR FOOT WILL TREAD UPON I HAVE GIVEN TO YOU" (JOSH. 1:3)

In Joshua the forty years of wandering in the wilderness comes to an end. The Exodus instructions concerning contact with the inhabitants of Canaan are about to be enacted in Joshua. These are reiterated in the familiar Exodus language of melting (2:8, 24; 5:1), utterly destroying (2:10), driving out (3:10), and handing over (6:1) the native inhabitants of the promised land. The narrative world of Joshua carefully connects its plot and story world with the book of Exodus. To Joshua, God says, "Every place that the sole of your foot will tread upon I have given to you, as I promised to Moses" (1:3).

Joshua then leads Israel "to go in to take possession of the land that the LORD…gives" (1:11). The entrance and contact with different races and towns begins with Jericho and proceeds systematically to Negeb, until "Joshua took the whole land, according to all that the LORD had spoken to Moses" (11:23). Israelite troops proceed methodically. Beginning with Jericho, they attack and commit "to destruction by the edge of the sword *all* in the city, both men and women, young and old, oxen, sheep, and donkeys" (6:21, emphasis mine) and set the city on fire. But "the silver and gold, and the vessels of bronze and iron, they put into the treasury of the house of the LORD" (6:24). Alongside these treasures, Rahab the prostitute is spared, a point that will be revisited below. Ai is the second target. The Lord says to Joshua, "Do to Ai, and its king as you did to Jericho and its king" (8:2), but this time they may keep its livestock for themselves as well. Joshua's troops then "entered the city, took it, and at once set the city on fire" (8:19). They "utterly destroyed all the inhabitants of Ai," saving "the livestock and the spoil of that city" (8:26–27). With this pattern of attacking cities, burning them, destroying people, but saving treasures, livestock, and land, thirty-one kings and their people are attacked and dispossessed (12:7–24).

Basically, the contact zone seeks to "utterly destroy" the inhabitants of the land. It is a strategy of depopulation by annihilation in order to weaken and control. In this clean-out approach we glean the rhetoric of the colonizers' cultural purity claim at its best. Its claim of maintaining rigid boundaries of purity is, in fact, nothing but the rhetoric of power. Just as colonized victims borrow from their colonizers, colonizing powers borrow cultural ideas, artifacts, and practices from their victims. They come to live with their colonized populations. For rhetorical reasons of power, however, they maintain the claim of a clean-out contact zone. This is evident in Israel's retaining of some cities, some populations, silver, gold, and vessels of bronze and iron that are put into "the treasury of the LORD," even though the projected contact zone prescribed a clean-out approach. Needless to say, these retained cultural artifacts preserve the culture that is supposedly dangerous. The contact zone, therefore, never completely wipes out native culture and populations, but for reasons of retaining power over the land, native culture and people are allowed to survive as suppressed entities.

Joshua 11:12–20 best summarizes the shape of the contact zone, showing its overt material interests and its anti-conquest ideology grounded in God and glory. It reads:

> And all the towns of those kings, and all their kings, Joshua took, *struck them* with the edge of the sword, *utterly destroying them,* as Moses the servant of the LORD had commanded. But Israel burned none of the towns that stood on mounds except Hazor, which Joshua did burn. All the spoil of these towns, and the livestock, the Israelites took for their booty; but *all the people they struck down with the edge of the sword, until they had destroyed them, and they did not leave any who breathed.* As the LORD commanded his servant Moses, so Moses commanded Joshua, and so Joshua did; he left nothing undone of all that the LORD had commanded Moses. So *Joshua took all that land.* (11:12–16; emphasis mine)

Conclusion

As the above analysis shows, the story of Israel's trek from Egypt to the land of Canaan is in every way a God, gold, and glory narrative. The Israelites were enslaved in Egypt, and thus they move to a land flowing with milk and honey (gold); due to their bondage, Moses was divinely commissioned to free and take Israel to the promised land (God). Finally, they are set free from Egypt by the sheer might of God, demonstrated in the ten plagues, in the whole journey to the promised land, and in the taking possession of the land (glory). In every way, Israel's story in Exodus–Joshua highlights the literary-rhetorical strategies of colonial subjugation of distant lands.

The Exodus–Joshua story is an imperializing rhetoric because it is expressly focused on taking and maintaining power over foreign and inhabited lands. Consequently, the above postcolonial analysis has illumined its methods of creating myths of power by showing the literary characteristics of the anti-conquest and the contact zone. The story of Exodus–Joshua shows that lands are not only physical geographical spaces. They are in every way webs of intricately woven literary structures, whose people, like the scrolls, equally bear on their bodies these geographical tales.[19] The colonizers narrativize themselves as exceptional chosen beings, while they also construct tales of derogation against their targeted victims as beings who deserve to be invaded, dispossessed, subjugated, and annihilated if need be.[20]

Given that imperialism is an unequal relationship of different lands and people, written on both paper and human bodies, how does its power discourse use gender representation to articulate relationships of domination and subjugation? What are the roles of women in imperializing narratives, and how do they reflect the use of gender to articulate colonial ideologies?[21] In texts such as Exodus and Joshua 1–12, which are so promise-oriented—that is, imperialist-geared—how must, or can, a feminist reading claim the female figures for feminist commitments? These questions seek to highlight gender and the rhetoric of imperial subjugation and domination.

Gender, Method, and Empire-Building in Exodus

"Their daughters...prostitute themselves to their gods" (34:16b)

Gender analysis of the books of Exodus and Joshua has been done in some feminist works.[22] Danna Nolan Fewell and David M. Gunn, in their book *Gender, Power, and Promise,* offer an excellent analysis of the use of

---

[19]See Homi Bhabha, ed., *Nation and Narration* (New York: Routledge, 1990), 1–8, on the idea of "nation as narration."

[20]See Anders Stephanson, *Manifest Destiny: American Expansion and the Empire of Right* (New York: Hill and Wang, 1995), for the use of Exodus ideas of chosenness and promised land in the colonization of America. He holds that the Puritans reenacted the Exodus narrative and America became "the new Canaan, a land promised, to be conquered and reworked for the glory of God by his elect forces," 6–7.

[21]For further works on gender in postcolonial theories see Ashcroft, Griffiths, and Tiffin, eds., "Feminism and Postcolonialism," in *The Postcolonial Studies Reader,* 249–73; "Theorizing Gender," in *Colonial Discourse and Postcolonial Theory,* 191–257; Donaldson, *Decolonizing Feminisms.*

[22]See Setel, "Exodus," 26–35, and Danna N. Fewell, "Joshua," 63–66, in *The Women's Bible Commentary,* ed. Carol A. Newsom and Sharon H. Ringe; Peggy L. Day, ed., *Gender and Difference in Ancient Israel* (Minneapolis: Fortress Press, 1989).

gender representation from Genesis to 2 Kings. By linking gender and the promise, their book is pertinent to a postcolonial quest. Indeed, after analyzing the characterization of women in Genesis, they conclude that

> In the beginning God involves women directly: he insists that Sarah bear the child of promise; he assures Hagar that she too will become a great nation; he explains to Rebekah that she will mother not one nation but two. Taking her revealed knowledge to heart, Rebekah becomes the voluntary guardian of the promise, ensuring, through whatever dubious means, that Jacob (Israel) inherits the choice land and prosperity rather than Esau (Edom). After Rebekah, however, God deigns not to speak to the other women of Genesis...Israel (Jacob) has been born. From this point on the women (as mothers) become unwitting caretakers of the promise. Leah and Rachel (Genesis 29–30), together, "they build up the house of Israel"...Tamar (Genesis 38), in an effort to secure her own economic well being, keeps Judah's line intact, holding in trust the future monarch David...By the beginning of Exodus the twelve sons of Israel with their families (seventy in all) are living in Egypt, becoming so numerous...Israel is well on its way to becoming a "great nation."[23]

Fewell and Gunn's analysis shows that women's stories of motherhood in Genesis are primarily about the nation of Israel over against other nations in a very promise-intended quest.[24] What these women do and what happens to them and their children is ultimately in the service of the promise. Their stories are not simply about women, but allegories of the "promise." Their baby boys, too, are not just children, but those who will either move, claim, or lose the promise. The same trend is evident in Exodus. The disobedient midwives (1:15–21), the courageous mother and sister of Moses (2:1–10), the compassionate daughter of Pharaoh (2:5-10), and the wife of Moses (2:15–22; 4:24–26) all serve to move the plot toward the realization of the promise.

Despite this overt centrality of the promise or imperializing ideology to the cultural texts of the Hebrew Bible, Fewell and Gunn's reading fails to ascribe equal importance to gender and promise. For instance, Fewell and Gunn are resisting critics who "read wondering what the story of promise might look like to those excluded people, in particular the women, who stand on the 'other' side of a *gender* divide."[25] They read with "a

---

[23]Danna Nolan Fewell and David Gunn, *Gender, Power, and Promise: The Subject of the Bible's First Story* (Nashville: Abingdon Press, 1993), 89–90.

[24]See Randall C. Bailey, "They Are Nothing but Incestuous Bastards," in *Reading from This Place*, vol. 1, 121–38, ed. Fernando F. Segovia and Mary Ann Tolbert, who finds negative sexual activities associated with foreign nations, to dehumanize and discredit these people, and to sanction Israel's oppression of them.

[25]Fewell and Gunn, *Gender, Power, and Promise*, 13.

commitment to see radical reformation in gender relations in our own society."[26] Yet Fewell and Gunn do not read wondering what the promise looks like to those who are the original inhabitants of the promised land. The "excluded people" single out women and do not empathize with those who have been marked for dispossession and death. Neither do they read with a social commitment to see radical transformation in the international relations of our own world. In short, for Fewell and Gunn, gender concerns override the promise, which, as shown earlier, is the biblical technical term for the act of claiming and possessing distant and inhabited lands: imperialism. Fewell and Gunn's definition of the promise and patriarchy also indicates that imperial critique is peripheral to their analysis. They recognize the centrality of the promise, pointing out that there is the

> promise to Noah regarding sustaining the creation, to Abraham regarding land and progeny, to Moses and the people of Israel regarding the covenant of law and security as a nation in exchange for exclusive allegiance, and to David regarding the maintenance of a royal dynasty. The counterpoint to the story...of Israel is to live up to the promise.[27]

Certainly, their definition captures the importance of the theme of promise in the Hebrew Bible. However, it falls short of naming the promise for what it is. Similarly, Fewell and Gunn's definition of patriarchy does not provide a sufficient naming and analysis of the promise. They use Gerda Lerna's words to define patriarchy as

> the manifestation and institutionalization of male dominance over women and children in the family and the extension of male dominance over women in society in general. It implies that men hold power in all the important institutions of society and that women are deprived of access to power.[28]

This excellent definition does not translate to a sufficient understanding of the promise, imperialism. The promise and patriarchy overlap, but they are not identical. Imperialism is not just about male power over women and children. Rather, it is the power of one nation, consisting of men and women, over men and women of distant lands and nations. In the story of Exodus–Joshua it is exemplified by the power claims of the Israelites over the Canaanites, while patriarchy would be found in both nations.

Needless to say, the category of imperialism in cultural texts, including the Bible, needs to be recognized for its reality. It should not be subsumed under patriarchy, first, because imperialism is not identical to patriarchy; second, because like gender relations, imperialism describes oppressive

---

[26]Ibid.
[27]Ibid.
[28]Ibid., 15.

power relations that since ancient times have continued to characterize international relations. That being recognized, we can then ask, How has patriarchy served imperialism, or, biblically speaking, served the promise?

Colonizing and Colonized Woman

Because of patriarchy, imperialism is to a large degree a male game. Yet women are always its active participants as travelers, revolutionists, sellouts, benefactors, and victims of its power relationships.[29] In imperial settings, women can be categorized into the colonized and colonizers: those who must rule and those who must be ruled. This great divide connotes differences of class, race, and culture consistent with the earlier mentioned dualisms that mark identities of colonizer versus the colonized. The dualisms always have a category of womanly and manly nations or lands; that is, imperialism employs gender relations to articulate ideologies of subordination and domination.[30]

Women often become the indicators of different lands and cultures.[31] In his discussion on aspects of race contact, Rene Maunier notes that in imperialist settings "native women have often been the first agents of contact. This provides the classic literary motif of the tragic romance between the European man and the native woman."[32] The meeting foreshadows the desires of the colonizer and the fate of the land. A good case in point is Pocahontas, one of the latest Disney reproductions of white, North American settler-colonizers' myth.[33] The white British settlers arrive, pronounce everyone an ignorant savage, and pitch the Union Jack flag, claiming the land, but Pocahontas falls in love with John Smith. She defies her father and everyone else to take the side of the enemy. Pocahontas undoubtedly belongs to the creative pen of the colonizer.

Through these classic literary motifs, women's bodies, therefore, become the prescripts and guide maps upon which the identity and desires of the colonizer, and the colonized too, are written and can be read. This is the discursive colonization of women, which while different from the actual colonization, is not independent of historical colonization and oppression of women. It is, therefore, important to highlight how gendered imperial

---

[29]See Alison Blunt, *Travel, Gender, and Imperialism: Mary Kingsley and West Africa* (New York: Guilford Press, 1994); and Alison Blunt and Gillian Rose, eds., *Writing Women and Space: Colonial and Postcolonial Geographies* (New York: Guilford Press, 1994).

[30]See Quint, *Epic and Empire*, 22–48, on the identification of Eastern nations with the fleeing Cleopatra inscribed in the shield of Aeneas and its reappropriation in the history of epic and empire. Using this scene, subsequent epics identified nations targeted for conquests with feminine figures and leadership.

[31]See Williams and Chrisman, eds., "Theorizing Gender," in *Colonial Discourse and Post-colonial Theory*, 193. See also Margaret Strobel, *European Women and the Second British Empire* (Indianapolis: Indiana University Press, 1991), 1–15, 49–51, on British wives and the women of colonized lands.

[32]Maunier, *Sociology of Colonies*, vol. 1, 70.

[33]The reference is to the movie *Pocahontas*.

rhetoric is expounded through the characterization of women in Exodus and Joshua 1–12 by examining the roles of women in the text.

Colonized and Colonizer Women in Exodus

Narratively speaking, the position of Israelite women changes from the colonized, in Egypt, to the colonizer as the journey to the promised land begins. As colonized women, they share in the oppression of their men. Israelite women and men are both slaves; they have no human rights in Egypt. To this degree, imperialism is gender blind, though, of course, colonized women suffer more because they also have two patriarchal systems superimposed on them. Because they are under oppression, the colonized usually overlook some gender roles in the struggle to gain independence.[34] In Exodus, for example, the struggle for independence is pioneered by women: midwives, mothers, sisters, and daughters defy the king's instruction to annihilate Israelite children (Ex. 1:15–2:1–22). Thus, they sustain the survival of Israel, leading to the survival of Moses, who later joins their long struggle against Pharaoh's imperial oppression.

Before the exploited Israelites leave Egypt, they want to reclaim the labor of their hands. They do not want to leave Egypt without indemnity.[35] This task is primarily assigned to women: "You will not go empty-handed; each woman shall ask her neighbor and any woman living in the neighbor's house for jewelry of silver and of gold, and clothing, and you shall put them on your sons and on your daughters; and so you shall plunder the Egyptians" (3:21–22; see also 11:2; 12:35–36). The narrator reports that they indeed "plundered" the Egyptians prior to departure. How this plundering was actualized the narrator does not inform the reader, beyond mentioning that the Lord would put them in favor with the Egyptians. The reader can imagine that it was not a peaceful "asking" and receiving from the Egyptians. Some economic war of seizing the expensive items must have ensued, one that was no less bloody than the plagues of Moses. Later, after they successfully crossed the Red Sea, Israelite men and women sang war songs together, with Miriam leading the dance and song (15:1–21). The point accentuated here is that some gender roles among the colonized are temporarily suspended, especially during the struggle for independence. Women and men are both victims of imperialism; they fight to reclaim their human rights together. In the Exodus story, however, the position of the Israelite women changes from the colonized to the colonizer.

---

[34]See Robin Morgan, ed., *Sisterhood Is Global: The International Women's Anthology* (New York: Doubleday, 1984), 750–51, on Two-Thirds World women and the struggle for independence.

[35]See Leticia Guardiola-Saenz, "Breaking Bread Together: A Mexican-American Reading of Matthew 15:21–28," a paper presented at the Society of Biblical Literature 1995 annual meeting in Philadelphia, for the argument of the colonized claiming indemnity from their exploiters.

Israelite women assume the status of colonizers upon entering the wilderness and journeying to the promised land. Together with their men they become God's "treasured possession out of all the peoples" (19:5), and they enter a covenant with God (20–21). How does the role of Israelite women reflect the imperialist agendas of their nation?

Compared with their earlier role as the colonized, the women's role as the colonizer is almost nonexistent. Patriarchy emerges and they are submerged. Moses leads the journey, assisted by Aaron. He remains a privileged conversation partner with God; he chooses able male assistants at Jethro's advice; he receives the codes of the covenant, the ten commandments; and, finally, at his death, Joshua takes over and enters the promised land.

But at the launching of the law, patriarchal division resurfaces. For the first time a distinction is made between Israelite men and women. Moses says to the people, "Prepare for the third day; *do not go near a woman*" (19:15; emphasis mine). Women's purity is evidently suspect–they are sources of pollution. In Exodus 20–21, when the ten commandments are given, it becomes evident that patriarchy reigns, since the law expounds on relationships based on propertied male-headed households. Like God, who is jealous, men are commanded not to covet another man's house, wife, slave, ox, donkey, "or anything that belongs to your neighbor," tellingly listing women under men's property. In short, the contradictory social position of Israelite women as colonized patriarchal objects and colonizing race-privileged subjects emerges.[36]

As women from the colonizer's side, Israelite women become the measure and keepers of the purity or holiness of their nation. Thus, their role emerges clearly when the identity of the Israelites is pitted against the identity of the Canaanites (34:11–17). The Israelites must not

> make a covenant with the inhabitants of the land, for when they prostitute themselves to their gods and sacrifice to their gods, someone among them will invite you, and you will eat the sacrifice. And you will take wives from among their daughters for your sons, and their daughters who prostitute themselves to their gods will make your sons also to prostitute themselves to their gods. (34:15–16)

What is at stake is the purity of the sons of Israel. Women of the targeted land pose a serious threat. Because they supposedly prostitute themselves to their gods (sacred prostitution has proven difficult to verify, suggesting that it is rhetorical),[37] if they are allowed to live, they will lead the sons of

---

[36]See Donaldson, *Decolonizing Feminisms,* 6, on this position also occupied by white, Western, middle-class women.

[37]See Peggy L. Day, *Gender and Difference in Ancient Israel* (Minneapolis: Fortress Press, 1989), 5.

Israel to the same snare, to sin. Undoubtedly, the gods of all the people in the targeted land are dangerous, yet the narrative singles out their women. Clearly, the women of the colonized embody the status of their land. The flip side of the coin is the role of the Israelite women. Although not mentioned in the passage, they hold the key to the identity of their men. Because the Israelite women belong to a jealous God, they can keep intact the identity of the nation as a chosen and treasured people of God over the rest of the earth. Thus, the women of the colonizer embody the status of colonizing men.

It is often tempting to categorize women from both sides as equally oppressed. This approach, rightfully criticized by Chandra Mohanty,[38] characterized early Western feminism and alienated Two-Thirds World women from the feminist discourse. To be sure, patriarchy affects both of them, but the category of colonizer and colonized is a significant international class division.[39] The former is some form of a high class, rhetorically marked for all political, economic, and social benefits of the land of the latter. Men may be its major beneficiaries, but the colonizing women, too, partake of its colonial harvest. The latter class designates those marked as lacking and undeserving in every way—which means disgrace, dispossession, slavery, exile, or even annihilation.

Rahab: A Colonized Woman

The characterization of Rahab, to me, best highlights the varying degrees of oppression experienced by colonizing and colonized women. A brief elaboration on Rahab will highlight the dangers of reclaiming women's roles without naming its imperialistic agendas. It is, therefore, proposed that this flexible, yet recognizable and reoccurring, pattern of the use of gender in imperializing rhetoric should be recognized as a literary type-scene of land possession in the rhetoric of God, gold, glory, and gender.

Lands are often represented by a woman in imperializing narratives. In general, if a woman is met, her affections won, then the land she represents will also be entered and domesticated by the colonizer, or it is at least available for the taking of the colonizer, if so desired. The characterizations of Pharaoh's daughter, Zipporah, and Rahab are thus different because they represent the colonizer and the colonized. Pharaoh's daughter is a princess, denoting the power of Egypt, and her affections are distant (she gives Moses back to his mother). Zipporah's affections are strenuously denied, her relationship with Moses is cold from the start and remains a labored one (2:20), indicating that Moses does not seek to win and

---

[38]See Chandra T. Mohanty, "Under Western Eyes: Feminist Scholarship and Colonial Discourse," in *Colonial Discourse and Post-colonial Theory,* ed. Williams and Chrisman, 196–220.

[39]For this point, see Gayatri Chakravorty Spivack, "Can the Subaltern Speak," in *Colonial Discourse and Post-colonial Theory,* ed. Williams and Chrisman, 66–111.

domesticate Midian.[40] The story about entering the promised land, embodied in the encounter with Rahab the prostitute, is completely different.

"THEY WENT, AND ENTERED THE HOUSE OF A PROSTITUTE" (JOSH. 2:1B)

Unlike Pharaoh's daughter and Zipporah, Rahab represents a land to be colonized. In a very brief and direct plot, the narrator tells us that Joshua sent two spies to view the land and "they went, and entered the house of a prostitute whose name was Rahab, and spent the night there" (Josh. 2:1). Beyond entering the house of a prostitute and spending a night with her, they do no further spying of the land. Rahab is the only land they enter and spy. The two Israelite men, who should avoid any covenant with the native people of the promised land, given the prostitution of their women, seem to demonstrate their vulnerability. Surprisingly, when Joshua hears about it, there is no indication that he regards their actions as a gross violation of the law.

Of course, Rahab's story is a prescript bearing the projected desires of the colonizer. Accordingly, Rahab is a prostitute: a woman open for any man's taking, a woman entered by any man and committed to none. Yet something drastically different happens. By the time the two Israelite men leave Rahab, the prostitute unconventionally seeks a commitment from them. She says, "Swear to me by the LORD that you...will deal kindly with my family. Give me a sign of good faith" (Josh. 2:12). And the men respond by saying, "Our life for yours!" (Josh. 2:14). They commit themselves to her as she has committed herself to them. Henceforth, Rahab is no longer going to exchange hands. She is committed to Israel and they are committed to her. And so it happens, Jericho is invaded, burned down, and men and women are destroyed, "but Rahab the prostitute, with her family and all who belonged to her [are] spared" (Josh. 6:25). Rahab's affections were sought by the Israelite men and were given with oaths made. The story of Rahab is a script about the domestication of the promised land. She reflects the colonizer's desire to enter and domesticate the land of Canaan.

As a script about the domestication of the promised land, the characterization of Rahab is loaded with colonizing ideologies. First, as a representative of her land, she is characterized as a prostitute. It denotes her inadequacy, her wildness, and her need to be tamed by those with superior morals, those who must save her. Second, Rahab's deeds and words reflect colonizing ideologies of subjugation. She wants her life and those of her family to be safe, but she does not believe her safety is in the hands of her people. Therefore, when the king's messengers come to inquire about the spies, informing her that they are enemies, Rahab takes sides with the enemy. She misleads her own people in order to hide and save the enemy.

---

[40]From this perspective, the concerns of Zipporah's story resonate with the story of Dinah's rape (Gen. 38).

Through her actions, Rahab is portrayed as one who totally believes in the superiority of the colonizer; one who totally wants the rule of the colonizer over her own people and land; and one who does not believe in the strength of her own people. With her words, she must proclaim their superiority and their beliefs; hence, she says,

> "I know that the LORD has given you the land, and that dread of you has fallen on us, and that all the inhabitants of the land melt in fear before you. For we have heard how the LORD dried up the water of the Red Sea before you when you came out of Egypt, and what you did to the two kings of the Amorites that were beyond the Jordan, to Sihon and Og, whom you utterly destroyed. As soon as we heard it, our hearts melted, and there was no courage left in any of us because of you. The LORD your God is indeed God in heaven above and on earth below. Now then, since I have dealt kindly with you, swear to me by the LORD that you in turn will deal kindly with my family."…The men said to her, "Our life for yours!" (2:9–14)

Fewell and Gunn note that Rahab's words sound as if she has been reading Deuteronomy. Her words also resonate with the Exodus and Joshuan projections of the contact zone, where themes of melting and utterly destroying first appear. Similarly, when the spies report back to Joshua they also say, "Truly the LORD has given all the land into our hands; moreover all the inhabitants of the land melt in fear before us" (2:24). Rahab's voice is notably one with the colonizer. As a literary creation of the colonizer's pen, she is the mouthpiece of their agendas. The colonizer's ideal dream is that the colonized will proclaim the colonizer's superiority, pledge absolute loyalty, and surrender all their rights voluntarily—an ideal met by the Gibeonites, who became slaves of Israel. Rahab's story contains the somewhat hidden agenda of the colonizer that proceeds by characterizing the colonized as people "who *require* and beseech to be dominated."[41] The latter point reflects the textual fantasies of colonizers, where they imagine themselves as highly demanded by their targeted victims. This pattern is evident in *The Odyssey* and *The Aeneid*, where imperial traveling heroes, Odysseus and Aeneas, are constantly detained by women and goddesses of foreign lands, who want them to stay in their lands.

The critical question, therefore, is, can Rahab's story in all its parts be reclaimed for feminist subversive purposes without subscribing to its overwhelming imperialist agendas? To use Audre Lorde's words, can the master's tools dismantle his own house?[42] If so, how?

---

[41]Said, *Culture and Imperialism,* 9.
[42]See Audre Lorde, *Sister Outsider,* 110–13.

In both *The Women's Bible Commentary* and her book with Gunn, *Gender, Power, and Promise*, Fewell makes attempts to employ the story of Rahab for feminist concerns. In the latter book they hold that

> the overall effect of this picture is to question the clear cut notion of insiders and outsiders. In other words, it seriously disturbs the patriarchal notion of the world as a set of binary opposites. When foreigners can quote Deuteronomy with more facility than Israelites can, what does that say about the grand theological ideas of chosenness and exclusivity? When foreigners show themselves to be more courageous and dependable than Israelites, what does that say about the integrity of Israel? In the context of imminent holy "war," where everything and everyone foreign is to be utterly destroyed, the story leads us to ask, how many Rahabs, how many prophets, how many protectors, indeed, how many innocents, are out there in Canaan, doomed to die on account of their Otherness. The bellicose rhetoric of Moses and Joshua—and YHWH, too, for that matter—is irreparably undercut. [43]

This is an admirable attempt to reemploy Rahab for feminist liberationist aims. It is a reading that attempts to subvert hierarchical dualisms and promote coexistence of differences. Nevertheless, it proceeds by writing into the imperialist agendas. The major problem, I would insist, is the use of the patriarchal category, where we are dealing with something bigger, or different: imperialism. As I will show, Fewell and Gunn's well-intended efforts demonstrate that patriarchal criticism does not translate into imperialism critique.

To start with the issue of insiders and outsiders, though the law of Israel is given to mark their chosenness from the rest of the earth, it provides for alien residents (Ex. 20:9–10; 22:21; 23:9). Rahab and Gibeonites live among Israelites (Josh. 6:25; 9:1–27). This clearly shows that the insider-outsider identity in imperializing texts is never meant to be absolute, but to maintain the power of the colonizer over the colonized. The primary aim of most colonizers is not so much to annihilate the inhabitants of the land, but to control the land, the people, the resources, and the culture. The ideal is embodied in the Pocahontas, Gibeonite, and Rahab types: those who will willingly and openly accept and proclaim the colonizers' superiority and pledge their loyalty to them.

Fewell and Gunn also read Rahab's surprising familiarity with Deuteronomy and faithfulness to Israel as an attestation of many prophets and protectors doomed to die due to their difference. For them, her echoing of Deuteronomy, her betraying of her own nation, and her siding with

---

[43]Fewell and Gunn, *Gender, Power, and Promise*, 120. See also Danna Nolan Fewell, "Judges," in Carol A. Newsom and Sharon H. Ringe, eds., *The Women's Bible Commentary* (Louisville, Ky.: Westminster/John Knox Press, 1992), 67–77.

the enemy not only ranks her with prophets and protectors, but also irreparably undercuts the dualistic rhetoric of Moses, Joshua, and God. Indeed, Rahab's actions are said to show her "to be more courageous and dependable than Israelites." Fewell and Gunn's reading lacks sufficient suspicion and resistance: They seem to overlook that Rahab is a literary creation of the author of Joshua, the colonizer. The question to ask is, Why would the author of Joshua, who carefully links the book with the aims of Exodus and Moses, write a story that undercuts his aims?

Far from undercutting the interests of the Israelites, Rahab embodies their interests. She does not resist their acts, aims, and dreams; she advances the promise. To regard her as a dependable, courageous woman when she can only do this by being party to the annihilation of her own city and people—a sellout—is to overlook that Rahab, like her dead people, is dead. Although physically alive, she is culturally and politically dead. From now on she can exist only as one who "can quote Deuteronomy with more facility than Israelites," that is, a perfectly colonized mind. Rahab is a literary phantom of imperialism's "cultural bomb," which, according to Ngugi wa Thiongo, works "to annihilate a people's belief in their names, in their languages, in their environment, in their heritage of struggle, in their unity, in their capacities and ultimately in themselves."[44] For the victims of imperialism, Rahab reminds us of our own stories—stories written about us, not for us, stories that are a nightmare to read.

I would, therefore, propose that before claiming any female characters, feminist readers should expose not only the patriarchal side but also the imperial agendas and ideologies in literary works. Many readers and readings that are committed to the struggle for the liberation of the oppressed will continue to subscribe to the agendas of imperialism unless they begin to recognize that imperialism is pervasive and persistent, and proceeds by adopting structured patterns that feature in most of our so-called canonical texts.

The persistence and pervasiveness of imperialistic colonizing patterns are evident not only in Jewish biblical literature but also in Western literature.[45] En route to highlighting its literary methods in *Heart of Darkness*, a twentieth-century novel, it is worth pointing out that *The Aeneid*, a Western classic, reflects literary strategies that closely resonate with the Exodus narrative. I will touch on *The Aeneid* to build a bridge from ancient to modern types of literature, and also as a strategy that counteracts anti-Semitism.

---

[44]Ngugi, *Decolonizing the Mind,* 3.

[45]To capture these reoccuring patterns of representations, Maunier, in *Sociology of Colonies,* vol. 1, calls them "organizations of ideas" or "worlds of feelings," 136; Mudimbe, in *Invention of Africa,* terms them a "colonizing structure," 2; and Said, in *Culture and Imperialism,* speaks of "the structure of attitude and reference," 75, 111.

The Aeneid: God, Gender, and Method in Empire-Building

The Roman Empire was already born when Virgil wrote *The Aeneid* between 31 and 19 B.C.E. His primary aim was to account for Rome's rise to power and to write away the shame of their defeat and destruction recorded in *The Odyssey*, in which the Greeks sacked Troy and burned it.[46] Thus, Aeneas, its hero and divinely sanctioned founder of the Roman Empire, survives and escapes with a sizeable company, sailing to Rome, where his ancestors supposedly originated. Three points highlight that, like Exodus, its imperial claims depend on divinely grounded anti-conquest strategy, intertextuality, and the gender representations that project the desires of the imperial heros.

To begin with the divine claim, Jupiter declares that "to Romans I set no boundary in space or time, I have granted them dominion, and it has no end…I will foster the nation which wears the toga, the Roman nation, masters of the world. My decree is made."[47] This promise was made after their defeat in Troy. According to Aeneas, when they escaped the war, they only wanted to search for an uninhabited land, but the divine powers instructed them to sail to Rome (Latium) where the Trojans' ancestors originated. A divine oracle informed him that "the house of Aeneas, the sons of his sons, and all their descendants shall bear rule over earth's widest bounds."[48] Nevertheless, Aeneas and his crew were detained from their destination by endless sea disasters. At the opening of the book, a hurricane has just redirected their route, wrecked their ships, and thrown them onto an African seashore by the city of Carthage, ruled by a woman, Dido. The latter brings into view the use of gender in imperial claims, a point I will revisit after highlighting the intertextuality of the Roman imperial myth.

Since Virgil wrote not only to explain the rise of the Roman Empire but also to address *The Odyssey*'s record of shame, *The Aeneid* is an intertextually conceived epic. It begins with the end of a battle described in *The Odyssey* between Greeks and Trojans, or Romans, and closely imitates its counterpart. Departing from the battle, Aeneas, like Odysseus, is a traveling hero who encounters and survives numerous terrifying dangers, disasters, and temptations, but whose final destination remains in focus regardless of hindrances. Aeneas' journey closely follows in the steps of Odysseus, encountering the same dangers (e.g., he also comes to the coast of Cyclops, and he visits Hades).[49] Like Odysseus and Moses, Aeneas is a traveling hero who is immensely favored by divine powers against all odds.

---

[46]Quint, in *Epic and Empire,* credits Virgil with the politicization of the epic genre, for his rewriting *The Odyssey* signaled the beginning of a long chain of imitation in the writing of epics to justify or counter various imperial powers, 1–18.

[47]Virgil, *The Aeneid,* trans. G. R. Wilson Knight (London: Penguin Books, 1956), 36.

[48]Ibid., 78.

[49]See Quint, *Epic and Empire,* 89–96, on how Virgil follows the plot of the *The Odyssey* while at the same time he subverts it in order to exalt his own hero, Aeneas, over Odysseus.

His arrival and reception at Carthage displays the divine favor on his side but, above all, demonstrates the use of gender rhetoric to project imperial desires.[50]

Gendered Imperialisms

Dido, like Pharaoh's daughter, is royal and much more. She is a widowed queen, founder and ruler of Carthage, who has decided against remarrying. The arrival of Aeneas and his crew, like that of the Israelites in Egypt, is also engineered by natural disaster and divine guidance. Jupiter has already declared that Carthage should "open and receive the Trojans as guests, and Dido must not forbid them her territory through ignorance of the ordained plan."[51] Mercury is thus sent "to put from them all thoughts of hostility," but especially to inspire "their queen with a tolerance for the Trojans and a kindly intent."[52] Thus, Dido not only welcomes the weary travelers and promises to help them with their journey but also immediately says, "Or would you rather settle here in my realm on an equal footing with me?"[53] Like the Pharaoh, who welcomes Joseph's family to the wealthy land of Egypt seemingly under his own initiative but who is in fact propelled by the divine will to push the plot of its chosen ones toward its ends, the implied reader knows that Dido is a helpless actor in the divinely decreed plot.

As if this were not enough, the divine powers of Aeneas' plan to "enclose the queen in such a girdle of flames that no act of divine power may divert her from submitting...to a fierce love of Aeneas."[54] They intend to "enflame her with a distraction of love, and entwine the fire of it about her every bone," even though they are set on sending Aeneas to Rome.[55] In short, Aeneas can never settle in Carthage. The two marry with the whole affair seemingly driven by Dido's excitement. Within a short time the divine powers recall Aeneas to rededicate himself to his journey and destiny. The heartbroken Dido, failing to retain Aeneas, curses him and commits suicide at his departure.

The story of Dido's availability (together with her land) and her attempt to detain the imperial hero, who is to be founder of "a nation that masters the world," closely recalls Odysseus' seven years of detention by Calypso, the demi-goddess in the island of Circe, who would not let him go until the divine powers intervened. As Quint points out, her curse recalls the Cyclops Polyphemus' curse on Odysseus for stealing his food and

---

[50]See Quint, *Epic and Empire,* on how the shield of Aeneas associated Eastern nations with the feminine figure of fleeing Cleopatra and the reproduction of this stereotype in subsequent epics, 28–31.

[51]Virgil, *The Aeneid,* 36.

[52]Ibid.

[53]Ibid., 45.

[54]Ibid., 48.

[55]Ibid., 47.

wounding his eye.[56] Through this intertextual approach of combining a lovesick Calypso and a cursing Cyclops to create a cursing and suicidal Dido, Virgil employs the imperial strategy of representing foreign lands. First, as feminine: yearning to be possessed by the imperial heroes, seeing no future without the imperialist powers, and foreign lands being simply available for the imperialist heroes' taking if they so wish. Second, the addition of the merciless, cannibalistic, and monstrous character of Cyclops reflects more than just availability. It is another imperial representation of foreign lands and people as dangerous and inhuman; hence, in need of the civilization/salvation of the imperial heroes. The latter point is precisely perfected by the character of a lovesick Dido, who offers to share her land with the strangers at their very first meeting. By equating the loving Dido with the cursing Cyclops, foreign lands are not only womanly and yearning to be possessed but also dangerous, barbarous, and inhuman to imperial traveling heroes.

In general, the indispensability of imperial heroes is thus underlined by employing gender representations to claim and justify acts of imperialism. These are evident in Dido's suicide, Rahab's betrayal of her city, Pocahontas' defiance of her father and alliance with John Smith, and, as we shall see in *Heart of Darkness*, an African woman's attempt to commit suicide as Mr. Kurtz, the master colonizer, is forcibly removed from the heart of Africa. Moreover, empire and method never stay away from godly claims but remain immensely intertextual, with constructions that reproduce certain images about the colonizer and the colonized. That such is the case is not only evident in ancient imperializing texts but also reflected in contemporary ones, as the poem "The White Man's Burden" and Joseph Conrad's *Heart of Darkness* will attest.

---

[56]See Quint, *Epic and Empire*, 108, for the character of a Cyclopean one-eyed giant as a colonial strategy of dehumanizing foreign lands and people. For the tradition of epic curse in the genealogy of the epic (that is, the resistance of the colonized) and how it loses impact as the world empires become more aggressive in contemporary centuries, see 106–25.

5

Method in Modern Imperializing Texts

Take up the White Man's burden.

Rudyard Kipling

Rudyard Kipling, who was designated "the greatest apostle of imperialism" of his time, captures the ideology that characterized the nineteenth and twentieth centuries' imperialism. He articulates what Rene Maunier described as the claim that "if you wish to rule, it is because you *ought*, because you *must*–to the benefit of the entire world."[1] The poem demonstrates how works of literature serve as instruments of imperialism. Metaphors, similes, and, indeed, the verse as a whole, not only reflect the imperialism of its time but are marshaled in the service of encouraging and sanctifying the system by comparing the colonizer and the colonized, by calling on the colonizer to travel to distant places and save the wild, sullen, silent, half-devil and half-child people. The poem participates by concretizing the vision of imperialism in a literary form that propounds its ethical claims, its ideology.

In Kipling's articulation of imperialism, we are a long way from ancient imperialism, with its overt admission of material interests and a conquest approach. The modern approach insists that imperialism is a duty, a burden, a cross that a white man must carry, not for his own sake but for another's profit, another's gain. The colonizer has become the liberator–a Moses, setting people free from the night of their own shortcomings. Despite

---

[1] Maunier, *Sociology of Colonies,* vol. 1, 33.

this shift in describing the intentions of imperialism, both Exodus and "A White Man's Burden" regard their act as a sacred sanction laid upon certain races, the Israelites and the British. They are both involved in a self-centered quest.

Heart of Darkness,[2] **Method, and Empire-Building**

If Kipling uses the genre of poetry, Joseph Conrad in his book *Heart of Darkness*, published three years after Kipling's poem in Britain (1902), does an effective job with a novel.[3] Conrad perfectly resonates with Kipling, though his approach emphasizes the economic side of imperialism and dismisses the godly claims rampant in the press as "rot" and "humbug" (p. 18). The story of *Heart of Darkness* is narrated by Marlow, its protagonist, and he tells his fellow travelers how he once traveled to the "farthest point of navigation" (p. 10), how he got there, what he saw, how he went up a certain river to a place where he met a poor chap, Mr. Kurtz. His narration makes no mention of the place directly, though it is clear that it was a journey to Africa, presumably the Congo area.

What are the literary-rhetorical strategies employed by *Heart of Darkness*? These will be examined thoroughly, beginning with the construction of its anti-conquest ideology, how it authorizes travel, and how it portrays the colonized lands and people in comparison with those of the colonizer. Second, its contact zone will be examined. Last is an assessment of how it employs gender relations to articulate relationships of subordination and domination. The first question, however, is, Does the implied author condone or reject the imperialism of his time?

Conrad and the Imperialism of His Time

Conrad's approach is best described as complicit criticism. A few pages into the story, the narrator says:

> The conquest of the earth, which mostly means the taking it away from those who have a different complexion or slightly flatter noses than ourselves is not a pretty thing if you look into it too much. What redeems it is the idea only. An idea at the back of it; not a sentimental pretence but an idea; and an unselfish belief in the idea—something you can set up, bow down before and offer a sacrifice to. (p. 9)

This criticism is tellingly placed where the narrator compares the Roman Empire with the British Empire. According to the narrator, the Romans lacked the British sophistication:

---

[2]All the quotations in this section are from Joseph Conrad, *Heart of Darkness* (Cambridge, Mass.: R. Bentley, 1981).

[3]For other postcolonial readings of *Heart of Darkness,* see Chinua Achebe, "An Image of Africa: Racism in Conrad's Heart of Darkness," in his book *Hopes and Impediments,* 1–20; Ngugi, *Moving the Center,* 16–18; and Said, *Culture and Imperialism,* 67–70.

They were no colonists; their administration was merely a squeeze, and nothing more…They were conquerors, and for that you want only brute force—nothing to boast of…They grabbed what they could get for the sake of what was to be got. It was just robbery with violence, aggravated murder on a great scale, and men going at it blind—as is very proper for those who tackle the darkness. (p. 9)

Marlow equates colonizers with "those who tackle the darkness," that is, those who bring civilization or light. Accordingly, he begins by declaring that Britain too "has been one of the dark places of the earth" (p. 6) until the Romans came to bring light. He holds that the Romans were "man" enough to face the British darkness and bring light to it. Therefore, he insists that "darkness was here yesterday" (p. 7) but holds that since light was brought "it is like a running blaze on a plain, like a flash of lighting in the clouds" (p. 7). And they, the British, "live in the flicker" (p. 7). Moreover, he hopes that their life in the flicker may "last as long as the earth keeps rolling" (p. 7). The overall picture is that he condones imperialism as a necessary evil. Both the Romans and the British are messengers of light who tackle darkness. Obviously, the writer authorizes travel, for the light must become "like a running blaze on a plain."

Inviting Travel

Marlow recounts how maps fueled his youthful dreams. He used to look for hours at South America, Africa, and Australia on the map and lose himself in the glories of exploration, for at that time, "there were many blank spaces on the earth" (p. 11). His attention was caught by the "biggest, the most blank" (p. 11), after which he began to yearn. This particular blank place, he maintains, was then "a white patch for a boy to dream gloriously over" (p. 11). In fact, Marlow's story, *Heart of Darkness,* recounts how he finally realized his dream.

Marlow's travel passions, no doubt, reflect their age. Yet the story also attests to the role of text in catalyzing imperialistic agendas. A map, a blank map, in those days was a rhetorical text that impassioned young men to find these places. The blank map was itself a colonialist discourse that held that any place that was not trodden and named by white European people was empty and up for grabs. It was these "inviting" maps that made young Marlow cry out and say, "when I grow up I will go there" (p. 11) to discover, to name, to light, and to claim the place.

Marlow's story, which purports to be a travel narrative, inevitably becomes another blank map. By constructing the land and people he journeyed to as immature and dark, he invites his readers back home to take up the white man's burden, so to speak. This is evident in the depiction of the colonized land and people.

Constructing and Mapping Lands

THE COLONIZER'S LAND

Since his tale begins while travelers are sitting on a ship on the Thames River, the implied author establishes the setting by describing the British land. According to the implied author, the land was "calm" (p. 4). Its "sea and the sky were welded together without a joint," and the day was ending in "serenity of still and exquisite brilliance" (p. 1). Moreover, "the water shone pacifically; the sky, without a speck, was a benign immensity of unstained light" (p. 4). When change came over the water, the implied author notes that its "serenity became less brilliant but more profound" (p. 4). The Thames, on the other hand, "spread out in tranquil dignity of a waterway leading to the uttermost ends of the earth" (p. 5). Even bad weather does not mar the beauty of England: The mist falling on the marsh of Essex looks like a "a radiant fabric" (p. 4).

In this brief description, the colonizer's lands are notably calm, perfect, complete, serene, benign. They have unstained light and tranquil dignity. The colonizer's land embodies holiness, beauty, roundness, and perfection. A look at the depiction of Africa reflects a sharp contrast.

THE COLONIZED LAND

The narrator effectively uses tone, allusions, and, of course, explicit descriptions to evoke an ever-increasing image of darkness, silence, and formlessness to describe Africa. The overall image that crystallizes is best captured by Genesis 1:1–2, which says, "in the beginning when God created the heavens and the earth, the earth was a formless void and darkness covered the face of the deep."

As indicated above, the narrator says this nameless place used to be "the biggest, the most blank" space on earth. At the time of his growth, however, it had moved from being a "white patch for a white boy to dream gloriously on" to become "a place of darkness" (p. 11). Hence, when he finally realizes his dream, he discovers that his journey has not taken him to the center of the continent but to the center of the earth. He finds this center "almost featureless, as if still in the making" (p. 20). He finds it with a "monotonous grimness," a "mournful stillness," and a "great silence" (p. 20). He finds it with "a smell of mud, of primeval mud…the high stillness of primeval forest" (p. 43). He finds its "great wall of vegetation…like a rioting invasion of a soundless life" (p. 49). Indeed,

> going up that river was like traveling back to the earliest begin-
> nings of the world, when vegetation rioted on earth and the big
> trees were kings. An empty stream, a great silence, an impenetrable
> forest. The air was warm, thick, heavy, sluggish. There was no joy
> in the brilliance of sunshine. The long stretches of the waterway
> ran on, deserted, into the gloom of overshadowed distances." (p. 55)

In short, Marlow and his fellow travelers discovered that they "were wanderers on a prehistoric earth" (p. 59); they "were travelling in the night of first ages, of those ages that are gone, leaving hardly a sign—and no memories" (p. 59).

The land, temperature, and vegetation of the colonized are subjected to the standard of the colonizer's home. Differences are then equated to deficiency. All this, however, is in the interests of power and subjugation. Ideologically, it authorizes the subjugation of those who are supposedly deficient. Accordingly, the people also bear their marks of the land, as the depiction of British and African people shows.

Constructing Identities of People

THE COLONIZERS

The characterization of people in the literature of the colonizer is consistent with the depiction of their lands. If the colonizer's land is serene, peaceful, powerful, so will be its people. Thus, white people, the colonizers in *Heart of Darkness*, are generally given divine characteristics. Marlow, for example, has an "ascetic aspect," he resembles an "idol," and he has "the pose of Bhudda preaching in European clothes" (pp. 4, 9, 131). The chief accountant of a trading company is described as a "vision," a "miracle" (p. 28). A group of other travelers in Marlow's steamboat are referred to as "pilgrims" (pp. 37, 39, 42, 86), though they are overt fortune seekers who constantly whisper and sigh the word *ivory*. Yet the most divine of the characters is Mr. Kurtz.

An elaboration on Mr. Kurtz is in order. The implied author meant to depict Mr. Kurtz as the ideal colonizer, a flat character. He is characterized as the embodiment of all colonizing powers and their strategies. Hence, Mr Kurtz's "mother was half-English, his father was half-French," his name was German, and "all Europe contributed to the making of Mr. Kurtz" (p. 83). As the personification of colonizing powers, Mr. Kurtz's divine characterization is the most pronounced. Mr. Kurtz is a "Voice!" a "magnificent eloquence," a "gorgeous eloquence" (pp. 10, 80, 102, 115, 124). He gives the word. Even when his body is totally wasted by tropical diseases, his voice continues its independent life. The voice remains alive. The identification of Mr. Kurtz with a persuasive and authoritative voice that makes things happen undoubtedly invokes an image of God. Thus, commenting on the relationship of Mr. Kurtz and his African followers, his disciple notes that "he came to them with thunder and lightning" (p. 94).

Mr. Kurtz's divinity is also underlined by comparing his capture and death to that of Jesus. First, though Mr. Kurtz is totally wasted by disease, his voice retains divine power. When he speaks, those carrying his stretcher stagger—an allusion to the capture of Jesus in John's gospel. Second, as they capture him, he swears, "I will return...I will return" (p. 104).

Meanwhile, the crowds of his native followers, who seemed ready to fight for him, scatter and hide in fear. A woman, however, follows his captors openly and fearlessly. Last, at his death the narrator evokes the death of Jesus directly: "It was as though a veil had been rent...he cried out twice" (p. 118). Darkness is then enacted by blowing out the candle in Mr. Kurtz's cabin. The plot intimates the passion of Christ. It suggests that Mr. Kurtz, the master colonizer, is a savior—a returning savior, one who cannot be kept away even by the power of death!

In evoking the image of Jesus' death and return to characterize Mr. Kurtz, the implied author makes one of his strongest statements on imperialism as a necessary evil that should continue. In fact, Marlow apologetically says he was entrusted with Mr. Kurtz's legacies, including his memories, and, if he had his way, he says, he would "choose for an everlasting rest in the dust-bin of progress, amongst all the sweepings and...all the dead cats of civilization. But then," he maintains, "I can't choose. He won't be forgotten" (p. 85). This may be a genuine acknowledgment of the powers that be, but does the narrator use his own power to create and characterize the colonized as fully human?

THE COLONIZED

The characterization of the colonized is based on four separate contacts Marlow makes on his journey: those he meets by the coast while journeying to his destination; the indigenous people at the trading stations of colonizers; members of his crew traveling with him from the station to bring back Mr. Kurtz from inland; and the people he meets in the interior. The depiction of those at the trade stations and the interior will illustrate how the colonized are portrayed.

Having reached the river of his destination, Marlow travels to the inland trading stations by a steamboat. Here he finds a lot of black people, but they move like ants, in a file, and a clink keeps time with their footsteps. They are enslaved. These "unhappy savages" or "raw matter," as he calls them, pass him, as he walks from the river to the station, "without a glance and with a deathlike indifference" (pp. 24, 26–27). Behind, they are driven by one of their own, what Marlow terms "the new forces at work" (p. 24). On their heads they are carrying baskets of earth; they are building a railway. On another side of the cliff Marlow says,

> black shapes crouched, lay, sat between the trees leaning against the trunks clinging to the earth, half coming out, half effaced with the dim light, in all attitudes of pain, abandonment, and despair...And this was the place where some of the helpers had withdrawn to die. They were dying slowly—it was clear. (p. 26)

The narrator paints a picture of subdued natives and collaborators who make no effort to resist their enslavement. There is no resistance. No war. Although the narrator doubts that the enslaved are criminals as claimed, he still makes no effort to portray them as fully human. They are lumped together with trees as savages, raw material, black shapes who have given in to the will of death and white man's conquest.

The inland natives, on the other hand, are not yet fully colonized. In resonance with his depiction of a land still in the making, Marlow presents the natives as almost indistinguishable from the trees, or part of the trees, and as a sea of disjointed body parts and shapes floating together, as making yells, uproars, shrills, screams, or just wild incomprehensible sounds.[4] He portrays them as ungodly devils, savages, niggers, simple, and childish people. He says,

> There would be…a burst of yells, a whirl of black limbs, a mass of hands clapping, of feet stamping, of bodies swaying, of eyes rolling, under the droop of heavy and motionless foliage. The steamer toiled along slowly on the edge of a black and incomprehensible frenzy…We glided past like phantoms, wondering and secretly appalled, as sane men would be before an enthusiastic outbreak in a madhouse…The earth seemed unearthly. We are accustomed to look upon the shackled form of a conquered monster, but there—there you could look at a thing monstrous and free…No, they were not inhuman. Well, you know that was the worst of it—this suspicion of their not being inhuman…the thought of their humanity—like yours—the thought of your remote kinship with this wild and passionate uproar. Ugly.[5]

The identity of the colonized assures the colonizer of his own humanity. The politics of superior race, or in this case, whiteness, is dependent on the adverse othering of Africans.[6] Indeed, the admission that they were human could only be conceived as something ugly.

Yet the narrator also provides for rebellious inland native people. These, however, are only dead and displayed heads around Mr. Kurtz's house (pp. 97, 99). They are called symbols of power, presumably a warning to

---

[4]See George Orwell, "Shooting an Elephant," in *Major Modern Essayists,* ed. Gilbert H. Muller and Alan F. Crooks (Englewood Cliffs, N. J.: Prentice Hall, 1994), 62–68; this essay, written in the 1920s, characterizes the people of Burma as a "sea of yellow faces." Evidently, Conrad's characterization of colonized African people as separate body parts that flow in crowds is applied to a different colonial setting, indicating the use of intertextuality in empire-building.

[5]Conrad, *Heart of Darkness,* 59.

[6]See Williams and Chrisman, *Colonial Discourse and Post-colonial Theory.* Their introduction points out that "the power valorization and experience of whiteness as a form of contemporary ethnicity needs serious theoretical and critical attention," 17. Toni Morrison, *Playing in the Dark: Whiteness and the Literary Imagination* (New York: Vintage Books, 1993); this is an examination of how the whiteness of American literature, as well as most European literature, has been dependent on the othering of Africans.

was your name," to which she responds, "I knew it—I was sure!" (p. 131), confirming Marlow's observation that she is without mental reservation and that she is completely incapable of understanding the colonial game and its players.

Even more seriously, the Intended is characterized as the insistent keeper of the memories and plans of Mr. Kurtz. As noted earlier, Marlow wished to dispose of Mr. Kurtz's memories into the dustbin of progress together with other dead cats of civilization. He thus visits the Intended because

> all that had been Kurtz's had passed out of my hands: his soul, his body, his station, his plans, his ivory, his career. There remained only his memory and his Intended—and I wanted to give that up, too, to the past, in a way to surrender personally all that remained of him with me to oblivion. (p. 124)

Marlow's wish, however, is denied by the Intended. She insists that Mr. Kurtz's memory and plans must be kept. Marlow, who during the conversation has been forced to pretend that he is a true admirer of Kurtz, quite angrily and helplessly agrees. In this visit, Marlow tragically discovers that Mr. Kurtz and his Intended are one: "I saw them together—I heard them together. She had said, with a deep catch of breath, 'I have survived'" (p. 126). With this assertion, British women are not absolved from the imperial game. Rather, they are shown to be tricksters who lead men to do what they really do not wish. Marlow's aunt and the Intended are shown to have trapped Marlow to identify with and to preserve Mr. Kurtz's memories and plans against his will and convictions.

Put differently, British women are discursively colonized bodies who are, nevertheless, significant participants in the colonizing culture. A look at the only African woman featured in the narrative indicates that she is also characterized as the image of her people and land.

An African Colonized Woman: "She Was Savage and Superb"

While the implied author tends to characterize the interior natives as crowds or masses of disjointed human parts indistinguishable from the forests, he nevertheless singles out one woman and describes her in detail:

> From right to left along the lighted shore moved a wild and gorgeous apparition of a woman. She walked with measured steps, draped in striped and fringed clothes, treading the earth proudly, with a slight jingle and flash of barbarous ornaments...She had brass leggings to the knee, brass wire gauntlets to the elbow,... innumerable necklaces of glass beads on her neck; bizarre things, charms, gifts of witch-men, that hung about her, glittered and trembled at every step. She must have had the value of several elephants tusks upon her. She was savage and superb, wild eyed

and magnificent…And in the hush that had fallen suddenly upon the whole sorrowful land, the immense wilderness…seemed to look at her, pensive, as though it had been looking at the image of its own tenebrous and passionate soul. (pp. 102–3)

It is when the rest of the crowd of worshipers remain hidden in the shadows, fearfully watching and resenting the capture of Mr. Kurtz, that she steps out to the open. She is more determined to challenge the capture of Mr. Kurtz than any of the male followers of her land. She rushes to the brink of the stream by the bank, raises her hands up, and shouts. As the steamboat blows its whistle to leave, the rest of the "masses of bodies" run away in terror of its sound, but "the barbarous woman did not so much as flinch" (p. 115). She was not only courageous, "her face had a tragic and fierce aspect of wild sorrow and dumb pain" (p. 103). She draws closer to the bank, seemingly contemplating suicide for Mr. Kurtz's departure! The narrator says, "She stood looking at us without a stir, and like the wilderness itself" (p. 103). The implied author, however, does not allow for suicide, because Mr. Kurtz does not leave the continent.

Her relationship with Mr. Kurtz is strangely intimate. The disciple of Mr. Kurtz reports that he struggled to keep her out of Mr. Kurtz's sickbed for two weeks. Now, as Mr. Kurtz leaves, she seems ready to drown herself. These are signs of an intimate relationship. Who is she? Unlike the British women, the "savage and superb" African woman's dress, her jewelry, her shouting, her raising of hands bespeak her wildness and extravagance. She displays immoderate passions. The implied author makes no secret in equating her to the wilderness, her land: She is like the "image" of the passionate soul of her land. The use of the figure of a woman as a representative of the colonized (as opposed to her colonizing counterparts, whom the narrator insists should be kept out of it) suggests that the colonized are wild and harmless. The woman's strong attachment to Kurtz, on the other hand, suggests that the colonized yearn and ask for subjugation and that they should indeed be subjugated to save them from their passions and wildness.

In sum, the savage and superb African woman is not unlike Rahab, the Jericho prostitute, nor is she so different from Pocahontas of the American myth of colonization, and Dido, the lovesick and suicidal queen of Carthage. All three women are creations of the colonizer's pen, writing their imperial desires on the bodies of their victims. Clearly, imperializing heroes write themselves as highly demanded by their victims, who beseech to be dominated.

Feminist attempts to reclaim the stories, therefore, should also be accompanied by a decolonizing reading. This begins with an acknowledgment that most of the so-called canonical texts are not only patriarchal but also imperial.

6

Method in Decolonizing Literature

This chapter highlights decolonizing literary strategies by analyzing *The Victims*,[1] a Botswanan novel, after first discussing the poem "May Imperialism Perish Forever." Literary-rhetorical methods of decolonizing are highlighted by asking the following questions:

1. Does the text name the imperial oppression of its setting?

2. What are its literary-rhetorical methods of decolonizing?

3. How is gender employed at the decolonizing zone?

"May Imperialism Perish Forever"[2]

I love reading about Chege[3]
About the time when he lived here on earth
I wish I was present
When he used to prophesy that
The colonialists would invade our country
And that they would be driven right out again
I shall be delighted when I see
The colonialists going back to their own country
So that our children will have their freedom
And live in peace in our own country,
The same way their children live in their country.
Imperialists may you vanish and perish forever!
Nature gave us this land

---

[1]Mositi Torontle, *The Victims* (Gaborone: Botsalo, 1993).
[2]Maina wa Kinyatti, ed., *Thunder from the Mountains*, 15.
[3]A footnote accompanying the poem explains that "Chege wa Kiburu was a patriot and a prophet," 15.

And provided us with rich black soils
Black like our skins.
He also provided us with many beautiful streams and great rivers
But now the colonialists have seized
All of them from us.
Those who have ears listen:
Hardship and suffering
Were experienced by our people in Olenguruone[4]
They endured heavy rains and severe cold,
But they refused to submit to the enemy's demands,
They firmly declared:
'We shall never surrender our land
To the foreign occupiers!'
Our people, let us welcome our heros home
With patriotic love.
Let us share with them land and livestock
We have snatched from the enemy.
Countrymen!
Our enemy has oppressed us,
He has stolen our land
And our livestock
But we shall never surrender,
We shall fight with heroism
Until we drive him out of the country.

"May Imperialism Perish Forever" was written in the 1950s, when most struggles for independence in Africa were beginning to take shape. It captures the sentiments that characterized the colonized. Two things are worth noting. First is the characterization of the colonizers. They are identified as invaders, foreign occupiers, thieves, and snatchers of the land belonging to others; they are imperialists and colonizers. For their crimes, perishing, vanishing, and driving them out and back to their countries is the plan of the colonized, who are determined never to surrender. The image of the colonists' role is drastically different from Kipling's portrait, when it is deprived of its anti-conquest veil of sanitizing the violence of imperialism.

Second, the goal of the colonized is to regain control over their land. The colonized want no more than the return of what belongs to them. They want a fair game: They seek to live in peace in their country just as imperialists have their own countries. They want their children to live in peace and freedom, just as the children of the colonizers have their own

---

[4]An accompanying footnote reads, "On October 29, 1949, 11,000 Gikuyu peasants were forcefully evicted from their land in Olenguruone to make room for the white settlers. Because the peasants put up a bitter resistance against the eviction, the majority of them were arrested and detained at Yatta." Ibid., 16.

country to live in. Their major concerns, therefore, are loss of control over a land that is rightfully theirs and the effort to regain it. While these sentiments characterized preindependence literature, postindependence texts continue the same theme, as will be evident in the following analysis of *The Victims*. The persistent concern indicates that the struggle over economic, cultural, and social independence is far from won. Moreover, it indicates that lands are more than just physical geographical bodies; they are spaces defined by political, economic, and cultural power.

The Victims: **Method and Decolonizing**

Background

The protagonist of *The Victims* is a young girl called Dineo. Her mother, Mmapula, is determined to educate her. Her father, Kgetho, works for the South African mines in Johannesburg and believes that a girl needs only basic education on an elementary level. Kgetho hardly ever returns home or sends money to his family in Botswana. He comes only to assert his authority as the head of the house and to impregnate his wife before returning to Johannesburg.

Dineo goes to high school determined to honor her mother's dreams. There she meets Tom, a young man determined to help her realize her dreams. Tom, however, impregnates Dineo and disappears, leaving her, like her own mother, to raise the child alone. Dineo later discovers that Tom's real name was Thabo, that he was not a Motswana but one of the 1976 South African Soweto student uprising refugees; that he was forced to flee from Botswana to Moscow, where he was receiving military training to confront the South African apartheid regime; and, last, that Tom was her half-brother, born to her father's South African consort.

Structurally, the novella has three parts. Part one covers Mmapula's marriage, her struggle to educate her children, and Dineo's departure to a boarding school. Part two covers what Dineo learns at school, how she meets Tom, and how their relationship progresses. It also covers Mmapula's turn to the African Independent Churches in an attempt to recall or recover Kgetho from the mines through ritual. Part three covers the expulsion of Dineo from the boarding school, the disappearance of Tom, and the revelation of his identity. The temporal setting of the novel spans the early sixties to the eighties. Spatially, it takes place between the South African metropolitan city of Johannesburg, a village, and a school in Botswana. Does this text name the imperial oppression of its time?

Naming Imperial Oppression

With its temporal and spatial setting, the novella covers preindependent to postindependent Botswana and apartheid in South Africa. It engages the settler colonial practices of the white apartheid regime and its effect on the whole region of Southern Africa. It addresses the breakdown of family life by placing the deeds and experiences of every character within the historical parameters of imperialism in the region. This is evident in the words of Kgetho's mother, Nala the history teacher, and Tom the South African refugee.

Kgetho's mother shares her life experiences with her sobbing daughter-in-law, Mmapula. Mmapula had gone to search for Kgetho in Johannesburg after five years without hearing from him. She found him living in a shack in Soweto with another woman and two children. Kgetho's mother comforts Mmapula, saying:

> I have been through the same journey and experience. I was married to Kgetho's father for fifteen years prior to his death. However, if I were to add up the years we spent together I doubt if they would even amount to one year. This pain that you feel my daughter is our pain. It is a pain felt by almost every woman and family in the southern region of Africa. We are together in this dilemma my child. Do not even begin to think that Kgetho is better off, or enjoying himself in the mines. We are all victims of our times and society. (p. 36)

Her words highlight labor immigration as a regional problem of several generations. Mr. Nala, on the other hand, expounds on its historical foundation. He points out that "labor immigration was a system of importing and exploiting labor from the whole region of Southern Africa" (p. 51). Mr. Nala informs the students that a method of hut tax was introduced precisely to force people in nonmonetary–oriented societies to work in the mines. He further recounts that "in other areas white settlers stripped people of all their farming land and reduced them to dependent laborers in the white farms or forced them to settle in agriculturally unproductive areas" (p. 52). This was another strategy of enforcing labor immigration.

Tom's perspective accentuates the continuing effects of labor immigration. He writes from Moscow to explain his mysterious disappearance and asserts that

> all people are wounded, both men and women alike. Mothers are separated from their husbands and children, men are separated from their wives and children, children are separated from their fathers and mothers. The whole society has been shaken, shattered, and scattered. Men and women cannot live and love each other again as they should…I and Dineo will probably never see each other again. (p. 122)

Tom's assertion that "the whole society has been shaken, shattered, and scattered" best summarizes the colonial strategies of the region. It entailed land dispossession, resettlement to unfertile areas, and coerced immigration. The depth of this displacement is reflected in Mmapula's determination to educate her daughter and the characterization of Mr. Nala. Mmapula encourages Dineo to pursue education to avoid getting married to an "empty space," that is, the imperially induced depopulation. Mr. Nala, one of the few men not captured by the labor immigration, is regarded as a "stubborn ghost" who refuses to remain at the graveyard. The very characterization of Dineo and Tom, children of the same father unknowingly falling in love and bearing a child, underlines the depth of the colonial displacement.

What, then, are anti-imperial literary strategies of decolonizing? These will be highlighted by focusing on concerns over losing control of one's land, subverting the literary genre and language of the colonizer, rereading the master's texts and retelling history, and gender at the decolonization zone.

Decolonizing: Anti-Imperial Literary Strategies

REGAINING CONTROL OVER LAND

What characterizes the literature of the colonized is the struggle to regain control over their own lands. The above poem about yearning for regaining their stolen land captures the sentiments of the colonized. Since colonization encompasses more than just the geographical and political domination, this struggle continues well after the colonized have regained their so-called independence.

Accordingly, *The Victims*, published twenty-seven years after the independence of Botswana, continues to express concerns over lack of control over land. For example, students conclude that Mr. Ronald, a white expatriate teacher who constantly refers to his students as "monkeys" (p. 6), "came to reassert before their very eyes that in spite of their so-called independence, the imperialist master was still enthroned" (p. 7). This conveys the sentiment that the imperialist shackles are yet to be broken, a concern that is also echoed in Mr. Nala, Mother Mary Magdalene, and Tom's views.

First, Mr. Nala the history teacher, who is also the school choir director, uses songs to make his students think about their land. In one dramatic urge to inculcate the message of a song in his students, he takes them to a hilltop in the middle of a village and says to them,

> "Do you see this land?"…"Yes," we chorused. "Look at it"…We bent half way, peeped through the thick air, and we began to see through his eyes. We turned slowly and saw the furthest point, down there, where the earth and the horizon kissed, where some blue meandering mountains lilted across the land, so lost and unknown to us, but they smiled and cried with us…"Now, listen to what this song is saying. I want you to say all the words." "Le ke lefatshe la rona," we began and he stopped us. "I want you to demonstrate the song"…"Le ke lefatshe la rona," we sang, as we

pointed to the ground and touched our hearts. "Lenkilwe ke ba ditshaba," we said, pointing towards the north. "Re fetogile makgoba, fatsheng labontata rona..." On this particular phrase, Mr. Nala stopped us several times and insisted that we should repeat the expressions until we grasped the meaning...How can we have our land, stand on it, and at the same time have it taken by foreigners? (p. 66)[5]

This question captures the paradox confronting most postcolonial subjects—to possess what they hardly control. Political independence deceptively suggested that total autonomy was won, but postcolonial subjects have painfully learned that political independence without cultural and economic control over their lands is a mockery of power. On these grounds, the contests over the empire continue to be voiced by postcolonial subjects. The land, insists the choir director to his students, is still in the hands of foreigners. The original inhabitants, goes the song, are now slaves in the land of their ancestors.

For Mother Mary Magdalene and Tom, the land is sick. The sickness, unlike the one construed in *Heart of Darkness*, is not inherent to the land but a consequence of imperial intrusion.[6] Mother Mary Magdalene was known to sing "Heal our land oh Lord, Heal our land, Bind our wounds, bind our wounds" (p. 60) repeatedly to all her patients, to the whole village, and to all the hearts that slept through the night. According to the narrator, she sang as a woman who "knew the pains and death of her land" (p. 61). Tom, too, said, "Ours is a sick land and a broken people...there is need for *Phekolo*, healing" (p. 122). For Tom and Mother Mary Magdalene, to regain control there must be healing.

The novel also uses anti-imperial literary-rhetorical strategies of decolonizing. Among many of these, I will highlight the subverting of the literary genre and language, the rereading of the master's texts, and the retelling of history. Last, I will discuss gender dilemmas at the decolonizing zones.

SUBVERTING GENRE AND LANGUAGE

Decolonizing literary strategies are at once a secret and a public code. They are secretive in their adoption of a language that is only understandable to the colonized. They are also open secrets in their adoption of the literary genre and language of the colonizer. Their double-faced character reflects autoethnographic constructions and, perhaps, the inevitable hybridity in the discourse of the colonized; it also reflects the intentions of

---

[5]The untranslated Setswana song says: "This is our land. The land has been taken by foreigners. We have become slaves in the land of our ancestors."

[6]See Tsitsi Dangarembgwa, *Nervous Conditions, A Novel* (Seattle: Seal Press, 1988), which is set in preindependence Zimbabwe and refers to sickness as "Englishness," 203.

anti-imperial literature. That is, on the one hand, it seeks to raise the awareness of   the colonized; on the other hand, it also seeks to counteract the colonizer's claims and to subvert the colonizer's imperializing methods.

For example, the novel genre evolved in the nineteenth and twentieth centuries and became an instrument of modern imperialism. English departments, too, developed primarily to serve the empire. Yet anti-imperial literature of most Two-Thirds World people adopted the same genre and language to decolonize. Can the master's tools dismantle his house?[7] This unresolvable question led to the subversion of the master's genre and language. The colonized do not reproduce the colonizer's literary forms. Rather, they interpolate them with various other literary genres unique to their contexts, thereby subverting the master's tools and using them at the same time. For example, in *The Victims*, local songs, poems, folktales, dreams, prophecies, and letters form a significant part of the novel.

Grammatically, stretches of Setswana sentences, phrases, and words are interpolated, some translated and some untranslated. In this way, the reader is rudely reminded that English is not the only or the standard language for all people. *The Victims* also openly problematizes English language through characterization. First, Dineo, who is selected to meet some dignitaries, forgets all her rehearsed proper English vocabulary when the moment arrives. Second, and more emphatically, in one of the African Independent Churches one uneducated old man begins to speak in tongues and speaks in English. The church leader "leaped up, pointed a trembling finger at him with anger and said, 'Unclean spirit, I command you to leave him now,' and the old man became silent" (p. 61)[8] When the whole church is stunned by this identification of English language with unclean spirits and its subsequent departure, the church leader simply retorts by quoting from Acts 2:7, "It is said they heard them speaking their own languages." Such characterizations highlight the unfinished discourse of decolonization. To use Laura Donaldson's expression, it highlights "the global theater of a world at war intertextually."[9]

REREADING THE MASTER'S TEXTS AND RETELLING HISTORY

As the above biblical quotation indicates, the literary strategies of decolonization entail rereading the colonizer's texts for liberation. This strategy is inseparable from the subversion of language because "both arenas—linguistic and cultural—are dialectically related. Language is culture."[10] Therefore, at the decolonizing zone intertextuality often reflects

---

[7]Lorde, *Sister Outsider,* 112.

[8]See also Ngugi, "Imperialism of Language: English, a Language for the World," in *Moving the Center,* 30–41.

[9]Donaldson, *Decolonizing Feminisms,* 105.

[10]Ketu H. Katrak, "A Theory for Post-colonial Women's Texts," in *The Post-colonial Studies Reader,* ed. Ashcroft, Griffiths, and Tiffin, 257.

cultural contests over land. The colonizers' texts are evoked in the texts of
their victims precisely to subvert the claims of the colonizer. *The Victims*
recalls Shakespearean and biblical texts and their respective institutions
quite interchangeably. The English language is subverted in the church,
and the Bible's complacency with colonialism is exposed at school. Both
the school and the church, both Jesus and Shakespeare, who brought light
to the darkest Africa, as Ngugi holds, are the focus of decolonizing
rereadings.[11]

With regard to Shakespeare, the author begins part two of the novel
by directly recalling Macbeth:

> The bell rang. "The bell calls me!" shouted a student. "To heaven
> or hell," replied another, with a quivering sorrowful voice that
> could rival a church minister by the grave side, as they quoted
> Shakespeare...the students gushed out of the grass thatched
> rondavels, popping out like soldiers towards the west. Their well
> polished shoes, shining like lightning across the dark stormy night,
> threatened to set the whole school ablaze. (p. 49)

Evidently, Shakespeare's words are now a common language among
students of the colonized. His words are notably associated with a church
minister in a burial service. The quotation itself recalls a scene in which
Macbeth is responding to his wife's signal to go and kill his own king—a
king that had come to promote him. Similarly, the tone of the above passage carries aggressive tones of invasion. Who must be murdered by the
students for their own well-being? The answer points to the school. The
school is problematized, for, as Jerry Phillips correctly notes, "the moment
of imperialism is also the moment of education," since education was a
central strategy of colonizing in modern imperialism.[12] To decolonize education is, therefore, an unavoidable anti-imperial stance. This is evident in
the events of Dineo's class, after the bell's call. Students sit down to write
examinations, but one boy begins to shake his head continuously and un-
controllably. When asked what is wrong, he gives a one-word answer:
"Everything" (p. 50). Two weeks later, the boy is reportedly still shaking
his head. The narrator never reports that the boy stopped, a device accen-
tuating that things are far from right.

The rest of the class, on the other hand, begins to write a history paper.
Students realize that those topics that seemed less important in the syllabus
are central to the examination. One question reads, "Reconstruct the conversation Kgosi Sechele had with missionaries when he discovered that

---

[11]See Ngugi, *Moving the Center,* 30–41, for the relationship of the English language and
the Bible in the colonial era.

[12]Jerry Phillips, "Educating the Savages," in *Recasting the World: Writing after Colonialism,*
ed. Jonathan White (Baltimore: Johns Hopkins University Press, 1993), 26.

Solomon, a man after God's heart, had many wives and concubines, or define the significance of Kgosi Sechele's defence of traditional doctors among early missionaries for our current world" (p. 50). Clearly, the question problematizes the biblical text, its readers, and its role in colonization. It revisits the cultural wars that characterized the colonial contact zone and activates them again.

Dineo answers the first part of the question, recounting how Kgosi Sechele of Bakwena was converted to Christianity and how he was advised to divorce his wives in order to get baptized. Kgosi Sechele reportedly complied, to the distress and disapproval of his whole kingdom. Later, however, Kgosi Sechele learned how to read, only to find out that biblical kings were polygamous. He confronted the missionary, saying, "Can you please make this passage talk to the Bakwena gathered here and tell us why you told us a different story?" (p. 50). Through Dineo's essay, the implied author underlines that the colonized subjects need to read and interpret the so-called canonical texts of the colonizer for themselves. The implied author also activates the colonizer's texts, perhaps, to demonstrate that the cultural demise that accompanied colonialism was unfounded, as well as to unveil its anti-conquest intentions.

The strategy adopted to set the school ablaze, therefore, is not a rejection of education. Instead, the school is an arena for problematizing education, for retelling history by teaching the seemingly unimportant but subversive things. Notable, too, is that the formerly colonized retell their own history, not as a history of the defeated, helpless, and indifferent victims who gave in to the imperialists, like those in *Heart of Darkness* and the silent and sullen people of Kipling's poem. On the contrary, "May Imperialism Perish Forever" retells how the Gikuyu people of Kenya, evicted from their land to make room for white settlers, passionately resisted the colonizer's demands. It depicts survivors who swear never to surrender. *The Victims* also documents resisting voices of Bakwena that questioned natives who believed the missionary gospel, as well as native believers who questioned their teachers right from the start.

Rereading the Canon for Decolonization

To return to the strategy of rereading the colonizer's canon for decolonization, biblical rereadings are championed in the African Independent Church. While the colonizing approach employed the biblical text to displace the cultures of the natives, to suppress difference, and to supplant it by some uniformity, decolonizing rereadings counteract the oppressive dualisms and hierarchies of imperialism. The Bible no longer goes against or above the culture. Rather, a method of putting it within and equal to the field of diverse flowers of the world is adopted. Unlike *Heart of Darkness*, nothing indicates that the colonized must be weaned of their supposedly horrid ways. These decolonizing rereadings of critical cultural affirmation are evident in quotations from Exodus and Daniel,[13] and African ancestral veneration, which will be examined according to the order of their appearance in the novel.

In the AICs the biblical text is also read to articulate the struggle for liberation and resistance. Thus, Mother Mary Magdalene delivers the much-needed healing by engaging the evil forces that break families apart and that keep people unemployed and poor. Basically, the colonial displacement is dramatically relived, confronted, and addressed within the spiritual space. According to the narrator, in her prayers it was

> obvious that she was fighting battles for the people and breaking the chains that held them...When Mother Mary Magdalene finally opened her eyes, she roared and groaned, commanding the invisible forces to depart. She walked around the room with a gourd of water, splashed it across the worshippers and said, "Let my people go! Let my people go! You have no right over them. Set them free," she said fiercely. (p. 73)

Mother Mary Magdalene quotes directly from Exodus to articulate a much-needed liberation. Interestingly, the colonized and the colonizer (Kipling's poem) both quote the Exodus narrative. At play here are the dynamics of intertextuality, the social location of writers/readers, and the ideology of Exodus. The story of Exodus, which embodies the colonized becoming the colonizer, serves the interests of both groups in the twentieth century.

Kipling holds that the colonizer is like Moses, facing the thankless colonized crowds he has liberated, crowds yearning for their precolonial night. But unlike the Moses of Exodus, Kipling's liberator is not a member of the oppressed: He comes from outside. Also, Kipling's poem purports to liberate people who are not necessarily enslaved by any apparent Pharaoh, except one of his own anti-conquest imaginations. Nevertheless, Kipling's claim of the Moses figure to portray the colonizer as the liberator to some degree reflects the imperial ideology embedded in the Exodus narrative. In both Exodus and "The White Man's Burden," a divine claim forms an anti-conquest veil that validates traveling to another land and dispossessing its inhabitants.

Mother Mary Magdalene's appeal to the Exodus story, on the other hand, is an intertextual approach that signals an anti-imperial discourse. How she uses the master's texts to decolonize lies in the intricate nuances of her social location and the difference it brings. She prays for the colonized to be liberated from their imperial oppressors. Like Moses, she is a member of her people sent to say, "Let my people go." But unlike the

---

[13]Another outstanding biblical rereading is the story of the Samaritan woman (John 4). See *The Victims,* 57–58.

Moses of Exodus or of Kipling's poem, she is not leading people out of one land to a land inhabited by other people. Neither is she coming into a land that is not hers. Her people are already in their own land though invaded by outside forces. Through saying "Let my people go" to those who purport to be saviors, she lifts the anti-conquest veil and shows the true colors of imperialists. Hers, therefore, is the voice of the dispossessed Canaanite, a Rahab, so to speak, coming out from the anti-conquest veil of imperialism's self-justification. Hers is a voice of the living dead speaking: a resurrected Rahab refusing to parrot the desires of the colonizer, as the latter's violent texts claimed. Unlike the Rahab of the colonizer's pen, she does not embody the colonizer's ideals, or, as observed by Fewell and Gunn, does not quote Deuteronomy with more facility than the Israelites can. Rather, as in the poem "May Imperialism Perish Forever," Mother Mary Magdalene names the violence of imperialism and seeks the restoration of what rightfully belongs to the colonized—culturally, economically, and politically.

The biblical text is also employed in a scene where Kgetho is finally brought home, suffocated to death by leaking gas in the mine. A preacher

> recounted the story of three young men who were thrown into a burning fire but were not burned because God was with them. As she…shouted about the tree and young men on fire who did not burn, it became obvious that these were people who would not be burned by the fires of their circumstances. (p. 119)

The AICs members preach about the burning bush of Exodus 3:2 and the blast furnace of Daniel 3:19–30 in which Shadrach, Meshach, and Abednego were thrown. They perceive themselves as engulfed by the fire of imperial oppression but resisting being consumed by its intense heat. The biblical text, like the Shakespearean one, has become the language of the colonized. However, they use it not in compliance with imperialism, but to articulate their distress as well as to counteract the atrocities of imperialism.

Be that as it may, the implied author by no means privileges the biblical religious stories over the local ones. The language and culture of the colonizer are not the only tools of communication and resistance. The same Mother Mary Magdalene concludes her prayer by dancing in a "traditional dance" and singing "a tune that closely followed that of a *sangoma,*" that is, a spirit medium and healer of local spirituality. Moreover, in prescribing medications for healing, she advises her patients to venerate their living dead ancestors. Mmapula, for example, is instructed to visit the grave of her late mother-in-law to plead for Kgetho's safe return. She is further instructed to break mud from the huts built by her mother-in-law, dissolve it in a bathtub, and wash all her children in the mixture. This is to reunite her mother-in-law's departed and protective spirit with them. Through venerating the spirit of Kgetho's mother, colonized Christian women resist denying themselves female divine symbols of power.[14] Unlike Marlow's aunt, Mother Mary Magdalene, the Christian colonized woman, does not subscribe to the colonial rhetoric of weaning the natives of their supposedly horrid ways.

Just like the strategy of subverting the master's genre and language, the critical twinning of biblical and indigenous religious stories is an anti-imperial decolonizing method. Because imperialism "took the form of destroying people's languages, history, dances, education, religions, naming systems, and other social institutions that were the basis of their self conception,"[15] Mother Mary Magdalene's approach is a radical transgression of boundaries. Her approach does not subscribe to the suppression of the life-affirming stories of the colonized.[16] She transgresses boundaries by not lingering within the confines of the imperializing texts, as the recent feminist biblical commentaries have tended to do, thereby maintaining the biblical imperializing power. Her approach cultivates "a new story field for feminism," called for by Laura Donaldson. Donaldson argues that in the postcolonial feminist space the new story field

> denies the privileging of any one plot (or gender identity) for women's lives in its affirmation of *stories* (and genders); *it also demands that each story negotiate its position in relation to all other stories* included in the field, which must in turn recalculate their own positions. This model aptly describes a solidarity in multiplicity.[17] (emphasis mine)

Given that biblical texts propound imperializing ideology (as shown in the analysis of Exodus) and that they served imperializing nations (as shown in chapter 1), Western biblical readers must not ignore the parameters of imperialism encircling the Bible or subscribe to its death-dealing rhetoric. By both content and use, biblical texts are not only patriarchal but also imperializing texts. Those who seek to read for liberation, therefore, cannot privilege the Christian stories over the religious stories of Others without subscribing to imperialism. Accordingly, feminist biblical rhetoric of liberation must transgress boundaries across texts, across genders,

---

[14]See Ifi Amadiume, *Male Daughters, Female Husbands: Gender and Sex in an African Society* (Atlantic Highlands, N. J.: Zed Books, 1987), on the erasure of female divine symbols of power with the coming of colonialism and Christianity. Colonial institutions such as administration, military, and trade collaborated with the missionary-owned schools in the suppression of native religious symbols that favored women by offering a religion that was profoundly patriarchal and educational training that was geared to supply the male colonial offices. In both cases, female symbols of power and their public role was relegated to a secondary position.

[15]Ngugi, *Moving the Center,* 42.

[16]As stated in chapter 1, this method is evident among the African, Asian, and Native American women readers, who insist on reading biblical stories together with their native ones. This is a refusal to accord the biblical text the final authority it claims for itself to suppress differences. In my opinion, their approach has not received the attention it deserves.

[17]Donaldson, *Decolonizing Feminisms,* 139.

across races, across cultures, across classes, across ethnicities, across nations, across sexual orientations to negotiate with the Other; that is, if it does not wish to invite them as colonized subjects–parroting Rahab, who quoted "Deuteronomy with more facility than Israelites." With this discussion, I have already begun to address the complex issue of gender at the decolonizing zone.

7

The Doubly Colonized Decolonizing Method

In this chapter, I shall draw from the historical experiences and strategies of resistance of Two-Thirds World women to propose a move toward decolonizing feminist practices in biblical studies by looking at the following:

1. Early feminism, imperialism, and Two-Thirds World women
2. Cultivating new spaces
3. Adding gender to the unholy three: God, gold, and glory
4. Type-scenes of land possession
5. Rahab's reading prism

Decolonizing feminist biblical practices describes the commitment and the methods of reading the Bible that resist both patriarchal and imperial oppression in order to cultivate a space of liberating interdependence between nations, genders, races, ethnicities, the environment, and development.

Early Feminisms and Imperialism

To a feminist reader, the decolonizing literary strategies discussed in the last chapter are familiar. Because feminist discourse also theorizes women as colonized landless citizens, subverts the master's genre and language, rewrites history, rereads the master's canonical texts, retrieves the excluded texts of women writers in order to subvert the patriarchal canon, and inter-rogates its textual representations, there are similarities in the strategies of resistance and liberation. However, feminist discourse, championed by white middle-class women, and decolonizing postcolonial discourse, articulated by the diverse Two-Thirds World masses, grew almost simultaneously, "their theoretical trajectories demonstrating striking similarities but rarely intersecting."[1] Their similar but uneasy discourse was/is due to a number of reasons, among them, the social location of the earliest artisans of feminist discourse of the twentieth century and the subsequent inevitability of conflict of interests with colonized subjects. White middle-class feminists regarded patriarchy as the foundational oppression, while colonized nations focused on imperialism, hence implicating the former as oppressors—and denying that patriarchy is also a problem.

The tendency to subsume imperialistic oppression under patriarchy and the lack of sufficient theoretical self-understanding among the exponents of early feminist discourse did not help the situation. White Western middle-class women hardly acknowledged that while they were discursively colonized patriarchal objects, they were also race-privileged colonizing subjects, thus collapsing the category of a woman into a monolithic entity; that is, a woman was regarded as a subject that is equally and universally oppressed by patriarchy (a stance well critiqued by Mohanty for limiting the complexity of the issues). In this way, early feminists overlooked the imperialist social position they occupied. This position pronounced them active participants and beneficiaries in the exploitation of Two-Thirds World people. This sore spot placed feminist and decolonizing subjects at loggerheads. That is, while the strategies of decolonization demanded a positive affirmation of native cultures precisely because the colonial contact zone entailed a systematic derogation of the cultural institutions of the colonized, feminist discourse, on the other hand, called for the rejection or reimagination of most cultures as patriarchal. Feminist discourse, true as it was in its intentions, resonated with the imperialist discourse, which dismissed native cultures on the basis of paganism or savagery. That feminist artisans were also from the imperialist metropolitan centers did not ease the tension.

Two-Thirds World Women in the Crossfire

Caught in this tension are Two-Thirds World women, for whom imperial oppression remains as real and persistent as the patriarchal one. Their male counterparts insisted on a "first things first" approach; that is, Two-Thirds World women were urged to prioritize the struggle against imperialism over patriarchal oppression. Early feminist discourse, on the other hand, insisted on patriarchy as the foundational oppression. Two-Thirds World women thus found uneasy peace among their male counterparts as well as among their white Western middle-class feminist sisters. This

---

[1]Ashcroft, Griffiths, and Tiffin, eds., *The Post-colonial Studies Reader,* 249.

conflicting position, sometimes termed "double colonization" (meaning they are oppressed by two structural systems: imperialism and patriarchy) has been changing the face of feminism and is still far from resolved, as attested to by *The Victims,* a novel that explores the impact of both patriarchy and the colonizing ideology of apartheid on women of southern Africa.

Some of the analysis of anti-imperial strategies of *The Victims* in the last chapter highlights the tension of gender and imperial oppression at the decolonizing zones. It illustrates the complexity of double colonization. For example, Kgetho's mother comforts her abandoned daughter-in-law, struggling to raise children alone, by cautioning her to avoid thinking that her husband, who works as an immigrant in the South African mines, is enjoying himself. "We are all victims of our own times," she asserts (p. 36). She implores her daughter-in-law to see her husband as an oppressed subject. Tom, a black South African student who was forced to flee South Africa and Botswana, leaving behind a pregnant girlfriend, Dineo, holds that "all people are wounded, both men and women alike" (p. 122).

In particular, *The Victims* narratively dramatizes gender and imperial oppression through the character of Dineo. She is the privileged hearer of her mother's story, Mr. Nala's historical perspective, Mother Mary Magdalene's spiritual approach, and Tom's South African perspective. She is forced to weigh their conflicting perspectives without any easy conclusion about what is the source of oppression: Is it patriarchy or imperialism, or both?

Her mother's story, covered in the first part of the novel, bears all the colors of precolonial patriarchal oppression. Mmapula informs Dineo that they have to sell vegetables and beer to raise money for her school fees even though her father is a working man. She informs Dineo of how Kgetho, her father, never comes home or sends money to support his family—a point later shown to be a result of imperial oppression. She also informs Dineo, however, that her father does not believe a girl needs to be educated beyond the elementary level—a point illustrating the persistence of precolonial patriarchy. When Kgetho comes home for one of his short and rare visits, Dineo experiences his oppressive male authority.

Kgetho, whom the implied reader is privileged to know is totally disoriented by his displacement and the degradation of the apartheid system at the Johannesburg mines, comes home to desperately reassert his male authority to his wife and children. "This is my home and my house. I am the master here and my voice must be heard," he says (p. 17). He informs Dineo that she has had enough education, that she must get married, for he wants to collect the bride price. Dineo pleads with him unsuccessfully to allow her to pursue her education: "Although I am away most of the time, I will have you and your mother know that I am still the head of this house. Things will have to be done my way," he asserts (p. 16). Dineo sympathizes with her mother and concludes that her father is an irresponsible and ruthless monster.

In the history class, however, Dineo is forced to reevaluate her conclusions about her father. The history teacher explains the origins of labor emigration and its impact on families. Dineo begins to understand that Batswana men did not send any money because they were indeed underpaid and, above all, that going to the mines was not so much a choice as a coercive strategy of imperialism. The latter point is dramatically brought home to her when in a history class Mr. Nala asks the students how, in their culture, major historical events are marked. The answer is that people born around such an event are given names that commemorate it. As the students list some of the names attesting to labor emigration, one of the names that comes up is Kgetho, which means "tax." To quote the narrator:

> The bell rang. Dineo's frozen mouth gaped. My father's name, she said to herself, shocked. Students were already walking out but Dineo remained on her chair, her heart rumbling softly, slowly, heavily, and threatening to stop, as she tried to accept that it was not necessarily her father's choice to go to the mines, nor her grandfather's. The knowledge seemed to request her to forgive and she found it unbearable. The suffering she and her mother had borne had to be blamed on someone. (p. 53)

Patriarchal or imperialist victims? Who is the victim and who is the victimizer? Dineo's bell rings, forcing her to reevaluate her conclusion about her father as a mere patriarchal victimizer, forcing her to see him as a victim too.

Tension of gender and imperial oppression is also dramatized through Dineo's relationship with Tom. Unlike her father, Tom encouraged Dineo to pursue her education to the highest levels. Tom "was different from all the men Dineo had known" (p. 96). When Tom disappears without a word, leaving her pregnant, Dineo is forced to see him through the image of her father. Yet even this conclusion is wrenched from her, when Tom's identity is revealed and the story of his departure explained. Tom, a South African refugee, fled one night with no prior notice or plan, save that he was warned that the South African apartheid regime had located his Botswana address and could attack him at any time. The narrator concludes the scene of the revelation of Tom's identity, noting that

> for the first time, Dineo fully agreed that it was indeed a sick land and a broken people as Mother Mary Magdalene had often said...Previously, Dineo believed that South African women were having the ball of their lives with all the men of the Southern region going to work in their country. But now, she knew that their sons, daughters, and husbands were fleeing and dying. "We are all caught under the same blazing fire," she concluded. (p. 123)

This constant replay of patriarchal versus imperialist oppression highlights the conflicts of double colonization, indicating their interconnectedness as well as the distinctiveness of each form of oppression. Continuing its adoption of decolonizing strategies, the novel closes with Mmapula sending Dineo back to school not only to avoid marrying an "empty space," that is, agreeing to live under the oppression of colonial depopulation, but also to be "educated enough to stand on her own if need be," a strategy geared to resist patriarchal subordination of women through economic deprivation (p. 123). To her mother's words Dineo responds, "I will hold the dream" (p. 124). She agrees to resist both patriarchy and imperialism. Schooling is, therefore, regarded as a degree of liberation for Dineo, in the sense that it allows her to understand imperial oppression in her region and it also empowers her to be a subject who does not need to depend on a man economically.

While we see a struggle to deal with both patriarchy and imperialism in the decolonizing zone—that is, among Two-Thirds World feminist discourse—this commitment has proved lacking among white middle-class feminist strategies. White Western feminist discourse has been thorough in its commitment toward unveiling and resisting all forms of patriarchy, yet imperialism is more often than not ignored. Similarly, biblical feminist discourses, articulated mostly by white middle-class women, also need to adopt decolonizing feminist practices, given the pervasiveness of imperial oppression in the global structures of the past and present. Unless feminist biblical discourse also strives to become a decolonizing practice, its liberation will be found wanting by Two-Thirds World women. I thus propose that decolonizing biblical practices should begin by making attempts to create new spaces to hear God anew.

Semoya: Cultivating New Feminist Spaces

Generally, gender at the decolonizing zones differs from gender at the imperial contact zone. In the latter zone, women appear as both colonizer and colonized. The colonizer women in Exodus and *Heart of Darkness* are thus among the chosen races, enjoying the harvest of imperialism, yet a little lower than their male counterparts. On the other hand, colonized women of the imperial contact zone appear as representations of colonial desires in imperializing literature. The likes of Rahab, Pocahontas, Dido, and "the savage and superb" African woman discussed in earlier chapters represent their lands as lands of people who yearn and beseech to be possessed by the colonizer.

At the decolonizing zone, therefore, Two-Thirds World feminist readers confront colonial representations that, despite their derogative strategies, are institutionalized as canonical texts in schools and churches—both Jesus and William Shakespeare remain enthroned and well girded. Jesus and

Shakespeare are both imperial and patriarchal symbols. To resist their imperial installation, colonized writers-readers have embarked on intertextual wars of decolonization by adopting a subversive hybrid approach. They weave cross-cultural discourse, drawing from the cultural banks of both the colonized and the colonizer. This subversive hybrid approach rejects the privileging of imperial texts and institutions as the standard for all cultures at all times, for such prioritizing characterizes imperialist ideology of claiming superiority in order to suppress differences.

Yet women at the decolonizing zones need to strive to cultivate new spaces for representing themselves more forcefully and more intently, to cultivate more anti-imperialist and anti-patriarchal structures of oppression by creating new spaces of articulating liberation against patriarchal and imperial oppression. This is precisely because the grind of imperial powers, through its ever-tightening control of world economy and distribution of ideas and goods, tends to mock any counterimperial discourse through reiterating its own validity. Further, patriarchy still mostly owns and controls the social institutions that maintain and reduplicate itself. On these grounds, decolonizing literary practitioners do not, and in my opinion, cannot, confine themselves to analyzing representations of the imperial constructions, or even spinning subversive hybrid rereadings of the colonizer's text. Rather, they must always insist on new spaces for cultivating new contextual and international readings-writings, which are both decolonizing and depatriarchalizing. As used here, new spaces, therefore, define new frameworks of imagining reality and building social, economic, and political structures that do not espouse patriarchal and imperial forms of relationships, or any form of oppression. Such new spaces demand the courage to constantly plant new seeds of critical assessment of social structures and build relationships of liberating interdependence. The vibrancy of such spaces will require embarking on a deliberate agenda of monitoring and resisting all forms of oppression.

I find a model of cultivating such new spaces offered by AICs women's biblical readings of *Semoya* (see chapters 2 and 9). The AICs readers recognize but override biblical oppressive claims by insisting on listening to what the Spirit says and holding that "God never opened the Bible to me." Thus a *Semoya* space reserves a critical and liberative reading of texts that have been instrumental in the colonization of Africa and oppression of women. It insists on hearing God afresh, in a new space—one that operates outside the oppressive structures and their symbols. The *Semoya* space insists on imagining a framework that enhances the lives of women and men and that does not embrace patriarchal and imperial oppression. Its resistance is articulated in its way of using and reading the Bible so that biblical interpretations that subscribe to the domination of women and of non-Christian nations are sidestepped in the service of seeking that which embraces the dignity of God's creation. The fact that *Semoya* resists dependence on the written biblical text, a book that is highly established in patriarchal and colonizing structures, means it stands a better chance of resisting assimilation into oppressive systems of perceiving relations. *Semoya* offers a framework that espouses a liberating existence of women and men in different cultures.

The authority of a *Semoya* space, as a new space, is indispensable for feminist decolonizing readers-writers, given the overwhelming power of the former colonizers' capacity to flood the market with their ideas and goods to the extent of silencing its resisting victims to a secondary status of consumers of Western goods, policies, and ideas. It is also indispensable in resisting patriarchy, which is deeply entrenched in our social, economic, and political institutions. To speak or to interpret the Bible from a *Semoya* space is to insist on hearing God anew—free from the often oppressive space of our current social structures. Methodologically, this chapter has insisted on this new creative space by reading the unknown and new counternarrative of *The Victims* side by side with the enormously canonized texts of the empire, such as Exodus, *The Aeneid,* and *Heart of Darkness.* Moreover, such a space offers hope not only to doubly colonized women but also to colonizer feminist biblical readers, whose discourse has often fallen into subscribing to imperial oppression.

God, Gold, Glory, Gender, and Method

The exposition on empire and method in earlier chapters capitalized on heightening the literary-rhetorical methods by which colonizing narratives construct and reproduce self-validating means of traveling to, entering into, and taking possession of foreign lands and people through intertextuality. Specifically, it highlighted how the narrative methods of imperializing texts depend on the intertextual reiteration of the following literary-rhetorical constructions:

1. authorizing travel through divine claims

2. representing the targeted foreign lands and people as in need or desiring the colonizing heroes and their nations

3. representing the colonizing nations as superior and exceptionally favored by divine powers to invade, help, or dispossess their victims

4. using gender representations to construct their claims

Because the exposition on empire and method finds "God," or divinely grounded claims, central to the narrative strategies of imperialism, it is crucial to carry out a postcolonial analysis of sacred texts. Such an analysis underlines that whenever divine claims appear in a narrative a reader must begin to use the postcolonial critical eye to interrogate its ideological motives. While I am not suggesting a transhistorical imperialism, our findings in Part 2 underline that across time, texts, and cultures, traveling heroes and their nations repeatedly present themselves as divinely sanctioned. Their economic and power interests are inseparably intertwined with or even subjected to godly claims. On these grounds, imperialism, as a systematic and persistent form of oppression inhabiting even biblical texts, demands postcolonial critical attention. To bracket it is to enter and to further the anti-conquest narrative strategies of these texts as well as to baptize the contemporary global relations of economic, cultural, and political inequality. Yet this inequality is often as divinely validated as it is narratively gendered.

Since the exposition on empire and method also attests to gender representations as central to the narrative strategies of imperialism, this chapter adds gender to the three "Gs" of God, gold, and glory. Like the God factor, the gender factor serves to remind biblical liberation readers and feminist literary readers of canonized texts that bracketing the presence and persistence of imperialism(s) is sustained at the cost of endorsing this oppressive institution. How, then, can feminist biblical literary practitioners avoid furthering imperialist agendas, and read for decolonization? How can biblical readers in general avoid subscribing to imperializing texts?

This section contributes to these questions and looks ahead to the last chapters in two ways: first, by proposing and arguing for the recognition of a literary type-scene of land possession. Under the latter, God, gold, glory, and gender can be recognized as central factors in the literary-rhetorical construction of imperializing texts. Second, it moves toward formulating a decolonizing feminist model titled "Rahab's reading prism." Under this umbrella, the postcolonial parameters can be kept within view, given the persistence of imperialism and the continued struggle of the subjugated in the face of neo-colonization/globalization.

Type-Scenes of Land Possession

As many scholarly works have observed, gender representations are central to literary-rhetorical strategies of imperializing texts. To validate and to veil the violence of imperialism, gender representations are a method of presenting victims of imperialism as those who love, need, or desire to be possessed by imperialist traveling heroes and their nations. In his study *The Sociology of Colonies,* volume 1, Maunier correctly notes that

> even where violent conquest was in progress, this factor was by no means absent. While the first contacts were still hostile, native women came to the conquerors; they it was who often formed the first links between the races. Cortes had a native mistress, Marina by name, who on occasion betrayed Mexicans and directed the Spaniards' strategy. This is no exceptional case; Chateaubriand used the subject for a romantic novel; native women have often been the first agents of contact. This provides the classic literary

motif of tragic romance between the European man and the native woman.[2]

Due to this persistent yet flexible pattern, I propose to call it a type-scene of land possession.[3]

Land or geography is integral to postcolonial reading strategies. Here land is not just a slab of a physical body, but a web of intricately woven tales of power and disempowerment—its pages are not limited to the books but also written on the bodies of people. Readers-writers and literary characters carry, perpetuate, or repudiate stories of certain lands.[4] Constructions of land are also gendered. Land representations, therefore, are subject to much critical examination in postcolonial studies. Similarly, readers-writers or people who are inscribed with these tales of power and powerlessness are subject to critical analysis in their literary practice about whether they endorse or resist imperialisms. Possession, in this case, describes the various levels of imperial and patriarchal domination. It covers the colonial control of foreign lands, the imposition of culture, economics, and political institutions of a foreign power on different lands and people, and how it functions through patriarchal ideologies.

The type-scenes of land possession are evident in the stories of Rahab, Pharaoh's daughter, Zipporah, Dido, Pocahontas, and the savage and superb African woman of *Heart of Darkness.* These are women of different empires, cultural backgrounds, times, genres, and cultures, with the status of harlots, princesses, queens, priestesses, and concubines. However, they are all products of imperializing pens projecting the desires of their designers. The following three features are central to all the stories: First, women characters are the contact point with the divinely sanctioned traveling heroes; second, the women desire, need, or love them in one way or another; third, the traveling heroes may respond positively or not. Whatever way the story goes, the type-scene portrays its victims as womanlike lands—people who are available for the taking and who also seek and beseech to be possessed by the imperialists. Since most of the time type-scenes of land possession represent the desire of imperialists, these women characters are often won over. Nevertheless, to underline that in the end it is not a relationship of equals, but one that seeks for devotees more often than not, the women characters are deserted and left crying for the traveling heroes.

---

[2]Maunier, *Sociology of Colonies,* vol. 1, 70.

[3]Although I cannot trace the origin of this literary convention, the attestation of biblical and ancient epics suggests an equally old literary convention. Through imitation, subsequent narratives employed its form in different contexts to articulate various relations to land.

[4]Whenever I talked to strangers in the United States, I was often reminded of colonizing stories associated with Africa and how I embody and evoke them. People immediately asked me, "How is it to live there? Is it dangerous? What kind of houses do you live in? Are there animals all over? Are you planning to go back?"

The departure of imperial heroes after winning everything by no means suggests disinterest in possessing the land; rather, it tends to highlight the availability of worlds to them and their freedom to go in and out. With the exception of Rahab, the latter point applies to all of the above women.

The inclusion of Zipporah stories under the category of the land possession literary convention suggests that this category includes but is not limited to betrothal type-scenes. Robert Alter's exposition on the main elements of the latter shows its reproduction and its flexibility and how the minor divergences in each story foreshadow the future carrier of the concerned patriarchy.[5] Alter's analysis covers stories reproduced in a wide range of Hebrew Bible books, attesting to the intertextual service in the reiteration of certain forms and ideology. He includes the stories of Rebekah and Isaac (Gen. 24:10–61); Rachel and Jacob (Gen. 29:1–20); Zipporah and Moses (Ex. 2:15–21); Ruth and Boaz in the book of Ruth; Saul and girls (1 Sam. 9:11–12); and a suppressed betrothal type-scene in David and Samson's story. However, Alter reads the form and reproduction of the ideology of these stories in terms of carriers of the protagonist or patriarchal figure in the "enterprise of Israel," or "the covenant God made with Abraham." The latter, as shown in Part 2, represents the origin of the promised land myth—a biblical expression for imperialism. The literary form of these stories contains and reiterates the beginning of Israel's promised land mythology, its progression, and its various players, who either maintain or lose it to other nations. In short, Alter's analysis supports my proposition of the type-scene of land possession as entailing a traveling hero who journeys to a foreign land, meets a woman, and forms some bond with her. The stories reproduce a narrative form that asserts unequal power between the concerned subjects, as will be seen in Matthew 15:21–28 (see also Jn. 4:1–42). Esther Fuchs analyzes the betrothal type-scenes from a feminist perspective.[6] Fuchs holds that the progression of the literary structure of a betrothal type-scene "constitute[s] a strategy that serves the Bible's patriarchal ideology, or the interlocking values and principles validating male political supremacy."[7] In particular, she notes how each story's progression consists of the diminishing status of the bride and the increase of the groom's power. For the purposes of my proposal, Fuchs's analysis also underlines a foundation of inequality upon which betrothal stories use gender to propose international relations.

On the other hand, Fuchs also brackets interrogating imperial purposes of these stories by not naming them. Her expression "male political supremacy" is a marginal admission of a form of oppression that is, in my

---

[5]See Alter, "Biblical Type-Scenes and Uses of Convention," in *Art of Biblical Narrative,* 47–62.

[6]Esther Fuchs, "Structure and Patriarchal Functions in the Biblical Betrothal Type-Scene: Some Preliminary Notes," *Journal of Feminist Studies in Religion* 3, no. 1(Spring 1987): 7–11.

[7]Ibid., 8.

opinion, too huge to be ignored. Fuchs's bracketing of imperialism, even when she detects it, is largely due to the collapsing of imperialism oppression into patriarchy.

Alter and Fuchs also note the suppression of a type-scene where one would have expected it. The stories of David and Samson are such examples. In my opinion, betrothal type-scenes in their early appearance in Genesis and Exodus became quite particular to the promised land myth. They become a plot that reiterates this desire in the Hebrew literature up to its realization. Fewell and Gunn's above observation somewhat captures this fact when they note that "in the beginning God involves women directly." Once the promised land dream is narratively realized, it is no longer as vital for the careers of the likes of David and Samson to be foreshadowed by a betrothal type-scene story. Nonetheless, the forms of these literary constructions remain instruments of proposing and naturalizing unequal relationships between nations and sexes. In the betrothal type-scene, therefore, we encounter a construction where patriarchal and imperialist desires overlap, interconnect, and appear normalized. The reproduction of their forms in various books also makes evident how intertextuality has served to reproduce and codify imperial and patriarchal relations of inequality across various times and people.

To return to the larger category of literary type-scenes of land possession, these often present foreign women welcoming the traveling heroes and their nations. Some feminist readers with genuine interests in reading for difference and against rigid and oppressive dualistic boundaries have easily fallen into the trap of reviving the imperialist projected desires. Fewell and Gunn's reading of Rahab is a good case in point. How, then, can feminist biblical literary practitioners read for liberation and difference without furthering imperialist agendas? To answer this question, I close this chapter by proposing a new reading strategy titled "Rahab's reading prism." It is a prism precisely because it seeks to read through multifaceted angles.

Rahab's Reading Prism

Rahab, a harlot whose body is open to any man's taking in Jericho, serves to remind the feminist and political gender readers that patriarchal oppression of varying forms and degrees is experienced by women of different cultures. It describes discursive colonization and precolonial patriarchy. Yet Rahab's body is also open to taking by foreign men, whose power includes taking possession of her permanently, destroying her native compatriots, and possessing her land—that is, historical imperial oppression, which includes colonized native males. The two forms of colonization overlap and intertwine but are not identical or translatable to one another. Women of different cultures may be able to speak of various forms of discursive colonization (patriarchy), but not all of them experience double colonization. For example, the social location of Israelite women in Exodus implicates them in the historical colonization of Rahab, just as white Western women of the One-Third World are today implicated in the oppression of Two-Thirds World women.

Rahab's reading prism, therefore, can help liberation and feminist readers of texts to grasp this tension of colonizer and colonized as inherent to a world ravaged by various forms and levels of imperial and patriarchal oppression. That is, it is inevitable for feminist reader-writers to avoid the parameters of colonizing and decolonizing practices that permeate feminist and liberation movements. In this way, Rahab's reading prism only highlights the historical fact of colonizing and decolonizing communities inhabiting the feminist space of liberation practices. Once this is recognized, resisting feminist readers of colonizing nations can choose to also read for decolonization. Doubly colonized women can continue to resist the pressure to read from "a first things first" position of privileging imperial oppression over a patriarchal one. Rahab's reading prism allows for political coalitions that go beyond one's immediate identity interests to a space that is subject to much negotiation between feminist practitioners of different classes, races, cultures, religions, nations, ethnicities, sexualities, and worlds.

Second, Rahab's prism does not consist only of a portrait of parroting or colonized Rahab. More importantly, the prism also consists of "Rahabs" who witnessed resurrection: bodies that rise against the imperial annihilation; bodies that speak with their own voices, and from their hearts and minds. Examples include the likes of Mother Mary Magdalene. The latter unveils the anti-conquest claims of imperializing texts by saying "Let my people go!" to those who purport to be saviors, thus exposing their true colors. The decolonizing Rahab, therefore, knows and recognizes the pen that constructed her and intertextually subverts it. She subverts it by recalling it and showing its lying fame; by subverting the master's genre and language; by retelling history; and by constructing radically decolonizing hybrid narratives, which refuse to privilege precolonial patriarchal oppression and the imperial claims of cultural, economic, and political superiority.

Third, the Rahabs of a resurrection experience name the imperial oppression and analyze the representations of its narratives, but they resist constraining themselves to these texts. They construct radically hybrid discourses of decolonizing, but neither do they confine themselves to these. Rather, they also insist on cultivating new postcolonial spaces for spinning new narratives of native and international relations of equity, difference, and liberation. One model of such a new space is provided by the *Semoya* reading grid of AICs women (discussed in chapters 2 and 9) who recognize the power of the Bible but still insist on listening to the Spirit of God speaking to them about the current needs of their society. The AICs women point out that when God spoke to them, *"God never opened the Bible."* Such a stance refuses to be confined to texts that are often patriarchal and imperialistic canons of those in power. Rather, it insists on the authority of a new creative space. It operates with the will to arise and to hear God anew, every day and responsibly.

To conclude, Rahab's reading prism is a postcolonial feminist eye of many angles and of seeing, reading, and hearing literary texts through resisting imperial and patriarchal oppressive structures and ideologies. It recognizes that women's feminist movements are inscribed within the parameters of those who read for, in collaboration with, or against imperializing narrative strategies; that some women are patriarchally oppressed beings who are nevertheless race-privileged colonizing subjects, while others are doubly colonized. Rahab's reading prism is a postcolonial feminist eye of many angles that enlightens women on how to form political coalitions that do not invite double-colonized women to the table as parroting Rahabs, but as Mary Magdalenes of the resurrection morning. It is a reading eye that demands the radical transgression of boundaries by embracing a multicultural canon, which does not continue to privilege imperializing canons, but demonstrates rather "the political willingness to take seriously the alternatives to imperialism, among them the existence of other cultures and societies."[8]

Finally, the most challenging function of Rahab's reading prism is how to boldly and responsibly begin to utilize postcolonial feminist new spaces without being content with reforming structures that are built on profound inequality and oppressive foundations,[9] but aiming at revolutionizing the structural oppression, at cultivating readings-writings of liberative interdependence, where differences, equality, and justice for various cultures, religions, genders, classes, sexualities, ethnicities, and races can be subject to constant reevaluation and celebration in the interconnectedness of our relationships. In short, the challenge at hand is how to seriously, responsibly, and effectively use the fact that *"God never opened the Bible to us,"yet we still hear God speaking to us as women and in our situations.*

Reading through Rahab's prism, I will in Part 3:

1. interrogate the narrative form and ideology of Matthew 15:21–28 and its other related verses such as Matthew 8:1–8, 10:1–22; and 20:18–20;

2. examine how various Western male and female biblical readers have inhabited the parameters of this highly imperialist and patriarchal world; and

---

[8]See Said, *Culture and Imperialism,* xx.

[9]See Mary Ann Tolbert, "Reading for Liberation," in *Reading from This Place,* vol. 1, ed. Fernando F. Segovia and Mary Tolbert, in which she holds that reforming profoundly oppressive structures is inadequate for mapping liberation.

3. engage AICs women readers as a move toward decolonizing feminist practices and to cultivate a vision of liberating interdependence.

PART III

A Postcolonial Feminist Reading of Matthew 15:21–28

> *Our knowledge of this Gentile woman does not come directly from her. Told in the Gospels of Mark (7:24–30) and Matthew (15:21-28) as part of the Christian canonical text, through the centuries her story has not been interpreted by her own people– Syro-Phoenicians who belong to other faiths–but by Christians, who appropriated her for their own specific purposes.*[1]

---

[1]Kwok Pui-lan, *Discovering the Bible*, 71.

8

Empire and Mission in Matthew

Part 3 applies Rahab's reading prism for a postcolonial feminist interpretation of Matthew 15:21–28 in two progressive chapters. Chapter 8 investigates Matthew's historical and ideological position on empire and mission. It undertakes a postcolonial feminist reading of Matthew 15:21–28 within the findings of the gospel's view on empire and mission. Chapter 9 investigates some Western metropolitan readings and how they confront the Matthean imperial setting and patriarchal ideology of Matthew 15:21–28. It presents the AICs women's readings of Matthew 15:21–28 as a move toward cultivating a postcolonial feminist space of reading for liberating interdependence.

The following analysis of Matthew's perspective on empire and mission is largely a literary reading that regards the presence of imperial power as central to the construction of the narrative. It is, therefore, a reading on and through the text that does not equate Matthew with historical facts. Rather, it is a reading that recognizes that Matthew is a rhetorical text engineered within and by a particular historical setting.[1] How the implied author narratively constructs reality in the text will be associated with the power struggles that pertain to the Roman imperial occupation. Postcolonial theories show that these struggles are usually not only between the colonizer and the colonized but also between various interest groups of the latter, which try to gain power to define the national cultural identity of the colonized as well as to compete for the attention of their collective

---

[1]See Michael T. Taussig, *Shamanism, Colonialism and the Wild Man: A Study in Terror and Healing* (Chicago: University of Chicago Press, 1987), for some of the most fascinating examples of how colonial narratives can hardly be equated with facts, while their rhetorical function and impact within a colonizing history cannot be denied.

oppressor.[2] Fortunately, it is not a debatable issue that the Matthean text was born in Roman imperial times. The city of Antioch and the date of 85–90 C.E. represent the general consensus of its date and place of origin. In some recent research, Capernaum has been suggested as a place of origin.[3] While exact date, place, and author remain inconclusive among scholars, the important issue is that the estimations are squarely within the time and geographical parameters of the Roman Empire.[4]

The exploration of empire in Matthew, therefore, seeks to establish the narrative's view toward imperialism by examining two aspects: its historical and ideological perspectives. The historical perspective seeks to establish whether the Matthean text is rejecting the imperialism of its time or seeking its favor. The ideological view, on the other hand, seeks to establish whether the Matthean intertextual perspective is geared toward rejecting or accommodating imperialism. The latter presupposes that Matthew stands within the Hebrew Bible foundation myth of the promised land, which was shown in chapter 4 to embody imperialistic values. Although the approach seeks to separate these two aspects, they are quite interconnected and reinforce each other.

Regarding the mission, defined here as the exportation of biblical religions to nonbiblical cultures, what are the reasons for examining it alongside imperialism in the reading of Matthew 15:21–28 from a postcolonial point of view? If one defines imperialism as an imposition of economic, political, and cultural institutions of dominant nations over foreign ones, then it becomes important to examine mission strategies for extending the biblical religions to foreign nations. First, since the mission is a cultural institution, it is important to determine whether its strategies advocate power relations that resonate with the model of liberating interdependence or embrace a model that is consistent with imperialistic impositions.

Further, the association of mission and empire reflects my social location as a reader of sub-Saharan African origin. As chapter 1 elaborated, the historical experience of sub-Saharan African people finds an intimate relationship between empire and mission. Popular African folklore and critical writers such as Ngugi wa Thiongo, Ali Mazrui, Canaan Banana, and Kwesi Dickson—as discussed in chapter 1—emphasize an ideological interconnection between biblical mission passages and imperialism. The

---

[2]On the theorizing of the colonialist self and colonized Other, see Frantz Fanon, "On National Culture," 36–52; Amilcar Cabral, "National Liberation and Culture," 53–65; Homi Bhabha, "Remembering Fanon: Self, Psyche and the Colonial Condition," 112–130, all in Patrick Williams and Laura Chrisman, eds., *Colonial Discourse and Postcolonial Theory: A Reader* (New York: Columbia University Press, 1994). Also see Horsley, *Jesus and the Spiral of Violence*, 1–33, who shows how the colonizer-colonized power struggles were operative in first-century Roman Palestine.

[3]See Andrew Overman, *Church and Community in Crisis* (Valley Forge, Penn.: Trinity Press International, 1996), 17.

[4]See David E. Garland, *Reading Matthew: A Literary and Theological Commentary on the First Gospel* (New York: Crossroad, 1993), 3, for the wide range of scholarly propositions on its place of origin.

relationship of empire and Christian mission is also attested by missionaries of colonial times (Pringle) and church historians of modern time (Walls). In his sociological analysis of colonies, Maunier holds that "it was the desire to convert the heathen which lured colonizers of modern times to seek to conquer the universal empire. Sometimes this was the chief motive."[5] He finds that "the salvation of the conquered became the inspiration which underlay colonization. Expansion was carried out in order to convert."[6]

Within the above sub-Saharan African historical understanding and experience, the testimonies of colonial missionaries, and the conclusions of various Western scholars, biblical texts propound values that are compatible with imperialistic tendencies. Historical evidence of modern imperialism thus categorizes the biblical texts as imperializing texts: texts that authorize the imposition of foreign institutions on one nation by another. To examine the basis of this effect, I shall apply the questions outlined in chapter 2 for measuring whether a text is imperializing or not. These are applied to Matthew as follows:

1. Does the Matthean text have a clear stance against the political imperialism of its time?

2. Does the Matthean text encourage travel to distant and inhabited lands and how does it justify itself?

3. How does the Matthean text construct difference: Is there dialogue and liberating interdependence, or is there condemnation and replacement of all that is foreign?

4. Does the Matthean text employ gender and divine representations to construct relationships of subordination and domination?

As stated, an analysis of Matthew's view on mission and empire includes an analysis of its intertextual constructions. The findings of intertextuality highlighted the fact that various genres of imperializing narratives tend to reiterate their right to dominate through imitations and allusions to classic texts. Decolonizing narratives, on the other hand, use intertextuality to counter the imperial claims, though sometimes it involves collaboration. Chapter 4 also highlighted that the foundation mythology of Israel—namely, the divine claims of a promised land that are narratively realized in the Exodus–Joshua story—articulates imperialist values. The question, therefore, is what do the Matthean intertextual constructions tell us about the text's perspective toward the empire and mission? Do they attempt to revive and reiterate ideologies of the Hebrew Bible to assert Israel's right to be an autonomous nation or to be an empire as well, or do they reinterpret them to collaborate with the contemporary empire? The overall perspective of Matthew toward imperialism will be drawn from its stance

---

[5]Maunier, *Sociology of Colonies,* vol. 1, 22.
[6]Ibid., 158.

toward the Roman Empire and the promised land foundation mythology of Israel in the Hebrew Bible.

Matthew and the Roman Empire

The imperial setting in Matthew is attested by some of its characters, by tax issues, and by the trial of Jesus. To start with characters, Matthew features a centurion (8:5–13), a Roman official and a commander of soldiers ensuring that the colonized do not rebel; several soldiers (27:27–31, 54, 65; 28:11–15); tax collectors (9:10); Pilate and his wife (27:1–26, 57–66; 28:11–15). Pilate is the governor and the highest imperial official mentioned representing the authority of the emperor. In addition, Matthew discusses the issue of imperial tribute. The Roman Empire was known to export its cult religion and its agents, while it imported taxes from its subjects.[7] Matthew attests to imperial tribute in 22:15–22, where a rival group confronts Jesus, asking if it is lawful to pay taxes to the emperor. Jesus inquires whose head the coin bears. With the answer "the emperor's," Jesus says to them, "Give, therefore, to the emperor the things that are the emperor's" (v. 21d). That such a question could arise or that the implied author felt obliged to address it and that a coin bearing the emperor's head was used in Palestine attest to the fact that Matthew's gospel was born in an imperial setting—where the colonized had to express their loyalty to the imperial power by paying tribute. The arrest, trial, and death of Jesus also attest to the imperial setting of Matthew (26:36–27:66). Local authorities—a council consisting of the high priest, chief priests, and elders—apprehend, try, and sentence Jesus to death (26:65–66). Nevertheless, they still take Jesus to Pilate, the Roman governor, to try him and pass the same judgment (26:1–27). Apparently, power was no longer solely in their hands. It seems that the accusation they presented to Pilate was that Jesus had claimed to be the "king of the Jews," since this is the first question that the governor puts to him (27:11). The kingship claim is tantamount to a challenge to the emperor's sovereignty. Thus, when Pilate hesitates to sentence Jesus to death, the local authorities insist that he must be crucified, and finally Pilate concedes (27:14–25). The trial, the accusation, and the verdict attest to powers of imperial domination that vigilantly guarded against any rebellious individuals in order to maintain its political sovereignty in a foreign land.

What does the presentation of the imperial characters, tax issues, and court system tell us about Matthew's perspective toward the imperial domination of its time? Assuming that Matthew is a Jewish text arising from imperially occupied Palestine in the wake of post–70 C.E. temple destruction, where are the sympathies of the implied author? The following will now be examined: the text's presentation of imperial agents and issues

---

[7]See Peter Garnsey and Richard Saller, *The Roman Empire: Economy, Society and Culture* (Berkeley: University of California Press, 1987), 20–40, 163–77.

such as the centurion (8:5–13), imperial tribute (22:15–22), Pilate and Pilate's wife in contrast to the presentation of local authorities and people (27:1–26), the faith of the Israelites (8:8–12), the temple tax (17:24–27), and Herod's wife (14:1–12).

The Roman Centurion (8:5–13)

The Roman centurion approaches and asks Jesus to heal his servant, who is in terrible distress at his home. Jesus responds to the critical situation by offering to come and cure the servant right away.[8] The centurion declines this offer, holding that his home is unclean given Jesus' racial background. Instead, the centurion expresses confidence in the power of Jesus to heal his servant by pronouncing him healed from a distance. The centurion states that he is also a man of authority, who gives commandments to his soldiers and servants and makes things happen through his word (v. 9). Similarly, Jesus could use his authority to pronounce healing on the sick servant without coming to the centurion's house (v. 8). In response, Jesus highly commends him, saying, "Truly, I tell you, in no one in Israel have I found such faith. I tell you, many will come from east and west and will eat with Abraham and Isaac and Jacob in the kingdom of heaven, while the heirs of the kingdom will be thrown into the outer darkness" (vv. 10–12). Jesus then sends the centurion away, pronouncing his wish fulfilled according to his faith.

Several points in the characterization of the centurion indicate the gospel's stance toward the Roman Empire. First, Jesus responds immediately without any hesitation: "I will come and cure him" (v. 7). Jesus is not concerned about the uncleanness of the centurion's home. The story is featured in a section that history-of-salvation scholars have designated as a period in which Jesus' ministry was exclusively for Israel. Yet there is no hesitation in meeting the request of the centurion. Although many scholars hold that the story "served the purpose…of showing Jesus breaking down boundaries which separated 'outsiders' from the religious community of Israel," that is, the beginning of the mission to Gentiles, there is more to it.[9]

The story also indicates the implied author's accommodating stance toward the Roman Empire. This is evident when the centurion is compared with the Canaanite woman (15:21–28), the only other Gentile featured in this section who makes a similar request. The Canaanite woman is also an outsider, she also seeks healing for an ailing dependent, and she too is commended for her outstanding faith. Yet she does not receive the same response from Jesus when she pleads on behalf of her sick daughter

---

[8]Bruce M. Metzger, *A Textual Commentary on the New Testament* (Stuttgart: United Bible Societies, 1975). This edition does not list the textual variations that suggest that Jesus asked, "Should I come and cure him?" (8:7). The question would imply surprise and unwillingness to go to the house of an outsider. The rest of the conversation makes it unlikely that Jesus responded with a question of surprise and reluctance.

[9]Elaine Wainwright, *Towards a Feminist Critical Reading of the Gospel According to Matthew* (Berlin: de Gruyter, 1991), 110.

(v. 22). After remaining silent to her request, Jesus informs his disciples that he was sent only to the lost sheep of Israel (v. 24). Then he informs her directly that he cannot give children's bread to the dogs (v. 26). Only after she has humbled herself, accepting that she is not equal to the children or does not wish to be treated like one, but only to be offered what is normally given to dogs, is she granted her request on the basis of her great faith. The divergent receptions accorded to the centurion and the Canaanite woman reflect the imperial and patriarchal currents at work in Matthew. Clearly, the positive reception that Jesus gave to the centurion from the start indicates the implied author's anxiety to present Jesus (his followers or Matthean community) positively toward the imperial powers.[10] If it were only a case of welcoming outsiders, then the open and positive reception would have applied to the Canaanite woman as well.

Second, the comparison between Jesus and the centurion also highlights the gospel's stance toward the empire. The implied author presents both of them as men of authority who make things happen by the words of their mouths (vv. 8–9). This may seem insignificant, but the paralleling of Jesus' divine authority with that of the imperial powers has the effect of sanctifying the imperial powers. The praise accorded to the centurion for his faith also indicates that the implied author's sympathies tilt toward the imperial powers. Jesus pronounces the centurion's faith as surpassing the faith of all in Israel, a statement that undoubtedly compares him with the colonized and exalts his righteousness above them. Further, Jesus says that the heirs of Israel will be overtaken by outsiders. The statement places imperial officials in a favorable light, casting them as holier beings as well as predicting that they, and other groups, will have more power. Although one cannot claim that the colonized are without social evil, such a characterization not only disguises what imperial agents represent, an institution of exploitation and oppression, but also pronounces imperialism as holy and acceptable.

Imperial Tribute (22:15–22)

With regard to the issue of imperial tribute, the presentation indicates a similar inclination. A group of Pharisees and Herodians, seeking to test Jesus, sought his perspective concerning paying tribute to the emperor. The gospel's stance toward the powers of imperialism is summed up in the words of Jesus, "Give therefore to the emperor the things that are the emperor's, and to God the things that are God's" (v. 21). This statement has solicited mixed commentary from Western scholars, ranging from overt omission to apologetic readings.[11] As Mazrui maintains, for those who have

---

[10]The centurion's refusal to let Jesus come into his house also indicates the implied author's allegiance to Jewish tradition.

[11]For an example of omission see Richard A. Edwards, *Matthew's Story of Jesus* (Philadelphia: Fortress Press, 1985), 77; and for an apologetic reading see Horsley, *Jesus and the Spiral of Violence*, 306–17.

experienced the historical colonialism of Western Christian nations, however, "the idea of giving to Caesar what is Caesar's and to God what is
God's was often a call to obedience and submission to Caesar—in the name
of God"; that is, the verse has sustained a partnership between imperial
powers and Christianity over the ages.[12]

Seemingly, the rivals of Jesus expected his answer to be negative or at
least to be a labored one. On the contrary, the answer parallels the things
of God with the things of the emperor, as things that can be smoothly
saddled together. It recognizes both powers without suggesting any incom-
patibility. If Israel was supposed to be under the sovereignty of God alone,
then certainly the implied author's suggestion indicates collaboration. The
implied author is anxious to present the imperial powers as acceptable and
the Matthean community as faithful to Rome.

The implied author's perspective on the temple tax further highlights
its perspective toward the empire. Jesus holds that his followers "are free,"
not bound to pay the temple tax, but he proceeds to encourage them to
observe it for the sake of peace (17:24–27). On the imperial tribute, however, the implied author makes no conditions—there is no hesitation or
conditional paying. Instead, there is an equal recognition of the things of
God together with the things of the emperor.

No doubt, the implied author, writing in the post–70 C.E. period, wishes
to present the Matthean community as a nonsubversive community to the
Roman imperial powers and, perhaps, to thereby counteract possible alle-
gations from rival interest groups. Nonetheless, paralleling faithfulness to
an imperial institution, one that is fundamentally oppressive and exploitative, with faithfulness to God not only disguises its evil character but also
sanctifies it. Given that "the history of effects shows that texts have power
and therefore cannot be separated from their consequences"[13]—just as chapter 1 has shown that biblical texts have informed many Western Christian
followers to serve the imperial interests of their countries with little or no
reservation—Matthew's perspective has far-reaching implications for international relations.

Pilate and Jesus' Passion

Pilate, the trial, and the death of Jesus (26:57–28:1–15) also highlight
the gospel's stance toward the Roman Empire. The implied author points
out that Israelite intellectuals and the elite ruling class had long plotted to
kill Jesus (12:14; 26:66). They only present Jesus to Pilate to push for a
judgment they had already reached. The implied author seizes this stance
to distance Pilate from the death of Jesus, while she/he increasingly shows
the ruling elites' desperate insistence on his death. First, Pilate, supposedly

---

[12]Mazrui, *Cultural Forces,* 22.
[13]Ulrich Luz, *Matthew in History: Interpretation, Influence, and Effects* (Minneapolis: Fortress Press, 1994), 33.

detecting their jealousy rather than a case against Jesus, attempts to release him by offering them a choice between Jesus and Barabbas, a notorious prisoner. The rulers insist on Jesus' death, opting for the release of Barabbas. Second, the implied author brings a divine revelation that confirms Pilate's conviction that Jesus is an innocent man: His wife receives a dream and warns him to "have nothing to do with that innocent man" (27:19) (this warning is notably the opposite of Herodias' request for John's head [9:18–26]). Third, when Pilate fails to persuade the insistent rulers to release Jesus, he takes water and washes his hands, saying, "I am innocent of this man's blood; see to it yourselves" (27:24). The religious leaders, who had also persuaded the crowds to support their quest, accept responsibility.

Even at the crucifixion of Jesus, the construction of the plot continues to implicate the religious leaders in the death of Jesus. As soldiers take Jesus to his death with dramatized torture, the religious leaders follow him to the cross and mock him (27:41–44). The religious leaders insist to Pilate that his grave must be heavily guarded against his disciples, who may steal his body (27:62–66). Last, when the soldiers testify that Jesus rose from the dead against all the forces of annihilation, the implied author insists that the religious leaders paid the guards to spread a lie that his disciples came and stole his body (28:11–15). On the other hand, the Roman soldiers who mocked and crucified Jesus notably receive a revelation and experience a change of mind. Thus, at the death of Jesus, which is accompanied by wonders of earthquakes and the darkening of the earth, "the centurion and those with him, who were keeping watch over Jesus…were terrified and said, 'Truly this man was God's son' (27:54).

On the whole, the implied author's literary construction presents the religious leaders, the rival group, as flat characters incapable of discerning the truth of God, and getting worse.[14] The imperial agents—Pilate, his wife, and the soldiers—are depicted as better and holier human beings. They show improvement and even become divine channels of revelation. Indeed, they are divine emissaries of God's truth. As Elaine Wainwright's gender-inclusive reading correctly observes, in Pilate's wife "we encounter another woman who plays a prophetic role," because "in Matthew, the dream is the means for conveying divine message: what to do or what to avoid. In the case of Pilate's wife it is the second."[15] However, Wainwright's gender-inclusive reading displays no suspicions of the implied author's motivations in characterizing Pilate's wife as a divine messenger. Similarly, Jack D. Kingsbury also observes that in "the soldier's confession of Jesus as Son of God…in vs 54, the Roman Soldiers are, properly, the receipts of an epiphany."[16] The point, however, is that this portrait of imperial agents is

---

[14]See Jack D. Kingsbury, *Matthew as Story* (Philadelphia: Fortress Press, 1986), 17–24, on the depiction of religious leaders in the text of Matthew.

[15]Wainwright, *Towards a Feminist Critical Reading,* 285, 286.

[16]Kingsbury, *Matthew as Story,* 75.

not innocent of collaborative stance and competition with its rival groups. Pilate, his wife, the centurion, and the soldiers are favorably compared with the local leaders, the crowds, Israel, and Herodias.

In sum, the presentation of the centurion's faith versus Israel's faith; the imperial tribute versus the temple tax; and Pilate, Pilate's wife, and the Roman soldiers at the trial, death, and resurrection of Jesus versus local religious leaders, Herodias, and the crowds all depict a recognizable perspective. The implied author repeatedly endows imperial agents with the capacity to perceive the Divine, thus hiding that they represent and participate in an institution that is inherently oppressive and exploitative.

Second, the implied author characterizes the local leaders (with crowds being sympathetically likened to "sheep without a shepherd" [9:36] or termed "the lost sheep" [15:24]) as increasingly becoming evil and incapable of changing their minds. This reflects rivalry and competition for power over the crowds between the Matthean community and local religious rulers. Matthew is, therefore, an example of a collaborative postcolonial narrative that arises from among the colonized but that deflects the focus from the root cause of oppression, the imperialists, and focuses instead on other victims. In this case, the religious leaders are portrayed as the source of oppression, while the Matthean implied author seeks the favor of the empire for his/her community. Similarly, scholars who bracket the category of imperialism in their reading hardly escape from sanctifying this oppressive institution.

Could one posit that the implied author's attack on religious leaders reflects a castigation of the empire itself, given that religious leaders collaborated with the Roman Empire and exploited their own people too?[17] Such a thesis cannot hold in the light of the above analysis. Clearly, the Matthean text seeks the favor of the Roman Empire by presenting the empire as righteous and holier than the Israelites.[18] The Matthean text, therefore, is one of those postcolonial texts written by the subjugated that nevertheless certifies imperialism.

How does Matthean intertextuality construct the empire and the mission? With this question Rahab's reading prism will scrutinize the intertextual constructions of Matthew.

---

[17]The conflict and competition between the Pharisees and the Matthean community is perhaps the most apparent and well-analyzed aspect of Matthew from various methodological perspectives. From a literary perspective, see Kingsbury, *Matthew as Story;* from a social science perspective, see Anthony J. Saldarini, *Matthew's Christian-Jewish Community* (Chicago: University of Chicago Press, 1994); and Overman, *Matthew's Gospel.* The latter book is one of the most informative for showing the wide range of competition, involving more than just the Matthean community and local religious groups. Overman also shows how seeking the favor of the empire was part of this conflict and competition.

[18]See Shaye J. D. Cohen, *From the Maccabees to the Mishnah* (Philadelphia: Westminster Press, 1987), 27–34, who argues that the prophet Jeremiah laid the theological foundation that encouraged collaboration with imperial subjugation rather than absolute resistance.

Intertextuality, Empire, and Mission

The genealogy of the gospel of Matthew intertextually grounds the whole gospel within the wide parameters of the promised-land foundation myth of Israel. This is evident in the very opening of the gospel: "An account of…Jesus the Messiah, the son of David, the son of Abraham. Abraham was the father of Isaac, and Isaac the father of Jacob, and Jacob the father of Judah and his brothers" (1:1–2). The opening not only recalls Abraham and David and a line of their male descendants, which is deeply patriarchal, but also grounds the narrative within the foundation myth of Israel from its beginning to its realization and its maintenance, which became epitomized by the successful reign of King David, and Israel's subsequent subordination to other empires. The narrative of Matthew is thus a thorough intertextual weave.

Matthew's intertextual perspective will be assessed by elaborating on the traditions of Abraham, David, and Rahab. My goal is to examine the meaning they assume within the Matthean setting of a Palestine dominated by the Roman Empire and how they relate to the narrative's perspective depicting the empire as acceptable. I shall be putting the following questions to its intertextual constructions: Are they a reproduction or a reinterpretation of an old text to reject the imperial power and reiterate the autonomy of Israel? Do they serve to collaborate with the contemporary powers of domination? These will now be assessed by looking at the traditions of Abraham and David first, and then that of Rahab, who in turn will pave the way to another Canaanite woman in Matthew 15:21–28.

Abraham

Matthew identifies Jesus as "son of Abraham" (1:1). Scholars hold that the intent is not only to name his ancestorship but also "to recall God's promise to Abraham that by his seed all nations of the earth shall gain blessing (Gen. 22:3). Jesus Christ is that seed…in whose name the gentile will find hope."[19] Evidently, scholars seem to regard the mission to the Gentiles as "the blessing" to the nations, promised to Abraham. Indeed, the implied author's next two references to Abraham, in the stories of John the Baptist (3:7–10) and the centurion (8:5–12), seem to strongly support this interpretation. John the Baptist warns the Pharisees and Sadducees to desist from taking their descent from Abraham for granted, since "God is able from the stones to raise up children to Abraham" (3:9). In the centurion's story, Jesus commends his exceptional faith, noting that "many will come from east and west and will eat with Abraham and Isaac and Jacob in the kingdom of heaven, while the heirs of the kingdom will be thrown into the outer darkness" (8:11–12). Both statements point to the extension of boundaries beyond the bloodline of Abraham.

---

[19]See Garland, *Reading Matthew,* 16.

The blessing of nations through Abraham, however, is a mixture of several other items (Gen. 12:1–7). First, God instructs Abraham to leave his country and kindred and to journey to the land that only God would show him. In obedience, Abraham journeys and comes to Canaan, where God appears to him and says, "To your offspring I will give this land" (vv. 6–7). In Genesis 15:7, the promise is repeated: "I am the LORD who brought you from Ur of the Chaldeans, to give you this land to possess." This marks the earliest construction of the promised land foundation mythology in the Pentateuch. The promise is then followed by the foretelling that his descendants will be enslaved in a foreign nation prior to the realization of this promise. In the books of Exodus–Joshua, the promise of land is narratively fulfilled. And, as chapter 4 has highlighted, this mythology espouses imperialist values. In short, Matthew's appeal to the figure of Abraham also invokes the divine authority to travel, enter, and possess foreign nations and lands–a literary trait that is characteristic of imperializing texts.

Accordingly, the implied author closes the gospel by sending the followers of Christ to the nations (28:18–20). The disciples meet with the resurrected Christ, who has been given all authority in heaven and earth, and he commands them to "Go…and make disciples of all nations," and to teach them to "obey everything" that he has "commanded" them.[20] Like Abraham, who is commanded by God to leave his own land and travel to a foreign land, the scene also gives divine authority to the disciples to travel to foreign nations with the authority of Jesus, who will be with them to the very end.

Moreover, the task of the commissioned disciples hardly embraces a model of liberating interdependence. Their commissioner notably holds "all authority in heaven and on earth" and commands them to go and disciple the nations, "teaching them to obey everything" that he had commanded them. The words "all," "obey," "command," and "everything" are absolute terms that leave little or no room for exchange and negotiations. Nothing suggests that the disciples of Christ will also need to be discipled by the nations. Nothing suggests they will need to recognize the existence of other powers of the earth and heaven, outside the Matthean vision of the Divine. Rather, it posits a universally available world, and it advances the right to expand to other foreign nations, to teach them, and to include them without necessarily embracing equality.

Because it depicts the non-Christian cultures as empty vessels that wait to be filled by the divinely commissioned disciples, the mission to the nations hardly posits a relationship of liberating interdependence between the disciples of Christ (read Christians or Christian nations) and the nations

---

[20]See Maunier, "Spiritual Imperialism: Motives," in *Sociology of Colonies,* vol. 1, 154–63, where he argues that religious ideas are among the earliest driving forces in the most ancient forms of imperialisms and have remained the validating motives up to the modern empires.

(read non-Christian nations). Because this model is expressed in absolute terms of superior, traveling teachers and dependent, student nations, the mission to the nations hardly makes room for working with and for differences among different nations. Rather, it advocates imposing sameness on a world of differences, for surely discipling nations to "obey" all that Christ commanded makes little allowance for diverse teachings of other cultures.

Therefore, when one asks, "Does the gospel of Matthew encourage travel to distant and inhabited lands?" one finds that both the appeal to Abraham and the subsequent great commission lead to a positive answer. When one asks, "How does the gospel of Matthew construct difference: Is there dialogue and liberating interdependence, or condemnation and replacement of all that is foreign?" the answer is positive rather than negative. In short, Matthew's intertextual use of the figure of Abraham has been read along the lines of "blessing to the nations" by Western scholars, without examining the power relations it advocates.

David

Another Matthean intertextual weaving is in the figure of David. What can the employment of the figure of David tell us about the gospel's stance on empire and mission? Scholars hold that by introducing Jesus as "the Messiah, the Son of David" the implied author recalls God's longstanding promise to raise up David's offspring and to establish the kingdom of his throne forever (2 Sam. 7:12–16; 1 Chron. 17:11–14; Ps. 89:3; 132:11; Isa. 11:1–5).[21] Throughout the various imperial dominations, ranging from the Babylonian to the Roman Empire, the successful reign of King David was fondly remembered, and it was believed that God would raise up a royal figure from his line to restore the sovereignty of Israel. The hope crystallized itself in what became the tradition of the Messiah-Christ figure. An intertextual weave that introduces Jesus as "the Messiah, the son of David," therefore, evokes a strong anti-imperial stance. Could it be that Matthew is making a strong statement against the Roman empire?

The nativity stories of the Magi and Herod indeed suggest that the implied author portrays a subversive political understanding of Jesus.[22] The Magi come inquiring about the whereabouts of Jesus, saying, "Where is the child who has been born king of the Jews?" (2:2). The question portrays Jesus as an expected royal figure. Herod's response indeed reinforces this interpretation. He gathers intellectual and spiritual leaders, inquiring "where the Messiah was to be born" (v. 4). His question indicates that he interprets the "king of the Jews," as mentioned by the Magi, along the lines

---

[21]Garland, *Reading Matthew,* 15.

[22]From these traditions, a historical approach can reconstruct the original/historical Jesus, who may have been more subversive than the implied author of Matthew is willing to permit for his/her own political setting of post-70 C.E.

of the long-awaited "Messiah." The answer confirms his fears: the Messiah was to be born in Bethlehem, where Jesus was born (2:1–16).

Herod's method of dealing with this royal Davidic figure is another intertextual reinforcement of the political image of Jesus. Herod decrees that all children who are two years or younger should be killed. But Jesus has already fled to Egypt in order that what God said may come to pass, "Out of Egypt I have called my son" (2:15). All these intertextual weavings are strong allusions to an earlier political figure, Moses, who led the Israelites out of the oppression of Egypt. The model of Moses and the trek from oppression to liberation is further buttressed by a replay of the wilderness temptation of Jesus (4:1–11), where he is tempted by the devil but remains faithful to God. Finally, the image of a subversive political figure is evoked in the Sermon on the Mount (5:1–7:28), which recalls Moses receiving and giving the law to the people at Mount Sinai (Ex. 19:16–24:18). Yet the appeal to Moses and the Exodus model of liberation cannot be taken for granted, since it is a reversal that embraces the right to travel to foreign lands and subjugate their natives economically, culturally, and politically. To return to the son of David image, does the implied author's intertextual portrait stand up to its expectations? The answer can be determined by looking into other occurrences of son of David titles. Some of these appear in the mouths of two blind men (9:27), of the Canaanite woman (15:22), and of the other two blind men (20:30). Notably, Jesus' Davidic sonship is recognized by marginal individuals rather than by the whole nation, as one would expect with regard to the long-awaited Messiah for a politically dominated people. This immediately alters the political power that should surround the Davidic Messiah, suggesting a reinterpretation rather than a reiteration of the Messiah tradition. In fact, reinterpretation was indicated in the very inquiry of the Magi—instead of rejoicing at the arrival of their long-awaited Messiah, the narrator reports that Herod and "all Jerusalem with him" were frightened (2:3).

That the intertextual allusion to the "son of David" is a reinterpretation that underplays the political position of Jesus is clear in his entrance into Jerusalem (21:1–11). This is the only time the Davidic royal sonship of Jesus is publicly recognized by "a very large crowd" rather than by individuals. Jesus enters Jerusalem riding a donkey, and crowds welcome him by laying down their cloaks and tree branches on the road while shouting, "Hosanna to the Son of David. Blessed is he who comes in the name of the Lord!" (v. 9). The whole city is shaken by his arrival and asks, "Who is this?" Then, Jesus goes straight to the temple, a political as well as a spiritual center, and overturns the tables of money changers, throwing them out. These seemingly political subversive tones are given a twist in the following ways:

First, Matthew quotes a scripture in Zechariah to explain Jesus' royal entry, but as Eugene Boring notes, it "omits Zechariah's characterization of the king as righteous and saving (LXX; MT, 'triumphant and victorious') in order to place all emphasis on Jesus as the humble...king who redefines the nature of kinship."[23] The arrival of Jesus "is not the triumphant entrance into Jerusalem of a powerful and victorious king—as the omitted words would have expressed, and quite possibly as his readers might have understood it. Rather, it is the entrance of someone who is meek and lowly."[24]

Second, that Matthew reinterprets Jesus' royal kingship is evident at his trial. Here Jesus is surrounded by all the important parties: the crowds, the religious leaders, and the Roman colonial officials—that is, the colonized, the collaborators, and the colonizers are all gathered. Pilate, the Roman governor, questions Jesus about his alleged royal and political stance: "Are you the king of the Jews?" (27:11). From Herod's interpretation of the Magi's question, "Where is the child who has been born king of the Jews" (2:2), it is an inquiry about the long-awaited Messiah. In fact, Pilate then confirms this interpretation by switching from "king" to the phrase "Jesus who is called Messiah" (27:17, 22). If one expected Jesus to seize this opportunity to reveal his duties and set the oppressed free, the implied author constructs a character who reluctantly and ambiguously says to Pilate's question, "You say so" (27:11), and who is a victim of the petty jealousies and false accusations of religious leaders.

Finally and ironically, Jesus gets crucified because of the insistence of the very people he has come to save (27:20–23) and by the very people a messiah is supposed to overcome, the colonizers. Every sight of a triumphant and militant Davidic messiah has been sharply reinterpreted to a "meek and lowly" king who dies silently on the cross. It is only after the image of a politically harmless Jesus has been established that Jesus is resurrected and he announces that "all authority in heaven and on earth has been given to me. Go therefore and make disciples of all nations...teaching them to obey everything that I have commanded you" (28:18–20).

Conclusion

What is the implied author's overall stance toward the Roman Empire? From the assessment of the Roman colonial agents and matters, the implied author presents them as holy and acceptable in comparison with local religious leaders, Israel's faith, the crowd's faith, Herodias' request, and the temple tax. From the intertextual weaving, evoking Abraham, Moses, and Davidic figures, Matthew sanctions the traveling to and entering foreign nations by divinely authorized travelers. It also constructs an

---

[23]M. Eugene Boring, "Matthew," in *The New Interpreter's Bible, A Commentary in Twelve Volumes* (Nashville: Abingdon Press, 1995), 403. For similar interpretations see Daniel Patte, *The Gospel According to Matthew: A Structural Commentary on Matthew's Faith* (Philadelphia: Fortress Press, 1987), 286.

[24]Patte, *Gospel According to Matthew,* 286.

apolitical rather than a political, subversive son of David and opts for a humble king rather than a triumphant king. Yet Jesus is resurrected with "all power in heaven and on earth." Does this power work against or with the imperial powers?

Ideologically, the mission advocates relations that sanction authoritative traveling teachers and reduces nations to the position of students who must be taught to "obey" all that Jesus commanded. Since the exportation of the gospel is a nonnegotiable cultural good to its potential consumers, it passes as an imposition. On its own, the great commission is a highly imperial statement; it has been noted that "it signifies…the exaltation of Jesus Son of God to *absolute and universal authority, or dominion"* [25] (emphasis mine). Moreover, the universal authority of Jesus is not limited to him, rather, the "disciples…share in Jesus' authority, a universal authority which applies to all nations." [26]

Since imperialism is a package of political, economic, and cultural impositions of social institutions of one nation on another, some may argue that Jesus' claim of "all power in heaven and on earth" and the command to disciple nations is just a cultural imposition, since the original Matthean readers and writers had no such power to impose on the world. This position does not hold for several reasons: first, from Judaism's cultural position, religion was inseparably tied to politics and economics. Second, the implied author has already distributed the contents of the imperialism package by willingly recognizing the political and economic powers of the Roman Empire and claiming for the empire a cultural role. In this way, the implied author creates a partnership that works with rather than against imperialists. The position of Matthew's text on empire and mission is a partnership approach that is best summarized in "Give therefore to the emperor the things that are the emperor's and to God the things that are God's" (22:21).

With this conclusion, I turn Rahab's reading prism to scrutinize the figure of Rahab in Matthew 1:5. Rahab's intertextual reappearance and analysis will pave the way for the examination of the construction and the relationship of empire, mission, gender, and race in the analysis of Matthew 15:21–28. The Canaanite Rahab of Joshua's conquest and the Matthean intertextual Rahab stand in continuity with the Canaanite woman of Matthew 15:21–28, whose story foreshadows the mission to the nations. This interconnection emphasizes the need to interrogate the implied author's ideological allusions to Rahab: how she paves the way to the mission and what this allusion implies for international and gender relations.

---

[25] Jack D. Kingsbury, *Matthew: Structure, Christology, Kingdom* (Minneapolis: Fortress Press, 1975), 77.

[26] Patte, *Gospel According to Matthew,* 400.

Rahab in Matthew

Rahab of the promised-land conquest (Josh. 2:1–24) reappears in Matthew (1:5). She is featured with three other women: Tamar (1:4), Ruth (1:5), and the wife of Uriah (1:6). Various theories have been advanced to explain their presence, yet as Jane Schaberg notes,

> the inclusion of Rahab…in Matthew's genealogy cannot be fully explained from the traditions now available for us. The statement that Boaz was her child by Salmon and that she was the ancestress of David (cf. Ruth 4:21; 1 Chr 2:11) has no support in the Old Testament or elsewhere, and it is strange since the biblical Rahab… lived at the time of conquest, nearly two hundred years before Boaz. Rahab is not mentioned in the apocrypha, or Philo. The name spelled *Rachab,* does not appear elsewhere in the New Testament, nor in the LXX or second-century Fathers…In spite of the difference in the Greek spelling and the dating difficulty, most scholars conclude that it is virtually certain that Matthew means the Rahab of the conquest.[27]

Amy-Jill Levine also points out that

> Rahab and Ruth were Gentiles, so their presence, along with that of Uriah the Hettite, foreshadows the welcome of Gentiles into the church (see Matt. 8:5–13). But this explanation, although correct, is insufficient…Nor can a Gentile association explain Mary's presence.[28]

Offering another explanation, Levine holds that "the genealogy is best interpreted as presenting examples of 'higher righteousness': Tamar acts when Judah unjustly refuses; Rahab recognizes the power of the Hebrew God and so protects the scouts…they demonstrate Matthew's recognition of those removed from power."[29] According to Levine, "Judah, the King of Jericho, David, and Boaz—all of whom had the power to act but who either failed to empower others or succeeded in exploiting them—are taught the lesson of higher righteousness by Tamar, Rahab, Uriah, and Ruth."[30]

While Levine's explanation is helpful, it subscribes to the conflict and competition for power among various interest groups, a phenomenon characteristic of colonized societies—one that is often accompanied by collaboration with the colonizer.[31] To start with, the theory of "higher

---

[27]Jane Schaberg, *The Illegitimacy of Jesus: A Feminist Theological Interpretation of the Infancy Narratives* (San Francisco: Harper and Row, 1987), 25.

[28]Amy-Jill Levine, "Matthew," in *The Women's Bible Commentary,* ed. Carol A. Newsom and Sharon Ringe (Louisville: John Knox Press, 1992), 253.

[29]Ibid.

[30]Ibid.

[31]See Almar Cabral, "National Liberation and Culture," in *Colonial Discourse and Postcolonial Theory,* ed. Williams and Chrisman, 53–65, and Horsley, *Jesus and the Spiral of Violence,* 3–22, for an application of the theory on intertestamental contexts of the Bible.

righteousness" (sometimes referred to as "greater righteousness") is a term used by several scholars to describe Matthew's tendency to set higher values (5:33–48). But in actual fact it reflects colonized people's competition for power among themselves, where they no longer have it, as well as their fight for the favor of the colonizer.[32] For example, the implied author uses "higher righteousness" to encourage the Matthean community members to be holier than the Pharisees (5:19), more law-observant (5:17–19), correct interpreters of the law, who also keep God's justice and mercy (23:1–39). The Matthean community is virtually commanded to "be perfect," as their "heavenly Father is perfect" (5:48). Yet, as shown above, the implied author is not critical of the real oppressor but pledges loyalty to the oppressive empire and seeks its favor just like the rival interest groups. Furthermore, to hold that "Rahab recognizes the power of the Hebrew God and protects the scouts" is to overlook that Rahab's story is not her own—it is written by her oppressors to project their own agendas as well as to validate the conquest.

Finally, Levine's categories of those who had the power to act and those who did not indicates an application of a patriarchal analysis. The former group consists of men and the latter is largely of women. The problem, however, is that there is more at play than just patriarchal oppression. Consequently, the listing of the king of Jericho (who of course was a man of a high class) among those who had power is tantamount to listing the colonized victim as a colonizer victimizer, and it also overlooks the fact that in the story, which, once again, is not his own, he actually acted to protect both Rahab and the whole city (Josh. 2:2–7). Rahab, however, is only a construct of her subjugators, and she can only respond according to their projected agendas. Thus, she is portrayed as trusting her safety to people she knowingly identifies as enemies of her country and city (2:8–21). In short, both the king of Jericho and Rahab are victims of colonizing powers by virtue of their racial and cultural difference and regardless of their gender.

According to Schaberg, Rahab and the other women "are exalted for their acceptance of the patriarchal status quo because it is believed that within that status quo the covenant promises to Abraham and David are being kept."[33] For Garland, "the stories behind these names prepare us for the kind of tenacious faith we will see in the gentile centurion (8:5–13) and the Canaanite woman (15:21–28)."[34] Like Levine's interpretation, they also illumine an important meaning in the recall of Rahab. However, by not naming the imperial ideology at play in the text, they fall short of

---

[32]See Overman, *Matthew's Gospel*, 6–34, for an excellent exposition on how the imperially occupied Israel of 165 B.C.E–100 C.E. resulted in conflict and competition among the various factions and sects of Israel, based in part on who best interpreted the law and lived a holier life.

[33]Schaberg, *Illegitimacy of Jesus*, 33.

[34]Garland, *Reading Matthew*, 19.

capturing the frightening implications of recalling her in anticipation of the mission. Schaberg limits her analysis to the use of the category of patriarchy, but the story also involves imperialism. Garland, on the other hand, overlooks that while the centurion and the Canaanite are both outsiders who foreshadow the mission to the nations, the difference in their stories reflects currents of collaborating with the empire and the use of gender in asserting power of domination–textual constructions that validate the oppression of some nations by others and the marginalization of women in the society.

Basically, the intertextual recall of Rahab, like that of Abraham, embodies a reassertion of the authority to dominate.[35] Through the character of Rahab, the ideology of presenting the targeted groups as womenlike people who require and beseech domination is reasserted in the articulation of the mission. In the book of Joshua, Rahab's story is ideologically matched by the Gibeonites' giving up their power, proclaiming the superiority of the invader, and voluntarily assuming the position of slaves (Josh. 9:3–27). In Matthew, it is matched by the Magi from the east, coming to bring gifts and to worship a king who is not their own (Mt. 2:1–2). The power relations that characterize the mission to the nations are engraved in these intertextual weavings, which employ patriarchal and imperial strategies. The use of the figure of Rahab, a woman, to articulate domination, however, also comes to serve, reinforce, and naturalize the subjugation of women in societies in which these narratives are used.

Decolonizing Matthew 15:21–28

This section brings Rahab's reading prism to bear upon Matthew 15:21–28. The passage is regarded as a type-scene of land possession. This decolonizing feminist reading therefore seeks to illumine and problematize the power relations entailed in the construction of mission, empire, gender, and race. It will investigate whether the story proposes relationships of liberating interdependence or whether it advances imperial and patriarchal relations of imposition and suppression of difference. The model of Rahab's reading prism presupposes that most of our current canonized texts were born in a world of varieties of persistent imperial and patriarchal settings and in turn became participants in justifying these social evils over various centuries and on different people and lands. The reading, therefore, is an endeavor to address the makeup of international and gender relations by interrogating some of those power relations that have become so normalized and are hardly questioned even by the most critical and liberation-oriented scholars.

Keeping in mind that the story of the Canaanite woman is a construct of the implied author of Matthew (who is collaborating with the empire,

---

[35]See Maunier, *Sociology of Colonies,* vol. 1, 70, on how the first contact in colonial literature usually features a woman character.

competing with other local interest groups for the attention of Rome, and propounding a patriarchal and imperial perspective of his/her own), the presentation of the geographical settings, characters, and plot, will be examined for patriarchal and imperial perspectives.

Geographical Setting

Land and people are always closely interconnected. Different lands have come to largely symbolize different people and the cultural narratives ascribed to them. Geography is therefore not just a physical body, but a page of intrinsically intertwined narratives of power and disempowerment. Depending on the author of a narrative and the reasons motivating her/him, foreign people and their lands can be characterized as inferior in all aspects, while the writer's race is endowed with all that represents goodness and excellence.[36] Land representations are, therefore, subject to much critical reading in postcolonial studies.

A new geographical identification thus opens Matthew 15:21–28 and sets it apart as a new unit. Verse 21 states that "Jesus left that place," that is, his own land and people, "and went away to the district of Tyre and Sidon." In verse 22 the narrative brings a person who bears the image of the land Jesus and his disciples journeyed to, identified as "a Canaanite woman from that region." A new geographical area in verse 29 also marks the end of the unit by stating that "after Jesus had left that place, he passed along the Sea of Galilee, and he went up the mountain." With these geographical markers of Tyre and Sidon, the Sea of Galilee, and the mountain, the story has introduced different people and the varying degrees of power and disempowerment associated with them, and it has demarcated Matthew 15:21–28 as a complete and coherent unit of its own, as will be shown by its characters and plot.

Matthew 15:21–28 is also placed within a larger context by geography and the identification of people. It opens by stating that "then Pharisees and scribes came to Jesus from Jerusalem," to ask him about the conduct of his disciples concerning purity issues (15:1–2). The Pharisees and scribes are the prominent members of an interest group with which the implied author of Matthew is in a vicious competition for power over the crowds and for the favor of the Roman Empire. After responding to their question, Jesus departs to Tyre and Sidon. Once there, the narrator says, "a Canaanite woman from that region came out" to him (v. 22a). The "Canaanite" identity marks her as a person associated with or who originates from the land of Canaan.

---

[36]See Blaut, *Colonizer's Model;* Alison Blunt and Gillian Rose, eds., *Writing Women and Space;* and Edward Said, *Orientalism* (New York: Vintage Books, 1978), for some of the intricate and genderized geographical constructions that have accompanied imperialism over the ages.

Jerusalem and Canaan are not only place names but also ideologically loaded geographical markers. The former represents Israel's political and cultural center, controlled by the implied author's rival group, and the latter recalls memories of conquering and possessing a foreign land. The rhetoric of the unit is encoded in these characters, who bear the tales of power and disempowerment associated with these geographical areas. Therefore, that Jesus is characterized as going to meet an outsider woman whose identity recalls those who must be subjugated is linked with the competition and rivalry that the Matthean community has with the Jerusalem religious leaders and the teachers of law and its own move to map for itself areas of power. This leads me to the analysis of the characters of the story.

The Characters

The story has three active characters: Jesus, the Canaanite woman, and the disciples. The demon-possessed daughter and the children of Israel are passive characters whose interests shape the progression and events of the story while they are absent. The interaction of all the characters brings the rhetorical agenda of the story to the fore, highlighting that its form and ideology are founded on the type-scene of land possession. The form of land possession is attested by the following literary aspects: First, a woman is the contact point with divinely endowed traveling heroes; second, the woman desires, needs, or loves them in one way or another; and lastly, the traveling heroes may respond positively or not.

The characters of a land possession type-scene can be put in two categories: first, the imperializing characters; second, their foreign victims. The former belong to a group that writes the story to authorize its own agendas, exemplified by Moses of the Exodus, Aeneas in *The Aeneid*, Mr. Kurtz of *Heart of Darkness*, and John Smith in the Pocahontas story. The second group consists of those who appear in stories written by their subjugators, exemplified by the likes of Rahab in the book of Joshua, Queen Dido of *The Aeneid*, the savage and superb African woman of *Heart of Darkness*, and Pocahontas, who are all constructs of the imperializing pen of their subjugators. How does the presentation of the Matthew 15:21–28 characters embody the form and ideology of a land possession literary type-scene? To answer this question, I shall begin by investigating the construction of Jesus, the Canaanite woman, and the disciples.

JESUS

Jesus is undoubtedly a traveler, whose divinity, class, race, and gender endow him with privilege and authority. As a traveler, he can leave his own geographical boundaries, travel to another land, and return at his own will (vv. 22, 29). This short journey to a foreign land anticipates the end of the gospel, where Jesus rises with authority in heaven and on earth and commissions his disciples to go to all nations (28:18–20).

The divine authority of Jesus as a traveler is already evident in this short journey to Tyre and Sidon. The Canaanite woman who comes to ask Jesus to heal her demon-possessed daughter highlights his divine power (v. 22). His capacity to heal is further underlined through the reluctance of Jesus and the subsequent begging of the Canaanite woman (vv. 23–26). Her persistence and her willingness to receive her request at any price (v. 27) emphasize her confidence in the divine power of Jesus. When Jesus finally heals the Canaanite woman's daughter through his word and from a distance (v. 28), the divine authority of Jesus is confirmed (v. 28).

In addition, the divine authority of Jesus as a traveler is girded by his privileged class and race. The Canaanite woman's address and Jesus' own statements indicate his social standing. From her words, "Lord, Son of David" (v. 22), the reader gathers that Jesus belongs to a respectable royal class. This is further underlined by her statement in verse 27, when she repeats the term "Lord" and assigns Jesus and the children of Israel the social class of the "master's table." From Jesus' response to the disciples and to her, one also gathers that Jesus has been "sent" to the lost sheep of the house of Israel. But it soon becomes clear that the "lost sheep" are also the privileged "children," who not only sit at the master's table but also deserve the bread. The Canaanite and her daughter, on the other hand, are undeserving "dogs" who can only pick crumbs that fall from the table. These statements assert the racial and class superiority of Jesus as a member of the house of Israel and, conversely, the racial inferiority of the Canaanite woman and her daughter. This leads us to the characterization of the Canaanite woman and its rhetorical function from a postcolonial perspective.

THE CANAANITE WOMAN

In Matthew 15:21–28 the Canaanite woman and her daughter represent foreigners who appear in stories they did not write. The woman character is notably the first point of contact, thus highlighting the reoccurrence of the type-scene of land possession form and its ideology. That the form serves to reiterate the ideology of foreign lands and people as those who require and beseech subjugation is evident in the implied author's intertextual allusions as well as in the characterization of the Canaanite woman in general. In the light of the promised-land foundation myth, to intertextually characterize a foreign woman as a "Canaanite" is to mark her as one who must be invaded, conquered, annihilated; or, if she is to survive, then, like Rahab and the Gibeonites, she must parrot the superiority of her subjugators and betray her own people and land.[37] Basically, she must survive only as a colonized mind, a subjugated and domesticated subject.

---

[37]See Maunier, *Sociology of Colonies,* vol. 1, 29–36, 53–63, on the centrality of race in colonial settings and the different ways in which race has been constructed by different empires over the ages. For contemporary centuries see Blaut, *Colonizer's Model,* 50–102.

Even more seriously, for a story that foreshadows the mission to the nations, to feature a foreign woman characterized as a "Canaanite" indicates that the Christian mission is proposed as subjugation. Three aspects attest to mission as subjugation: the great commission; the redaction introduced into Mark's story to build on the character of the Canaanite woman; and the plot of Matthew 15:21–28. To begin from the end (28:18–20), the above analysis has shown that the implied author's so-called great commission presents a Christ figure that has "absolute and universal authority or dominion" and who commissions his disciples to teach the nations to obey all that he commanded them. This mission discourse does not underline a model of liberating interdependence, but one of subjugation, of conquest, of students, of authoritative teachers, and of travelers.

The second point is the redaction introduced to Mark's version (7:24–30) in order to build on the character of the Canaanite woman. While Mark had identified the woman as "a Greek, by race a Phoenician from Syria,"[38] the Matthean implied author's editorial hand changes it to "a Canaanite woman from that region." Through this change, the mission to the nations is foreshadowed not by featuring Greek characters, who were never mythologized as conquest targets of Israel. Instead, there is an option to feature a Canaanite, a character whose very image alludes to those who must be conquered and dispossessed. Undoubtedly, the mission is constructed as a relationship of unequals. The image of a Canaanite in the foreshadowing of the mission is a discourse that espouses imperialistic values of imposition and that puts the empire on a par with the Christian mission to the nations. The mission is constructed on a model of subordination and domination, of unequal subjects.

The implied author's redactional hand has also intensified Mark's text to characterize foreigners as evil and dangerous. While Mark's narrator reports that "a woman whose little daughter had an unclean spirit" (7:25b) came and asked Jesus "to cast the demon out of her daughter" (7:26c), in Matthew the story is not narrated; it is a direct speech. She comes and says, "My daughter is severely possessed" (v. 22d, author's translation). Notable here is that Mark's "unclean spirit" or demon has assumed an adverb of intensification–the daughter is "severely possessed." The addition presents the foreign people, represented here by the Canaanite woman and her daughter, not only as womenlike but also as intensely evil and dangerous. This, of course, paves the way for the ideology of those who are in desperate need of divine redeemers and justifies travel and entrance into foreign nations.

Third, the plot of the story, which continues to build on the character of the Canaanite woman, is another major instrument in presenting the mission as subjugation. The plot of Matthew 15:21–28 embodies the form

---

[38]See Robert W. Funk, *New Gospel Parallels,* vols. 1 and 2 (Sonoma, Calif.: Polebridge Press, 1990), 127, for this translation.

and ideology of a land possession type-scene. It is also mainly moved by the actions and words of the Canaanite woman and her request to Jesus. Her role in the progression of the story is a good example of depicting the targeted foreign people as those who beseech and need subjugation. To start with, while the narrative says Jesus went to the region of Tyre and Sidon (v. 21), the story does not state the reasons for his journey. The readers assume from the context that Jesus was in his usual business of teaching and healing.

Furthermore, while Jesus went to this district and while it seems he entered into this district, it is the woman who "came out to meet" to him (v. 22a, author's translation). Her coming out indirectly implies that Jesus may not have entered the district at all; rather, it was the woman who came seeking him. The depiction immediately provokes the reader to wonder about Jesus' reasons for going toward the region. Ambiguity regarding who followed whom remains evident in the division that translators and scholars assume.[39] The ambiguity, however, effectively underlines the initiative of the woman in seeking, needing, and following Jesus.

Proceeding from this ambiguous encounter that downplays the initiative and the agenda of Jesus, the plot intensifies the desperation and initiative of the foreign woman. Upon arrival the woman does not make a composed request to Jesus. Rather, she started "shouting" or "crying out" to Jesus for mercy from the onset. The characterization emphasizes her desperation, her need, and her belief in the power of Jesus to help her. The progression of the story capitalizes on heightening her desperation, while it increasingly underlines disinterestedness on the side of Jesus.

Accordingly, Jesus' response to her "crying out" and request for mercy is a classical case of disinterest. Jesus simply ignores her. Jesus is characterized as not even informing her whether the request can be granted or not. The woman, however, continues to follow them and to cry out for mercy, since verse 23b says she was crying out behind them to the point where the disciples requested to be relieved from what must have been an embarrassing scene. The disciples say to Jesus, "Send her away, for she keeps shouting after us" (v. 23d–e). Whatever way, either by meeting her needs or just dismissing her empty-handed, the disciples want to be relieved of this embarrassing and persistent woman.[40] Their request, like the silent

---

[39]For example, Wainwright, in *Towards a Feminist Critical Reading,* 110 and 124, holds that Jesus entered into the Gentile territory. On the other hand, Levine, "Matthew," suggests that the woman crossed over and met Jesus on his "own turf," 259.

[40]In comparison to the two feeding stories in Matthew 14:15 and 15:32, which also include the suggestion of "sending away," it seems in the Canaanite woman's case the suggestion did not include fulfilling her request. In 14:15, the disciples come and ask Jesus to "send the crowds away" hungry, but Jesus openly rejects this suggestion, insisting that the disciples must feed the crowds before dismissing them. In 15:32 Jesus openly expresses compassion for the crowds and his reluctance to send the crowds away hungry. In the Canaanite woman's story, however, Jesus does not negate the disciples' suggestion, nor does he express compassion for the woman.

response of Jesus, serves to underline the collective disinterest of these divinely empowered travelers to the needs of a desperate woman: they do not ask Jesus to assist her, as is his usual practice, but to "send her away."

At this point in the plot of the story, the reader expects that Jesus' heart will be softened and that he will at least speak to her. Instead, Jesus retorts, "I was sent only to the lost sheep of the house of Israel" (v. 24). While the woman is defending the interests of her "severely possessed" daughter (read by some to refer to the future of Gentiles), Jesus seemingly guards the interests of "the house of Israel"–a statement that can hardly be read literally, given that with the centurion Jesus responded quickly and positively to a foreigner's needs. With the latter, Jesus even proceeded to say that "many will come from east and west and will eat with Abraham and Isaac and Jacob in the kingdom of heaven" (8:11). Returning to the character of the Canaanite woman, even at this point Jesus is not speaking to her. He is responding to the disciples; basically, he is still ignoring her desperate cries.

The woman, undeterred by Jesus' indifference, comes closer and kneels before him, saying, "Lord, help me" (v. 25). This is the climax of her desperate request for help. Face to face with the pleading woman, Jesus is finally forced to respond to her, but only to firmly reiterate his stand to this desperate woman: "It is not fair to take the children's food and throw it to the dogs" (v. 26). The verse serves to underline Jesus' uninterestedness, and is a major statement about this woman and her people as foreigners. It adds to the characterization of the woman as a Canaanite who must be conquered; it adds to her characterization as mother of a daughter who is severely possessed by a demon, that is, as people who are full of evil and dangerous. The term *dogs* underlines the foreigners as "unworthy people"– those who must follow their masters, while they do not deserve children's food. These images ground the mission to the nations on a concept of unequal inclusion. It projects the mission as subjugation of differences rather than as a relationship of liberating interdependence between nations, races, and genders.

At this point, the reader would expect the woman to give up in the face of such an overt insult and rejection. The implied author, however, is still intensifying the Canaanite woman's desperate need for divinely empowered travelers. The Canaanite woman does not give up; she does not question the insult. The implied author constructs her as a native so desperately in need that she is prepared to get what she wants at any price. Hence, instead of disputing Jesus about the undeserving "dogs," she says, "Yes, Lord, yet even the dogs eat the crumbs that fall from their masters' table" (v. 27). The Canaanite woman is portrayed as accepting the social category of a dog assigned to her and as agreeing to stay under the table and pick up crumbs.

It is when the woman accepts the social status of a "dog" and requests mercy as such that the reticent and surprisingly unsympathetic Jesus thrills the reader with a positive answer: "Woman, great is your faith! Let it be done for you as you wish" (v. 28b). The narrator adds a confirmation that "her daughter was healed instantly" (v. 28c). This verse draws the reader to itself and gives the impression that Jesus changes his mind or that she changes his mind, as some have argued. Such interpretations, however, are inconclusive from the text. What is clear is that the woman did not dispute the categories of "dogs" and "children" but insisted on being helped as a dog. Based on the conditions laid upon her, which she accepted, Jesus included her among the children on the understanding that she did not threaten to eat the children's bread.

That the Canaanite woman is portrayed as accepting the "dog" social category assigned to her and that her request is granted on these conditions, however, has frightening implications for a narrative that foreshadows the mission. The non-Christian followers, who must be sought and taught to obey everything, are not integrated as equals who have something to offer. Instead they are welcomed as "dogs" who have come to follow, beg, and depend on their masters. With the healing of the child granted, the mysterious short story of Jesus' journey to Tyre and Sidon comes to an abrupt end. Jesus departs to Galilee, back to his own people and land (v. 29).

Despite the amazing indifference accorded to Jesus in this story, the postcolonial reader cannot help but wonder about Jesus' reasons for traveling to this land and its people if he did not have any vested interests. If Jesus clearly understood himself to be sent only to the lost sheep of the house of Israel, how can his journey to Tyre and Sidon be explained? In short, why does the implied author characterize Jesus in this fashion? Before I pursue the story's ideological motives, I must return to the characterization of the woman.

Although the woman character is portrayed negatively, she also has a second face. Indeed, she is a woman, a Canaanite, a mother of a daughter who is severely possessed, and she and her people are dogs, yet from the beginning of her cry for help she addresses Jesus as "Lord, Son of David" (v. 22). The former title may be read as a general term of respect, but its closeness to the latter title strongly suggests that they are both christological titles. Furthermore, she falls down before Jesus, or "worships him" (v. 25; see also 28:9, 17), and asks for help. A Canaanite Gentile, an outsider, is a worshiper who recognizes the lordship of Jesus. Evidently, the divinity of Jesus is underlined here. Nevertheless, this raises two questions: What does such a characterization tell us, and what does it serve?

The redactional hand of Matthew indicates that the story of the Canaanite woman and her characterization are products of the implied author's choice and construction. The purpose of her second face, therefore, can be found within the whole gospel's aim, from the beginning to the end. The appeal to the figure of Abraham (1:1), the four Gentile women in the genealogy (1:1–8), the Magi from the East (2:1–2), and John the Baptist's warning to the Pharisees that God can raise children to Abraham from stones (3:9) all highlight that the implied author had a vision of the gospel going to all the nations from the start. At the healing of the centurion's servant, this vision is explicitly stated (8:11–13). At the end of the gospel, the vision of including all the nations is finally commissioned (28:18–20).

Parallel to the extension of the kingdom to all other nations, however, is the vicious attack on the Matthean rival group, consisting of the Pharisees, scribes, Sadducees, and, at the end, the crowds who are won by the latter (27:20–25). From the beginning the implied author says, "all Jerusalem" was disturbed by the birth of Christ, instead of rejoicing for the arrival of their long-awaited political savior. John the Baptist is calling all people for the baptism of repentance, but when the Pharisees and Sadducees respond positively to his call, he immediately gives them a hostile reception. "You brood of vipers," says John the Baptist, and warns them not to say, "'we have Abraham as our ancestor'; for I tell you, God is able from these stones to raise up children to Abraham" (3:9). The whole text of Matthew gradually and consistently builds this tension. In chapter 23, the tension reaches its vicious point and the repentance of the rival group to the Matthean community is declared almost impossible. The ending of chapter 23 opens out to include Jerusalem and her children, declaring that her house is left "desolate" (v. 38). As the above analysis of the trial of Jesus indicated, this pattern of inclusion of outsiders and the increasing, vicious attack on the children of the kingdom is played out to the end in the arrest, trial, and resurrection of Jesus Christ.

It is therefore surprising that with all these signs, the implied author presents Jesus as saying, "I was sent only to the lost sheep of the house of Israel" (15:24; see also 10:5–6) and informing the Canaanite woman that it is not fair to deprive the children of their bread by distributing it to the dogs. The story characterizes Jesus as being exclusively for Israel and against Gentiles. The above evidence, however, necessitates a deeper suspicion of the exclusive statements of Jesus. I would argue that Israel and Gentiles are both at the mercy of the implied author's quest for power. No doubt, the Matthean community is beginning to painfully and unwillingly (23:34) define itself as distinct from its parent group (5:20–48; 16:18–20; 18:1–20; 23:1–12). Nevertheless, the implied author is including the Gentiles in his/her own terms of superiority (10:5; 15:24–26; 28:18–20).[41] In short, neither Israelites nor Gentiles are spared by the implied author's strategies of seeking power.

For the Israelites, the characterization partly reflects the competition between the two groups. As many scholars note, the characterization serves

[41]See Graham N. Stanton, *A Gospel for a New People: Studies in Matthew* (Louisville, Ky.: Westminster John Knox Press, 1994), 160, for the implied author's negative construction of Gentiles.

to underscore Israel's rejection of their Messiah in order to legitimate the extension of the boundaries of the kingdom to include outsiders. For Gentiles, it partly serves to reinforce the superiority of the divine travelers and their nations to foreign lands and people (considering that both Jesus and the disciples are the children of the house who deserve the bread). The Matthean community may be at odds with the leaders and crowds, but, once out of the bounds of their people and land, they need to play the card of superiority, a typical rhetoric for subordinating the foreign nations. (See also John 4 in which Jesus declares both Gerizim and Jerusalem cultural centers invalid, but not before stating that salvation comes from the Jews and that the Samaritans worship what they do not know [v. 22]). The strategy of subjugating foreign people resists placing the divine traveling heroes on a cultural par with the natives of a land they enter. The international relations are only established after the superiority of the traveling divine heroes and their nations have been expressed, acknowledged, and secured.

Under Rahab's reading prism, the statement that Jesus was sent only to the house of Israel is also shown to be consistent with the ideology embodied in the plot. That is, while the gospel has shown interest in the nations from the start, the rhetoric of subjugation resists any admission of its own interests. Rather, the outsiders must not only be characterized as evil and dangerous, womenlike, and worthless dogs but also be seen as those who beg for salvation from a very reluctant and nationalistic Jesus. In short, the implied author hides the agenda of the Matthean community while it projects its agenda on outsiders as people who seek and beseech subjugation. Pharisees, scribes, Sadducees, and crowds on the one hand, and the Canaanite woman on the other, representing the outsiders, are therefore constructed to further the aims and interests of the Matthean community. Yet the implied author weaves the narrative in such a style that it is easy for an unsuspecting reader to blame the victims and to miss the tactics of the narrative. The hiding of one's power and projecting it onto the targeted victims brings me to the characterization of the disciples.

THE DISCIPLES

In Matthew 15:21–28 the Canaanite woman is indeed after Jesus, ignored by him, told off by him, and, finally, granted her request by him. The disciples, on the other hand, are hidden—they are in the background of the story, an uninterested lot. The disciples only surface to say, "Send her away, for she keeps shouting after us" (v. 23). How she is to be dismissed or silenced seems to be of no particular interest to them. Yet if one veers into the historical sphere of the text, one may surmise that, quite to the contrary, this is the group that is at the center of the narrative. At the time of the text's composition, the disciples would most probably represent the Matthean church leaders or community. They would be the group that is deciding to take their gospel to the nations, since their rival group has won the leadership of the crowds (Israel) and the favor of the empire.[42] Last, the real author of Matthew should be located among the disciples. However, the story proceeds by hiding its interests: putting up a face of disinterest toward a Canaanite foreigner when it is interested, and stating an exclusive interest in Israel when it has already decided to include the other nations.

In this fashion, the discourse calls on the implied reader to fall prey to its tricks. That is, the implied reader is apt to conclude that, after all, the nations desperately wanted the gospel, and Israel was not receptive to a Christ who openly took an exclusive option for them. At the same time, the disciples or the Matthean church are easily excused for appearing to be somewhat uninterested spectators. In this way, the story mystifies oppression by displacing it from the appropriate sources (the imperial oppression being the root cause that instigates collaboration and the fight for power among different classes and interest groups) and projecting it to its textual victims, represented here by both the nations and Israel.

Hidden as they may be, the disciples are travelers. Together with Jesus, they leave their home area, travel to a foreign region, and return. They have a share in the power of their master; they are shown to be superior, privileged, and much sought after. This is evident in the request of a woman whose daughter who is severely possessed by evil/demons and who believes that their master has power to heal the daughter. The refusal to guarantee her the healing highlights the identity of the disciples. Together with Israel, they are defined as "lost sheep," children who deserve the bread, in contrast to the Canaanite and her daughter, who are undeserving "dogs." While they depict themselves as spectators in this visit to the nations, at the end of Matthew they surface to openly take their place at the center stage: They worship Jesus and are sent to all the nations by the Lord who has been given all power in heaven and on earth.

Conclusions

The examination of empire and mission and a decolonizing reading of Matthew 15:21–28 indicates the following constructions:

- The implied author's stance toward the imperial powers of his/her time presents the imperial rule and agents as holy and acceptable.

- Its intertextual weaving constructs a politically unsubversive Jesus and encourages travel to distant and inhabited lands.

- The positive presentation of the empire and the decision to take the word to the nations is born within and as a result of a stiff competition for power over the crowds (Israel) and the favor of the empire.

---

[42]See Overman, *Matthew's Gospel,* 2, 35–55, on the success of Matthew's rival group and how the Pharisaic tradition readily made them the most viable candidates after the destruction of the Jerusalem temple.

- In envisioning the mission to the nations, Matthew's model embodies imperialistic values and strategies. It does not seek relationships of liberating interdependence between nations, cultures, and genders. Rather, it upholds the superiority of some races and advocates the subjugation of differences by relegating other races to inferiority.

- Matthew's model employs gender representations to construct relationships of subordination and domination as attested to by featuring the Canaanite woman in a story foreshadowing the mission to the nations.

- The form and ideology of Matthew 15:21–28 reflects that of the land possession type-scene, thus embracing imperialistic values and strategies as well as employing gender images that reinforce the oppression of women.

With this summary of a decolonizing/postcolonial feminist reading of Matthew 15:21–28 within the larger context of the gospel, it is important to assess the stance of Western communities of readers.

9

Decolonizing White Western Readings of Matthew 15:21–28

How do white Western male and feminist scholars read Matthew 15:21–28 within its imperial setting? Do they problematize the power relations it proposes? This chapter is a postcolonial approach that regards critical literary practitioners as belonging to a world molded by imperialism—a world of colonizing powers and their texts; a world of decolonizing nations and texts; a world of collaborators dealing with the texts of the colonizer and the colonized.[1] Scholars, therefore, belong either to the community of readers who advance and collaborate with colonizing institutions of education by bracketing imperialism in texts, or to the community of readers who reject and decolonize the imperializing texts in their critical practices, or to the community of readers who negotiate their worlds between colonizer and colonized by reading multiple texts and spinning hybrid interpretations.[2]

Chapter 1 showed that African critical scholars and popular oral perspectives have found an interconnection between biblical texts and the ideology and practices of imperialism. Do Western biblical readers

---

[1] For theoretical perspectives, see the articles listed under Williams and Chrisman, eds., "Theorizing Post-coloniality: Intellectuals and Institutions," 269–359; Chandra Talpade Mohanty, "Under Western Eyes: Feminist Scholarship and Colonial Discourses," 193–96, in *Colonial Discourse and Post-colonial Theory.*

[2] For a thorough exploration of intellectuals and literary practices that resist or endorse imperialism, see Edward Said, *Culture and Imperialism,* 62–262, which contrasts the narrative texts of the Western and Two-Thirds World writers; *Orientalism;* and *Representations of the Intellectual* (New York: Pantheon Books, 1994).

problematize the interconnection between the Bible and empire building? Do they regard the imperial setting as central to the construction of Matthew? Do they problematize or normalize the power relations propounded in mission passages? These questions will be examined by looking at some white Western male and feminist interpretations of Matthew 15:21–28, mostly in conjunction with Matthew 8:5–13 and 28:18–20.

White Western Male Readers

The readings of Western male readers are assessed according to the following methods of reading: social-scientific readers, historical-critical readers, and literary-critical readers. The division according to methods is artificial because interpreters engage a number of methods at the same time. Most literary and social-scientific readers, for example, are also redactional critics.

Social Scientific Readings: Andrew J. Overman

Overman's sociological study of Matthew's gospel and formative Judaism is by far one of the very best in highlighting the conflict and competitions of various interest groups and communities among the colonized.[3] Numerous sects and factions emerged between 165 B.C.E. and 100 C.E., competing to define, reconstruct, and preserve culture, and to win the favor of the empire and the popular masses. According to Overman,

> the harsh treatment of many Israelites by the Seleucid rulers, the encroaching Hellenism and its appeal to some Israelites and abhorrence to others, and the abuses of later Hasmonean rulers all led to division. Among the elements that provoked fragmentation in the first century c.e. were Roman occupation, competing Jewish schools, and the destruction of the Jerusalem temple.[4]

Overman's study situates the Matthean tensions and competitions with its archrivals, the Jewish leaders and intellectuals, within this wider setting and social world of formative and Matthean Judaism. He shows that conflict and competition were, in fact, characteristic among various other interest groups, such as the Qumran community, the Pharisees, and other apocalyptic revolutionaries, most of which tended to launch vicious attacks on the Jewish leadership, charging them with dishonesty, corruption, and incorrect interpretation of the law. The attack, evident in Matthew, "was one of the several ways in which the community sought to discredit the leadership and to assert that they, the sectarian community, were in

---

[3]See also Saldarini, *Matthew's Christian-Jewish Community,* which uses conflict and deviance theory; Bruce J. Malina and Jerome H. Neyrey, *Calling Jesus Names* (Sonoma, Calif.: Polebridge Press, 1988), who use an anthropological approach that employs labeling and deviance theory to analyze the social and rhetorical function of calling Jesus names.

[4]Overman, *Matthew's Gospel,* 9.

truth God's chosen people."[5] Dissenting groups presented themselves as the chosen, holy people or the "true Israel," who interpreted and kept the law of God correctly, usually through "the presence of an agent or interpreter who receives the understanding from God and in turn imparts this insight and understanding to the communities."[6] Basically, these literary rhetorical strategies, found also in Matthew's text, were not unique to the Matthean community, but were widespread among other factions and sects in the social setting of the first century.

With regard to the ideological mission passages, whether they endorse or reject imperial values is not Overman's question. However, his treatment of the ministry, portrait, and role of the disciples brings this point to the fore.[7] Arguing that the disciples probably represent the audience of Matthew's text rather than just leaders, Overman notes that Matthew has significantly curtailed the mission and changed its nature. In chapter 10, for example, they are never sent out, while in the Canaanite woman's story there is a reluctance in admitting that Jesus entered a foreign territory (15:21–22). Thus, according to Overman, Matthew contains the geographical movements of Jesus within Galilee, while he transforms the Marcan version of mission as preaching, healing, and exorcism to mission as "teaching and education." The emphasis serves to "maintain and protect the community and its world" in the act of correct interpretation of scripture and competition with its rival groups.[8] As a result, "Jesus is portrayed as an authoritative and effective teacher in Matthew more than any other Gospel," a feature that, according to Overman, the "Matthean disciples inherit and perpetuate" as attested by the final commission in chapter 28.[9]

Overman describes the disciples as inheritors of Jesus' authoritative teaching, in the following terms, which, in my opinion, depict the degree to which the power relations they advocate intimates imperial values and agendas:

> The community and the unusual authority it possesses is seen also in the binding and loosing, granted to the community in 18:18 and to Peter in particular in 16:19. Here the decisions of the community and its leaders are depicted as possessing the authority and sanction of heaven. The decisions that are made in the community are at the same time made in heaven. The community members behave as does God, who is in heaven (5:48), and their decisions are consonant with the will of God, and indeed are the very decisions of the kingdom in heaven...They enact decisions

---

[5] Ibid., 23.
[6] Ibid., 28.
[7] Ibid., 125–40, on his analysis of the disciples.
[8] Ibid., 130.
[9] Ibid., 128.

within the community which in Mark and Luke belonged only to —
Jesus or his Father.[10]

The implications of the authority ascribed to the disciples for international relations is best captured by Overman's statement that "the Matthean
community's portrayal of disciples and the authority they possess is too
exclusive to allow for other authorities, such as teachers, judges, or arbitra-
tors of any kind."[11] Overman shows how it is far from a relationship of
liberating interdependence that makes room for differences, since its codes
were developed in the heat of competing groups that sought power to define their cultural identity where they basically had no power. Nonetheless, these are the codes by which the disciples are sent to the nations, and
as African critical writers and popular perspective have held, the ideology
of biblical texts have been instrumental in the colonization of foreign nations.

The problem, however, is that most biblical criticism and scholars tend
to enter and flow with the divine story world that Matthew constructs to
legitimate his/her power claims as if it were benign, and as if it were not a
thorough search for worldly power. Readers enter the "anti-conquest" rhetoric (the literary art of veiling violent means of seeking power by making it
seem innocent) and elaborate it as a supposedly divine and innocent story
world, as it claims itself to be.[12] Postcolonial readers, however, have
underlined that "*texts are worldly…even when they appear to deny it,* they are
nevertheless a part of the social world, human language, and of course the
historical moments in which they are located, and interpreted"[13]
(emphasis mine).

⊱ Second, biblical scholars' methods of interpretation have generally
consigned the texts to the past, reading them as if they belonged only to
ancient times and as if they did not continue to affect international relations
through the power relations they advocate. Postcolonial readers, however,
insist that these texts have informed and continue to mold the making of
our international relations; feminists, too, insist that the employment of
female gender to articulate relationship of domination and subjugation is
instrumental in the social oppression of women.[14]

— Third, although New Testament texts were born in an imperial setting
and participated in various other imperial projects over the centuries, biblical interpretation has so far lacked a thorough theoretical understanding
of how imperialism works and the complex chain reactions it catalyzes
from its victims. As a result, many readers can hardly begin to identify

---

[10]Ibid., 131–32.
[11]Ibid., 133–34.
[12]Pratt, *Imperial Eyes,* 7.
[13]Said, *The World, the Text, and the Critic,* 4.
[14]See Mazrui, *Cultural Forces, 1–61,* on how the texts of the so-called universal religions
are the foundation on which current international relations are based.

imperial agents with the tensions and competitions of the colonized even when they identify it. The capacity of imperial powers to rule from a distance through the local elites often hides the face of colonizers and makes it difficult to integrate their presence as a central trigger in the divisions and competition of the colonized. As will be shown in the analysis of other readers below, focusing on the symptoms of the imperial presence leaves colonial violence potent and the collaborative stance of the competing groups unexposed. In fact, this is evident in Overman's excellent study, which, while it identifies the source of conflict, hardly gives the imperial presence the attention it deserves. In his own words, Overman says,

> an important question which goes beyond the bounds of this study: What was the relationship of this consolidating Jewish body with the ultimate power and force in the region, the Roman Empire, and its clients and Lords in Palestine...One wonders whether the Roman rulers and authorities would even have been aware of the conflict we read about in Matthew's gospel.[15]

Historical-Critical Readers: Graham Stanton

Stanton's historical interpretation touches on other methods, though it is primarily a redactional approach. Does Stanton read Matthew 15:21–28 within the imperial setting of Matthew? Does he problematize the power relations advanced by the mission passages? In a recent book, Stanton proposes an alternative setting for Matthew's text. The setting he proposes is that "Matthew has recently parted company with Judaism after a period of prolonged hostility."[16] Consequently, "the evangelist is...coming to terms with the trauma of separation from Judaism and with the continuing threat of hostility and persecution."[17] On these grounds, Stanton suggests that "Matthew's anti-Jewish polemic should be seen as part of self-definition of the Christian minority which is acutely aware of rejection and hostility of its mother Judaism."[18] Stanton also holds that the "gradual acceptance of some Gentiles led to intolerable tensions between Christian and non-Christian Jews."[19]

Basically, Stanton's alternative setting for the Matthean text focuses on the competition and conflict of the interest groups of the colonized, without making the important interconnection with the presence of imperial powers. The imperial violence remains hidden because he proposes a setting that focuses primarily on "victim on victim" violence without handling its root cause just as seriously. Furthermore, his reading is apt to

---

[15]Overman, *Matthew's Gospel,* 154.
[16]Stanton, *Gospel for a New People,* 156.
[17]Ibid., 157.
[18]Ibid.
[19]Ibid., 281.

subscribe to the collaborative stance that the competing groups often adopt to win the favor of the empire in the cultural constructions they embark on to present themselves as legitimate rulers to the oppressors and the oppressed masses. A good example is Stanton's reading of the centurion within his suggested setting. He holds that the implied author "contrasts the faith of the Gentile centurion with the complete rejection of Israel."[20] Notable here is that Stanton's historical reading from a redactional perspective demonstrates no connection between the positive presentation of the centurion with the implied author's collaborative stance toward the Roman Empire. He only reads it as the tension between Matthew and the parent Judaism, without accounting for the root cause for the tension.

Regarding Matthew 15:21–28, Stanton does not deal with the whole story in detail, but the following quotes will elucidate his understanding and how he relates it to Matthew 28:18–20. Stanton places the passage of Matthew 15:21–28 under Matthew's creative expansion of the sayings of Jesus found in Mark. Thus, using a redactional approach, he argues that Matthew 10:5–6 (Mk. 6:6bff.) and 15:24 (Mk. 7:24ff.) should be read together because they are Matthew's expansion of Mark's words. Noting that the story of the Canaanite woman has been interpreted in association with the Gentile mission, Stanton says,

> I am convinced that in Matt 15:24 the evangelist is simply attempting to clarify the rather puzzling Marcan pericope. There is no suggestion in Matthew's interpretation of the incident that a strict "Jewish Christian" restriction of mission to Israel is modified. Matthew is stating as clearly as he can what he believes (following Mark) was the attitude of Jesus to the lost sheep and to non-Jews. For Matthew, Israel's rejection of her Messiah at the end of the life of Jesus leads to the acceptance of the Gentiles.[21]

Consequently, Stanton concludes his book by holding that

> the evangelist's juxtaposition of particularist (go only to the house of Israel) and universalist ("go to all nations") strands…would have been read and listened to "with awareness" by the original recipients. They would have known instinctively which parts of the story belonged to the past history, and which parts were important for their on-going Christian community life.[22]

In short, Stanton's redactional reading separates the original story of Jesus and the later developments of the Matthean community, assigning the particularist and universalist stance to each respectively. This redactional reading, in fact, holds that the particularist stance is an elaboration

---

[20]Ibid., 151.
[21]Ibid., 330.
[22]Ibid., 380.

of Mark's statement "Let the children be fed first" (7:27), while the historical rejection of Jesus as the Messiah of Jews by the parent groups led to the universal mission (implicit in this redactional reading is a salvation history framework, which I comment on below in the assessment of Kingsbury's reading).

Be that as it may, one seeks in vain for Stanton's critical assessment of the power relations advanced in the universal stance. This is attested to by Stanton's omissions in his redactional reading of the Canaanite woman as well as his comment on Matthew 28:18–20. As shown above, Matthew has indeed elaborated on Mark's story, intensifying the demonization of the daughter and reassigning the woman from a Greek to a Canaanite identity. Stanton's singling out of the particularist statement of 15:24 to the exclusion of the rest of the redactional changes introduced in Matthew is not innocent. Rather, it is an eloquent attestation to his unproblematic acceptance of the unequal foundation on which the mission to the nations is proposed.

Literary-Critical Readers

Two literary readers, Richard Edwards and Jack Dean Kingsbury, who represent different versions of literary criticism, reader-response and narrative criticism, will be examined.

READER-RESPONSE: RICHARD EDWARDS

Edwards' reader-response approach regards Matthew as a story with interrelated narrative parts (characters, plot, narrator, reader in the text, etc.) whose cumulative effect guides the reader to its meaning over time. Edwards thus pays attention to "the sequence of information and its relation to the earlier portion of the story."[23] Since Matthew 15:21–28 is in the middle of the narrative, what is Edwards' reading based on the cumulative effect? The following quotes reveal his interpretation and how it addresses or does not address the imperial setting and the construction of power relations of mission, gender, and empire expounded above:

> This is the second incident in which a Gentile approaches Jesus for help. The Centurion of Capernaum (8:5–13) asked for help, acknowledged Jesus' authority, and was sensitive enough to Jewish purity laws to avoid asking Jesus to violate them. Here in Chapter 15, however, Jesus is travelling in non-Jewish territory, apparently to get away from the Pharisees and Sadducees. Consequently, his response to the disciples (15:24) is not clear, except perhaps to remind them that he is not here in gentile territory for missionary purposes.[24]

---

[23]Edwards, *Matthew's Story,* 9.
[24]Ibid., 56.

In a second quote Edwards points to the accumulative effect on the reader and holds that

> the reader will contrast the understanding exhibited by this Gentile with the perversity of the Pharisees and Sadducees and the dullness of the disciples. Unlike the incident with the Centurion, the focus is not on Jesus' authority, but on the woman's ability to understand Jesus' elliptical teaching (in addition to recognizing his power). The narrator made it prominent by noting the change in location.[25]

The last quote, drawn from the last verses of Matthew (28:18–20), allows Edwards the full benefit of his method. He holds that

> the "authorized Son" commands the disciples to "make disciples of (or disciple) all nations," both the Gentiles and the Jews. Thus the narrator, in reporting the Son's final words, focuses our attention once again on the disciples. They are asked to go out and create more people like themselves…The second command is to teach the things which Jesus taught with the added emphasis that these people must be taught to "obey."[26]

Edwards compares the Canaanite woman, first, with the centurion and, second, with the disciples. His comparisons on the cumulative scale of reading, however, reflect an insufficient struggling with the apparent dissonance in the plots and a lack of consideration for the imperial setting as a significant factor in the implied author's construction of the implied reader. For instance, the Canaanite woman and the centurion are both outsiders who seek healing for their dependents and who receive healing on the basis of their exceptional faith. But the plots that lead to the final result are drastically different and call for interpretive attention. With the centurion, Jesus' response is immediate and positive, "I will come and cure him," followed by a positive comparison of the two as similar men of authority—men who make things happen by their word of mouth. The Canaanite woman, on the other hand, is forced to beg three times before her request is considered; there is a negative comparison between her, her people, and the people of Israel. The latter are "children" who deserve to eat bread from the table, while she belongs to the "dogs" who can only pick up the crumbs falling from the table. Only after she has accepted the degrading social status of a "dog" is her request granted. These differences in the plots make the whole difference in the meaning of the two stories.

What is the rhetorical function of these differences? How are they related to gender, mission, and empire? In short, is the centurion assisted

---

[25]Ibid., 57.
[26]Ibid., 94.

quickly because he is a man, an imperial official, or an outsider? Is the Canaanite woman ignored because she is a woman, a Canaanite, and an outsider? Obviously, the variable of "outsider" is struck out since it is common to both, leaving one with the categories of gender, race, and class (imperial agents). If one agrees that the latter factors are central to their divergent reception, one has to go further and ask: What are and what have been the implications of such a construction for international and gender relations?

Instead of raising the above questions, Edwards' reading is characterized by a bypassing of the apparent dissonance in the plots to a point where it borders on omission. The differences are dismissed by focusing on themes: one story is about the authority of Jesus and the other about understanding the teaching of Jesus. The positive and negative comparisons of social status, based on class, gender, and race, are swiftly passed over. However, this does not mean Edwards finds no relation of the stories to the mission, for he comments in the centurion story that "the contrast between Gentile and Jew" is "about the future kingdom" and suggests that in the Canaanite story Jesus' exclusive statement may be a disclaimer of "missionary purposes." Edwards' comparison of the woman with the disciples and his comment on the great commission make his position even clearer.

In comparing the Canaanite woman with the disciples, Edwards notes the dullness and inactivity of the disciples: The Canaanite woman begs, follows, and worships Jesus, while the disciples remain silent and then ask for her dismissal. Jesus, on the other hand, disclaims any missionary interests among the nations. But, at the end, the disciples worship Jesus and are commissioned by the same Jesus to go to the same nations that he had seemed to exclude. How does Edwards' cumulative scale of reading over time and sequence account for the function of this dissonance? How does he explain its meaning?

In the third quote, drawn from the last verses of the Matthew passage, Edwards has the benefit of playing all the cards of the cumulative scale of reading to work out the similarities and differences and their rhetorical function in the gospel as a whole. Yet he does not attempt to recall the earlier story of the Canaanite woman or to work out the striking differences that characterize the great commission and the mission disclaimer in the Canaanite story. Just as Edwards does not question the negative and positive comparisons of class, race, and gender in the Canaanite and centurion stories, he does not problematize the proposed power relations advocated by Matthew 28:18–20 between the disciples (read Christian) and the nations (read non-Christian nations). Instead, Edwards elaborates on them, pointing out that the disciples are sent to "create more people like themselves...that these people must be taught to 'obey.'"

In sum, Edwards does not question the model on which the mission is grounded; he brackets the outstanding dissonances between the centurion, the Canaanite, and the great commission. As a result, he leaves untouched and unexplained the function and interconnections between mission, gender, and empire. By serving as an elaborator of the implied author's agenda without problematizing the ideological implications, his bracketing of these issues endorses, maintains, and normalizes the proposed international relations, whose gender appropriations are also bound to authorize the subjugation of women in the society.

NARRATIVE READING: JACK D. KINGSBURY

Kingsbury's literary approach regards a narrative as consisting of a "story" and a "discourse." The story is the "what" of the narrative, while the discourse is its "how." The former focuses on the events, the plot, and the characters, the latter focuses on the ideology of the text through following how the text constructs its perspective (narrator, implied author, point of view). How, then, does Kingsbury as a white male reader confront the imperial setting of Matthew and the mission power relations it advocates?

Kingsbury describes the setting as "the place or time or social circumstances in which a character acts."[27] In elaborating on Matthew's setting, Kingsbury's description of the three aspects of the setting notably excludes the "social circumstances" of first-century Palestine as an imperially occupied territory. Accordingly, his analysis of characters does not consider that Matthew's story and discourse are informed and catalyzed by the Roman imperial occupation—an occupation that usually gives rise to collaboration, loss of identity, fierce competition, and conflict among various interest groups of the colonized as well as between the colonized and the colonizer.

Kingsbury, however, does not fail to document the fierce competition between the Matthean community and the religious leaders.[28] Yet, without taking into consideration the impact of an imperial presence on any colonized society and the complex response it elicits, Kingsbury leaves untouched the root cause of tensions and competition. His reading, therefore, focuses on the victims, a factor that makes it run the risk of embracing the collaborative approach of Matthew and leave intact the imperial exploitative agendas. For example, the failure to take the imperial setting seriously leads Kingsbury to make no separate list of imperial characters and how they are presented. Thus, Pilate is listed among the colonized religious leaders, though Kingsbury is forced to acknowledge that he is not really a "flat character," as his local counterparts are portrayed. Similarly, the centurion and the Canaanite woman are listed under "minor characters," who serve as foils for more elaborate characters in the narrative. The blanket listing, however, is problematic, as the quote cited below shows:

---

[27]Kingsbury, *Matthew as Story,* 28.
[28]See ibid., 115–26.

The "Magi" (2:1) and the "centurion" (8:5) serve as foils for Israel: the faith of these Gentiles contrasts with the unbelief of Israel (2:1–12; 8:5–13). The two "blind men" (9:27), "the Canaanite woman" (15:22), the other "two blind men" (20:30), and the children in the temple (2:15) also serve as foils for Israel: these "no accounts" see and confess what Israel cannot, namely, Jesus is its Davidic Messiah. Pilate's "wife" (27:19) serves as a foil for Pilate himself.[29]

While these characters serve as foils, Kingsbury's exclusion of the imperial setting as a central factor in the story of Matthew automatically limits his exploring other motivating factors behind the positive presentation of the centurion and Pilate's wife. Pilate's wife, for instance, is not a foil to Pilate in the same sense as the other foils. Her dream does not contradict Pilate's independent conviction that Jesus is not guilty (27:18). Rather, her words serve as a confirmation of Pilate's judgment, and to a certain degree, he acts on them by washing his hands (27:19–24). If anything, both Pilate and his wife serve as foils to the local religious leaders and crowds who insist on the guilt of Jesus (27:20–25). Similarly, if the Canaanite woman serves as a foil, then the degradation accorded to her makes no sense and demands attention, especially since it was not applied to the centurion. Last, the centurion, Pilate, and his wife may be outsiders to Israel's faith, but as imperial agents they cannot be easily categorized as "no accounts," for their class is indeed significant.

Kingsbury also holds that "Gentile cities…Tyre and Sidon" (15:21) lie beyond the purview of Jesus' own mission to the lost sheep of the house of Israel (15:24). Jesus' visit to them, however, portends the Gentile mission to come."[30] Basically, Kingsbury regards the Canaanite woman's story as foreshadowing the mission to come, without problematizing the foundations on which its power relations are laid. However, the question is, Why was it important to foreshadow the mission to the Gentiles through a portrait of a woman, a Canaanite, a mother of a severely demon-possessed daughter, who is regarded as a dog? What are the implications of such a characterization for women and international relations? These questions do not feature in Kingsbury's literary reading of Matthew's discourse, primarily because the imperial context is not regarded as central to the implied author's story and discourse.

Accordingly, in his reading of Matthew 28:18–20, Kingsbury displays no reservations regarding the model on which the mission to the nations is proposed. Kingsbury holds that "the disciples, whom the risen Jesus commissions to a worldwide ministry at the end of Matthew's story, understand this and so does the reader. It is apparent that the first evangelist, who wrote this story, would also have wanted any real reader both to

---

[29]Ibid., 26–27.
[30]Ibid., 29.

understand this and to act on it."[31] In short, Kingsbury not only fully embraces the model of Matthew 28:18–20, but also recommends that the real flesh-and-blood reader of today must act on it. It must be said, however, that Kingsbury's uncritical endorsement of the mission model is based on two concepts, salvation history framework and servant king christology.

From a salvation history perspective, Kingsbury can explain the rejection of the Canaanite woman as a period when the ministry of Jesus was still limited to Israel; after his resurrection, however, it was extended to include all other nations. From this perspective, Kingsbury's reading can avoid confronting the Canaanite woman and the great commission as two faces of the same coin, that is, as mission stories that are built on a model of inequality: a land possession literary type-scene model. The salvation history framework, however, should be read with suspicion and subjected to decolonization: First, it should be read as part of Matthew's tactics to claim power over other interest groups—by claiming to provide an absolute or final answer through the character of Jesus. Second, it should be decolonized because it is a model that propounds imperialistic values in itself by positing (in the words of Kingsbury himself) Jesus as "an absolute and universal authority, or dominion" and by positing a universally available world for the Christ-followers and the nations.

Similarly, the characterization of Jesus as servant king should be subject to a suspicious and decolonizing reading. As elaborated above, the construction of Jesus as a meek and lowly king is not innocent of collaborative interests in the empire. It is not a rejection or criticism of the emperor's universal and absolute power. Rather, it is the implied author's way of sharing in it as attested by his/her presentation of the empire as holy and acceptable as well as his own mission model, which characterizes Jesus as an absolute and universal authority.

Conclusions

The assessment of white Western male readers of Matthew 15:21–28 within the Roman-dominated Palestine setting and for its power relations leads to the following findings:

- There is little or no attention paid to colonial and postcolonial theories and era, often leaving behind as a result—unattended and unquestioned—the imperial setting, the violence of imperialists, and the collaborative stance of the colonized.

- Readers tend to enter the story world of Matthew and its rhetorical language of divine claims such as salvation history, servant king, universal mission, and absolute claims of power without any decolonization of its intentions.

---

[31]Ibid., 163.

- There is hardly any effort to investigate gender, mission, and empire construction on the side of male readers.
- Readers have used methods that render the gospel antiquated, in the sense that most Western biblical scholars can elaborate on biblical texts while completely avoiding dealing with how these texts have informed and continue to inform the international and gender relations of today's world.
- The social location of biblical studies in the Western metropolitan centers, which also represent the imperialist centers, is instrumental in the bracketing of imperialism as a systematic social evil that takes up organized forms of textual constructions and that depends on literary practitioners who maintain the power relations they propound. Similarly, their gender, race, and class privilege accounts for the lack of any problematizing of the power relations propounded by the story.

White Western Feminist Readers of Matthew 15:21–28

White middle-class Western feminist biblical readers of various social locations have used different methods to read Matthew 15:21–28. What distinguishes feminist biblical practice from its male counterpart is its insistence on reading for social liberation. Feminist readers have rejected the claims of scientific objectivity and a detached reading of texts and have insisted instead on reading as women, on behalf of women, and against all forms of oppression. As a result, feminist scholarship can be termed one of the most revolutionary and ethical movements of the century in biblical studies.

Methodologically, feminist practices have grown from a naive theoretical perspective to more theoretical depth and sophistication. Early feminism prioritized patriarchal oppression, viewing it as the fundamental and universal form of oppression. It theorized women as a monolithic group of universally oppressed beings. Current feminism acknowledges that it can no longer "appeal to some transparently universal grounds of being but rather must negotiate the meaning of feminine identity in relation to structures of language, sex, race, class, age, physical ability, nationality, religion and so forth."[32] The earlier analytical approach is now recognized for its shortcomings. Women of the world are now seen as a complex mix of people who are not totally oppressed or free from oppressing other women and men of different races, classes, sexual, and religious orientations.

The story of the Canaanite woman has enjoyed popularity among white Western feminist readers. Sharon Ringe hails her an "uppity woman," who "wins the argument with Jesus" and opens "the way for Jesus' (and the

---

[32]See Donaldson, *Decolonizing Feminisms*, 137.

church's) mission beyond the Jewish community."[33] For Elisabeth Schüssler Fiorenza, she is the woman who "overcomes Jesus' prejudice," the "foremother" of all Gentile Christian women; she is "a paradigm for feminists who transgress intellectual and religious boundaries in their movements towards liberation."[34] Gail O'Day celebrates her "robust faith."[35] In general, she is the woman who "won" an argument with Jesus, changing his mind about limiting his mission to the Jews and hence opening the way for the Gentile mission.[36]

Yet as a black African Motswana woman and a Western-trained academic biblical reader, the more I read this story and its Western feminist interpretations, the more I identify with the Canaanite woman, not as a heroine but as a victim of patriarchal and imperial ideology. It is on these grounds that Rahab's reading prism is brought to bear on the feminist space of reading and its readings of the Canaanite woman. It will be used to examine:

1. how white women readers enter Rahab's space—whether they recall Rahab to inhabit the position of a colonized subject or allow her to walk out of a story that is written about her and not for her sake;[37] and

2. whether their feminist deconstructions permit Rahab to speak with her own voice, to tell her own story, or imprison her to a story that is written about her but nevertheless against her.

The feminist readings of Janice Capel Anderson, Amy-Jill Levine, Elaine Wainwright, and Elisabeth Schüssler Fiorenza will serve as sources for analysis. The interdisciplinary approach of feminist practices, however, makes it difficult to easily categorize each reader according to method.

Narrative Approach: Janice Capel Anderson

Anderson, who describes herself as a "feminist New Testament critic," a "white American middle-class Presbyterian mother trained in academic historical and literary biblical criticism,"[38] reads Matthew from a narrative

---

[33]See Sharon Ringe, "A Gentile Woman's Story," in *Feminist Interpretation of the Bible,* ed. Letty Russell (Philadelphia: Westminster Press, 1985), 65.

[34]See Schüssler Fiorenza, *But She Said,* 12, 97.

[35]See Gail R. O'Day, "Surprised by Faith: Jesus and the Canaanite Woman," *Listening: Journal of Religion and Culture* 24 (1989).

[36]The readings of Janice Capel Anderson, Sharon Ringe, Elaine Wainwright, and Elisabeth Schüssler Fiorenza, most of which are assessed in this section, all hold that she is the woman who championed the mission to the Gentiles. Amy-Jill Levine does not conclude this.

[37]See Kwok Pui-lan, *Discovering the Bible,* 71–72, which makes the point that the story of the Canaanite woman and the interpretations that have followed are not hers nor from her people.

[38]See Janice Capel Anderson, "Feminist Criticism: The Dancing Daughter," in *Mark and Method: New Approaches in Biblical Studies,* ed. Janice Capel Anderson and Stephen D. Moore (Minneapolis: Fortress Press, 1992), 104.

approach. She explores the symbolic significance of gender and the reading process in Matthew from a feminist standpoint.[39] With the exception of Herodias and her daughter, Anderson finds that the overall characterization of women in relation to Jesus in Matthew is positive. She observes, however, that gender still limits their role and inhibits their acceptance into the inner circles of male disciples. According to Anderson, the positive portrayal of women mainly serves as a foil for major characters such as Jewish religious leaders and male disciples.

Concerning the Canaanite woman, Anderson notes,

> Her faith and persistence lead him to expand his mission and to heal her daughter. Her confession of Jesus as Lord and Son of David cast the rejection of Jesus by Jewish leaders and crowds in a dark light. Together with direct narratological comments (4:4–16;12:18–21) and the Magi (2:1–12) and the Roman centurion (8:5–13) episodes, this episode makes a powerful argument justifying the mission to the Gentiles. This is an important theme coming to a climax in the great commission. Thus the Canaanite woman scene is more significant for the gospel as a whole.[40]

Anderson compares the Canaanite woman's story with that of the centurion and associates it with the great commission. The question, however, is whether Anderson's reading demonstrates awareness toward the imperial setting and how such a setting informs the implied author's construction of the implied reader on issues of mission, gender, race, and empire? Unfortunately, Anderson limits her exploration of the significance of women to their role as foils. She demonstrates little or no alertness to the imperial setting and its centrality to Matthew's story world. This is evident in her comparison of the centurion's and the Canaanite woman's stories without investigating the factors that led to the implied author's divergent comments and presentation of supplicants who are both outsiders.

Anderson's bracketing of the imperial setting is also evident in her reading of women in the passion narrative. Here she focuses on the woman at Bethany (26:6–13), the women at the cross and at the tomb (27:55–56, 66; 28:1–10), but notably omits Pilate's wife. This circle of women is enmeshed in a highly imperial setting of the colonized against the colonized and the colonized against the colonizer, yet Anderson demonstrates no sensitivity to the imperial context of the Matthean story world. She limits her reading to a view of women's characters as foils to the disciples who desert Jesus. In omitting the role of Pilate's wife, Anderson totally brackets confronting the imperial context and the implied author's consistent presentation of colonial agents as holy and acceptable.

---

[39]See Janice Capel Anderson, "Matthew: Gender and Reading," *Semeia* 28 (1983): 3–27.
[40]Ibid., 14.

Second, Anderson does not problematize the power relations proposed in Matthew 15:21–28 and its subsequent great commission. Anderson also holds that the story of the Canaanite woman is "a powerful argument justifying the mission to the gentiles." She associates it with the great commission and argues that it is much more significant to Matthew as a whole. Apart from the fact that gender inhibits women from entering the inner male circle that was finally commissioned to the nations, Anderson does not problematize the proposed power relations of the mission. Moreover, how gender is employed to represent foreign nations and to articulate relations of domination and subordination does not arise in Anderson's investigation of gender significance in reading. The implications of accepting Gentiles through characterizing them as women, Canaanites, evil, dangerous, and dogs who seek and desire the help of the divine traveling heroes thus remains uninvestigated.

Social-Scientific Approach: Amy-Jill Levine

Amy-Jill Levine, who describes herself as "a Jew," "a woman," a "student," and "a professor of religion," reads Matthew in two major works, using social-scientific and historical methods.[41] These will now be assessed for their view of the imperial context and the power relations advanced by mission passages.

In her book, Levine focuses on the mission passages of 10:5; 15:24; and 28:19. In fact, Levine states that "rather than locate Matt. 10:5b–6 and 15:24 on the periphery of the gospel, I have placed them at the center of Matthew's program of salvation history."[42] Levine's reading engages the traditional white, Western, Christian interpretations that have associated the "exclusive" statements of the mission verses with Jewish Christians and sometimes claimed that the great commission excluded the mission to the Jews—interpretations that have borne deadly conflict in Jewish-Christian relations. On the contrary, Levine argues that the exclusivist and universalist mission statements are not contradictory but complementary to each other; that the great commission does not deny Jews the privilege they have always had, but extends it to the nations; that the mission to the nations does not exclude Jews but includes them.[43]

Levine's interpretation is placed within a salvation history framework consisting of the time of Jesus and the time of the church. In the latter time there is neither Jew nor Gentile, and the criterion for salvation is no longer

---

[41]See "'Hemmed in on Every Side': Jews and Women in the Book of Susanna," in *Reading from This Place*, ed. Fernando F. Segovia and Mary Ann Tolbert, vol. 1, 175, for her self-identification. For her work, see *"Go Nowhere Among the Gentiles" (Matt. 10:5b)* in *The Social and Ethnic Dimensions of Matthean Salvation History*, vol. 1 (New York: E. Mellen Press, 1988), and "Matthew," in the *Women's Bible Commentary*, ed. Carol A. Newsom and Sharon H. Ringe, 252–62.

[42]Levine, *"Go Nowhere Among the Gentiles,"* 5.

[43]See ibid., 1–3, for this summary.

based on descent or relation to the centers of power but on "faith manifested in action," that is, "higher righteousness." Levine also holds that the Matthean community consisted of marginal individuals who built their community on an egalitarian principle that "dismantles all forms of hierarchies." According to Levine, this egalitarian principle is evident in its "mobility." That is, its feature of "refusing to locate spatially" is unique and is supposedly subversive to previous institutions of Jews and Gentiles.

Holding that the particularist and universalist mission statements are complementary and reading within a salvation history framework, Levine underlines the priority of Jews in the time of Jesus. She holds that "just as Jews had priority over the Canaanites in the past, so too they retain this priority in the present...The temporal subordination of the gentiles is not transcended but legitimized by the reference to the 'Canaanite' and by the dialogue that follows."[44] Levine underlines that

> Matt. 15:21–28 clearly indicates that the logion is consistent with the themes established in the Hebrew scriptures: it confirms the doctrine of election and supersession of Israel over Canaan. Nor are these concepts incompatible with universal salvation. For example, while Israel may be the "chosen people" conversion into this nation had become possible and not infrequent...One might argue that the replacement of Canaanite hegemony with the Israelite monarchy is repellent: the deity granted the Hebrews an exclusive claim.[45]

Unlike most Western feminist readers, Levine identifies herself not with the Canaanite woman but with the children, whom she argues have and must retain their place at the master's table during and after the time of Jesus. Keeping in mind that Levine's reading engages the white Western interpretations that nurtured anti-Semitism, her reading is a search for liberation. White male Christian interpretations have claimed racial superiority, religious superiority, universal right and duty to travel and suppress all other non-Christian cultures, which were held to be inferior and waiting to be fulfilled or civilized by Western Christian cultures. Levine, therefore, reads as a colonized subject, and her reading is an anti-imperial approach. Nevertheless, Levine's approach is problematic in two ways.

First, Levine's reading subscribes to the very ideology she wishes to counteract. Levine enters the concepts of "salvation history," "higher righteousness," dissolution of space or "mobility," "particularist," and "universalist" constructions, advanced by both Matthew and the white Western male interpreters, without sufficiently problematizing their power relations, their implications, and their impact on the contemporary world, a world that consists of diverse Other cultures. Through subscribing to the

---

[44]Ibid., 138–52.
[45]Ibid., 143.

universalist mission statement without problematizing the power relations it advocates, Levine seems to overlook that the Christian traditions are used not only against Judaism but also against all other non-Christian cultures in the non-Western world. Consequently, Levine's anti-imperial reading, which does not reflect on the impact and implications of "mobility" and the "universalist" constructions of Matthew on Other non-Christian cultures, subscribes to the oppression of the Other. Read and heard by a Two-Thirds World woman from a postcolonial non-Christian culture, Levine, too, speaks from the Western imperial metropolitan centers, which continue to assert their right to dominate the rest of the world culturally, economically, and politically.

Second, Levine's anti-imperial approach is compromised by her failure to fully acknowledge her conflicting identities. On the one hand, she seeks to counteract the oppressive interpretations that have polarized the differences between Jewish and Christian traditions; on the other hand, she asserts the divine claims of the Hebrew Scriptures without problematizing their ideology, even where they clearly depend on hierarchies to construct differences. In Matthew 15:25 Levine thus enters the story about the Canaanite woman, claims her place and bread at the master's table, and asserts her divine right to suppress the Other woman. In this way, Levine speaks as a doubly colonized subject who does not relinquish her right to oppress a triply colonized woman under the table. Levine's approach, as I read and hear it with the eyes and ears of a non-Western outsider, is an in-house struggle for power among Western races and classes: Levine "talks back" to white Western Christian men and women, who, while they claim racial superiority and divine destiny, derogate similar traditions. Levine's approach is, therefore, a rejoinder and a reversal, for it rudely awakens Western Christians to face up to their hypocrisy, but it does not seek to counter the terms of power they use. Rather, it seeks to share in it by uncritically adopting both the particularist and universalist mission statements.

Conversely, I adopted an interdisciplinary analysis of texts in chapters 4 and 5 that was meant specifically to highlight that classical and modern claims of racial election or superiority based on divine claims and the use of gender to construct relationships of subordination and domination are not unique to the Hebrew texts. Such practices are evident among the Romans, the Greeks, the British, the Spanish conquerors, the American founding fathers, the South African settler colonizers, or in just about any other group with a tradition of imperialism. Second, I highlighted the fact that claims of racial and cultural superiority are mostly constructed under imperial motivations and serve those agendas: to claim power over those races that are constructed as unchosen, unelected, evil, dangerous, inferior, and womanly. A Western feminist reading, be it Christian or Jewish, therefore cannot uncritically claim these traditions of election without subscribing to those ideologies that have characterized imperialism. A Western feminist biblical interpretation that claims these racial hierarchies and universalist constructions uncritically will certainly be heard by most Two-Thirds World women as seeking to share in the power of white Western males, who subjugated the whole world and suppressed other cultures by claiming racial, religious, economic, and technological superiority.

In her commentary on Matthew, Levine works in a similar framework. She regards the Matthean community as consisting of "persons removed from religious and political power in both the Roman and Jewish systems" and as a community that "attempts to eliminate all relationships in which one group exploits or dominates another."[46] The former statement takes cognizance of the imperial context of Matthew. The latter statement suggests that the Matthean text castigates patriarchal and imperial oppression of its context. My earlier analysis of the characterization of imperial agents, however, shows that the implied author of Matthew does not reject the Roman imperialism; rather, she/he engages in a vicious competition with religious leaders and elites to gain power over the crowds and the favor of the empire.[47] Levine certainly recognizes the imperial context of Matthew, but she does not sufficiently interrogate how it informs the implied author's construction of characters and how the Matthean story is in the service of seeking power. Levine's suggestion that Matthew consists of those removed from power, who seek to build a community that dismantles all forms of hierarchies, is therefore questionable. The inclusion of the centurion and Pilate's wife, for example, may foreshadow the mission to the Gentiles, but their position of power as representatives of people associated with the exploitative power of the Roman Empire contradicts a move toward building an egalitarian community, seeking to eliminate all relationships of exploitation and domination.

In her commentary on the Canaanite woman, Levine's reading is consistent with her earlier reading. It embraces a salvation history framework as well as higher righteousness and remains unsuspicious of Matthew's quest for power and the methods employed to attain it. Levine holds that

> The episode of the Canaanite woman recalls that of the centurion (8:5–13). These healings—the only two in the Gospel explicitly concerning Gentiles and accomplished from a distance—indicate both that the Gentile supplicants are worthy of Jesus' beneficence and

---

[46]Levine, "Matthew," 252.

[47]See Overman, *Matthew's Gospel,* 113–22, on the presence of scribes, prophets, and missionaries in the Matthean community; the amount of power allocated to the Matthean disciples (read community) hardly suggests that they were powerless or egalitarian, 124–36. See also Kingsbury, *Matthew as Story,* 152–53, which holds that the value of coins Matthew mentions indicates that its intended readers were a "well-to-do" community, which cannot be easily theorized as powerless or egalitarian, for it probably contained people of different classes.

that the Gospel will eventually be extended to all peoples. Unlike Mark's account (7:24–30), Matthew's does not present Jesus entering Tyre and Sidon; rather, the woman leaves her native land to meet Jesus. Further, she is not identified as a Syro-Phoenician (Mark 7:26) but as a Canaanite. Her presence recalls the original struggle between the Hebrews and the indigenous population of the land. By meeting Jesus both on his own turf and on his own terms, the Canaanite woman acknowledges the priority of the Jews in the divine plan of salvation.[48]

Like most male and female readers assessed above, Levine does not problematize the gender and imperial factors at work in the characterization of the centurion and the Canaanite woman.[49] She notes Matthew's redaction of the Marcan text without questioning its ideological motivations and its implications for a text that foreshadows the universal mission. Further, the woman's acceptance of Jesus' terms, namely, "the priority of Jews in the divine plan of salvation," contradicts Levine's thesis that Matthew aims at building an egalitarian community, for the latter embraces racial hierarchies.

That Levine accepts both the particularist and universalist mission statements without problematizing the entailed power relations is also evident in the last part of her commentary on the Canaanite woman's story. Levine observes that

Jesus ignores her, and the disciples wish her to be sent away (cf. 10:5b–6; 15:24). The woman overcomes Jesus's reluctance by turning to her advantage his language about taking the children's food and throwing it to the dogs...The woman asserts her claim and demonstrates her faith not by protesting the insult to her ethnic group but by arguing that both Gentiles (dogs) and children (Jews) are under the same authority.[50]

Here, Levine observes that the inclusion of Gentiles does not entail or suggest equality, but she does not question it or its implications. There is certainly no doubt that "children" and "dogs" can be and have been under the same authority, but this in itself is not liberating as long as these categories

---

[48]Levine, "Matthew," 259.

[49]See Levine, "The Centurion and the Sons of the Basileia," in "*Go Nowhere Among the Gentiles*" in which her interpretation of the centurion story follows a textual variation that holds that Jesus' immediate response was not positive. Rather, it was a question anticipating a negative answer: "Shall I come and heal him?" 111. From this perspective, in both the stories of the Canaanite and the centurion, Jesus resisted helping them because his ministry was confined to Israel. This interpretation still does not explain the extended rejection accorded to the woman; neither does it consider that Matthew's relaxed resistance to the centurion possibly indicates collaboration with the imperial powers.

[50]Levine, "Matthew," 259.

construct racial privilege and derogation of some races on the basis of cultural differences. For postcolonial Two-Thirds World women, the principle of inclusion without equality is too familiar; it is too characteristic of an imperial ideology that disavows boundaries to include nations not as equal partners but as perpetual subordinates and devotees. Therefore, ideologies of racial election, chosenness, and superiority based on religious, racial, economic, political, and technological claims, which often accompany universal and imperial expansion, should be subject to a thorough postcolonial feminist decolonization, regardless of whether they appear in *The Aeneid,* Hebrew Scriptures, *Heart of Darkness,* the story of Pocahontas, or in poems such as "The White Man's Burden."

Literary-Historical Readings: Elaine Wainwright

Wainwright, who describes herself as "an Australian woman of Anglo-Irish origin who is affiliated with one of the mainstream Christian traditions,"[51] has also done extensive work on Matthew 15:21–28. This work appears in a book, a commentary on Matthew, and an article.[52] In all these works, Wainwright's feminist critical reading of Matthew is best described as a gender-inclusive reading that uses literary and historical methods. Holding that patriarchal and androcentric authors, texts, and histories have excluded women, Wainwright's feminist practice sets out to read women and men right to the center of early Christian texts and history. Wainwright's gender-inclusive reading is a remarkable feminist achievement in its clarity, its creativeness, and its persuasiveness, for it foregrounds the presence and centrality of women to Matthew's story without underplaying the patriarchal and androcentric cores that contain them.

The question, however, is, Does Wainwright take into consideration the imperial setting of Matthew? Does she problematize the power relations propounded in its mission texts? Does Wainwright decolonize the collaborative stances of Matthew? Does she read with decolonizing communities or among imperializing communities? When one brings Rahab's reading prism to scrutinize Wainwright's work for these questions, she demonstrates blindness to the imperialist setting of the text. Her reading provides an excellent example of how patriarchal categories of analysis do not necessarily translate into imperialist criticism. Wainwright's comparison of the Canaanite woman with Rahab of the conquest and with the centurion highlights how her analysis brackets textual imperialist strategies and, hence, subscribes to it.

---

[51]Elaine Wainwright, "A Voice from the Margin: Reading Matthew 15:21–28 in an Australian Feminist Key," in *Reading from This Place,* vol. 2, ed. Fernando F. Segovia and Mary Ann Tolbert, 134.

[52]See Wainwright, *Towards a Feminist Critical Reading;* "The Gospel of Matthew," 635–77, in *Searching the Scriptures:A Feminist Commentary,* vol. 2, ed. Schüssler Fiorenza (New York: Crossroad, 1993); and "A Voice from the Margin: Reading Matthew 15:21–28," 132–53.

In comparing the Canaanite woman of Matthew with Rahab, Wainwright observes that "the woman's gentile origin is stressed as she is introduced. Calling the woman Canaanite (in Greek) also reminds the reader of another Canaanite woman, Rahab, who was instrumental in changing the course of Israel's history by facilitating their entry into the land of Canaan."[53] Wainwright continues,

> Just as the initiative of both Rahab and Ruth, foremothers of this Χαναναία woman, enabled God's [reign] to be made manifest beyond gender and ethnic boundaries so too the initiative of this woman will become the vehicle whereby the compassion of Jesus will be made manifest beyond the same boundaries.[54]

Wainwright's comparison uncritically embraces the two stories of Canaanite women. First, she identifies the association of the Christian mission with the conquest without problematizing its terms or implications. Second, she recognizes the featuring of a woman in both stories that concern entering into a foreign land, but she does not suspect that this may be a case of using gender to articulate relations of domination and subordination. Wainwright thus eulogizes Rahab as a woman who changed the course of Israel's history by facilitating their entry into the land of Canaan—Rahab is eulogized for betraying her land and people. Like Rahab and Ruth, her "foremothers," the Canaanite woman in Matthew also opens the way to the nations. Wainwright not only sanctifies and normalizes Rahab's colonization and her betrayal of her people, but also calls on Rahab to remain a colonized subject. Evidently, Wainwright enters and embraces the literary type-scene of land possession without deconstructing the imperial ideologies and agenda of the story.

Wainwright's feminist hermeneutics of suspicion are overcome by her reconstructive agenda of including women as they are limited by their categories of analysis. First, Wainwright's feminist project is so intent on including women that its deconstructive agenda is sacrificed for reconstruction purposes.[55] Thus, she easily overlooks that the stories of these two Canaanite women in Joshua and Matthew are not their own stories, nor do they serve the women's interests; rather, the narratives are projections about them to authorize the agendas of their subjugators. Second, her desire to "include" women in texts, centers, and histories without acknowledging that the latter are also imperialistic makes her reading party to the oppressive powers that she wishes to counteract. Her very association of the criteria of "inclusion" with liberation to a great extent overlooks that to include is also fundamental to the imperialist strategy of domination. A

---

[53]Wainwright, *Towards a Feminist Critical Reading,* 105.
[54]Ibid., 109.
[55]See Lone Fatum, "Women, Symbolic Universe and Structures of Silence: Challenges and Possibilities in Androcentric Texts," *Studia Theologia* 43 (1989): 61–80; Fatum also sounds the warning on the hurried feminist reconstructions that often forego their deconstructive stages.

liberative inclusion will need to be qualified in order to differentiate it from imperialist inclusions, which usually entail subjugation of difference and inequality of subjects.

That Wainwright unproblematically subscribes to imperialistic strategies of the text is also indicative of her own social location. Being herself a white settler of Australia, a country where the natives exist as subjugated subjects, or as Rahabs, so to speak, Wainwright presents the latter as instruments of God's agenda in the invasion and possession of the land. It is quite doubtful, however, if Australian aborigines, who can identify with Canaanite women more closely, would eulogize these women as foremothers of God's liberative agenda.[56] Needless to say, like many of us who have experienced imperialism and who know its violent textual strategies, the stories of these Canaanite women are representative of those stories and movies written about us, which are always a nightmare to read and watch, for it is not difficult to see that they are stories written not only about us but also against us. Thus, Kwok Pui-lan correctly notes that "like much information we have about Third World women, our knowledge of this Gentile woman does not come directly from her own people…who belonged to other faiths, but by Christians, who appropriated her for their own specific purposes."[57]

Wainwright compares the Canaanite woman with the centurion, Peter's mother-in-law, and the demoniacs in the Gentile territory, and, once again, the patriarchal category proves itself inadequate to identify some of the major factors at play. Thus, Wainwright asks,

> Why this rebuff?…Jesus has already healed the centurion's servant. Why not this woman's daughter? Is his silence a narrative device to draw the reader's attention to the ministry within the gentile territory? Yet, Jesus has already healed the demoniacs in the Gadarene countryside. There is no clear and definitive answer to these questions.[58]

Since she does not take into consideration the imperial setting and how Matthew participates in its power struggles, Wainwright is at a loss to explain the rejection of the Canaanite woman.

She thus turns to her inclusive reading and holds that the centurion story "served the purposes within the narrative of showing Jesus breaking down the boundaries which separated 'outsiders' from the religious community of Israel."[59]

---

[56]See Robert Allen Warrior, "A Native American Perspective: Canaanites, Cowboys and Indians," in *Voices from the Margin,* ed. R. S. Sugirtharajah, 287–95, which makes an association between Native Americans and Canaanites.

[57]See Kwok Pui-lan, *Discovering the Bible,* 71.

[58]Wainwright, *Towards a Feminist Critical Reading,* 106–7.

[59]Ibid., 110. In fact, within colonized societies, where the strategies of resisting foreign impositions of cultural, economic, and political institutions often require the tightening of local boundaries, breaking boundaries of the colonized can indicate collaboration.

Similarly, in her reading of Pilate's wife, Wainwright celebrates her inclusion, pointing out that "the stereotypical role given Herodias is here reversed when an unknown gentile woman, the wife of Pilate, becomes a prophetic messenger not to bring about the condemnation of Jesus."[60] Wainwright notes how a Jewish royal woman, Herodias, is given a negative role by Matthew while Pilate's wife, an imperial royal woman, is given a positive role. But she only reads the portrayal of Pilate's wife as one of the traditions that "authenticate the role of women in the Jesus Movement" in order "to highlight the role played by women during Jesus' final suffering," without suspecting Matthew's collaborative stance towards the empire."[61]

In sum, postcolonial theories on the methods of imperialism, such as its use of divine claims, construction of race, and employment of gender to articulate and authorize subjugation of foreign nations, as well as the various ways in which the colonized respond, could inform Wainwright's feminist deconstructive stance and guide its reconstructive agenda of inclusion. As it is, Wainwright's "hermeneutics of suspicion complicit with the agendas of imperialism" intimately befriends those feminist readers who "use anti-sexist rhetoric to displace questions of colonialism, racism, and their concomitant violence."[62]

Historical Reconstruction and Rhetorical Model: Elisabeth Schüssler Fiorenza

Schüssler Fiorenza employs the story of the Syro-Phoenician/Canaanite woman to illustrate the application of a feminist "rhetorical model of historical reconstruction."[63] The latter is a theoretical framework she designs to counter patriarchal exclusions and to write an early Christian history in which women and other suppressed groups can feature. This feminist historiography is guided by emancipatory goals, and it defines feminist hermeneutics as a rhetorical practice of liberation that reconstructs "a plausible 'subtext' to the androcentric text."[64] This model and agenda, in fact, continue to build on Schüssler Fiorenza's earlier and larger project, which sought to "reconstruct early Christian history as women's history," and employed historical-critical methods and some sociological theories.[65]

To apply the model, Schüssler Fiorenza underlines that "the androcentric text's rhetorical silences, as well as its contradictions, arguments, prescriptions, and projections, its discourses on gender, race, class, culture or religion, must be exposed as the ideological inscriptions of the

---

[60]Ibid., 286.

[61]Ibid., 287.

[62]See Donaldson, *Decolonizing Feminisms*, 11, 62.

[63]See Schüssler Fiorenza, *But She Said*, 80–101. In fact, the very title of this book is adopted from the story of the Syro-Phoenician/Canaanite woman, whom Fiorenza holds "represents the biblical-theological voice of women, which has been excluded, repressed, or marginalized in Christian discourse," 11.

[64]Ibid., 96.

[65]See Schüssler Fiorenza, *In Memory of Her*, xiv, 91–92.

Western politics of Otherness."[66] Schüssler Fiorenza underlines that the feminist model of historical reconstruction is not only for exploring "*what* the text excludes, but also for investigating *how* the text constructs what it includes."[67] If faithfully applied to Matthew 15:21–28, this model for reconstructing feminist history should thoroughly problematize the power relations advanced in the text before reclaiming the story.

Schüssler Fiorenza's application, however, indicates that she compromises the terms of her model in the interests of feminist reconstruction. For instance, Schüssler Fiorenza argues that the Canaanite woman "overcomes Jesus' prejudice" and "wins the controversy because Jesus, convinced by her argument (*dia touton ton logon*), announces her daughter's healing."[68] Schüssler Fiorenza holds that while "the Syro-Phoenician respects the primacy of the 'children of Israel,' she nevertheless makes a theological argument against limiting the Jesuanic inclusive table-community and discipleship of equals to Israel alone."[69] While it is certainly clear that the narrative makes a case for the inclusion of Gentiles, Schüssler Fiorenza does not elaborate on whether the categories of "dogs" and "children" suggest differences of subjects or a hierarchical inclusion. Schüssler Fiorenza does not explore or develop how she interprets "primacy" and how she reconciles it with equality. Even the fact that a woman supposedly "wins" an argument in a patriarchal and androcentric text is not subjected to sufficient suspicion for arguing the projections and prescriptions it may entail. This inadequate deconstruction of the issues of race, gender, culture, and projections entailed in the story compromises Schüssler Fiorenza's own terms of reading, and this is evident in her reconstruction, which embraces the oppression of the Other.

In her reconstruction, Schüssler Fiorenza holds that the Syro-Phoenician "gives us a clue to the historical leadership of women in opening up Jesus's movement to 'Gentile sinners' (Gal 2:15)."[70] Here, Schüssler Fiorenza employs the story as a historical window to make women's contribution in Christian beginnings "historically visible," for she maintains that "through such an analysis, the Syro-Phoenician can become visible again as one of the apostolic foremothers of Gentile Christians."[71] Schüssler Fiorenza maintains that if we move "her into the center of the debate about the mission to the Gentiles, the historical centrality of Paul in this debate becomes relativized."[72] Schüssler Fiorenza also holds that Luke's historical model excludes this foreign woman's story because it wishes to spotlight Paul and Peter as the characters at the center of the debate about the mission to the Gentiles.

---

[66]Schüssler Fiorenza, *But She Said,* 93.
[67]Ibid.
[68]Ibid., 96.
[69]Ibid., 97.
[70]Ibid.
[71]Ibid.
[72]Ibid.

Schüssler Fiorenza's goal is certainly to counteract patriarchal and androcentric exclusions by reconstructing women's participation in the early Christian history. Such a reconstruction is undoubtedly ethical and imperative, yet it proceeds by assuming that the mission to the Gentiles was and is in itself liberating, since it does not scrutinize or problematize the strategies of the mission nor the power relations it advocates. This is even evident when Schüssler Fiorenza moves to Matthew's version of the Syro-Phoenician woman. Here, Schüssler Fiorenza notes that "she is characterized with the archAICs term 'Canaanite,' which reminds the reader not only of Rahab, who facilitated Israel's entry into Canaan, but also of Israel's long struggle with Canaan's cultic heritage."[73] Schüssler Fiorenza then proceeds without asking why Matthew's redaction characterizes her as a Canaanite and without looking into the implications of such a characterization for a mission story. Schüssler Fiorenza notably interconnects the Canaanite woman with the Rahab of the conquest without problematizing the patriarchal and imperialist ideological agenda packed in the latter woman and what the allusion to her implies for a mission story. Rahab's colonization is, once again, embraced, normalized, and furthered.

Clearly, Schüssler Fiorenza compromises the terms of her model of reconstruction: that readers must not only investigate *"what* the text excludes" but also *"how* the text constructs what it includes." In assuming that the mission in itself is liberating–by not problematizing its intentions, its strategies, its impact as well as the power relations it advocates and entails–Schüssler Fiorenza's reconstruction is implicated in the very patriarchal and imperialist institutions of the West it wishes to counteract. Like the other female and male readers, Schüssler Fiorenza's feminist discourse speaks from the Western metropolitan centers and, ultimately, seeks to have a share of its power rather than to revolutionize its patriarchal and imperialist strategies of subjugation and domination.

Conclusions

The above investigation into the white middle-class Western feminist readings of Matthew 15:21–28 both from the point of view of its Roman imperial setting and the power relations it proposes, yields the following conclusions:

- Most readers do not consider how the implied author of Matthew, writing within a setting of imperial occupation, may be challenging the religious leaders, competing with other local groups for power, and seeking the favor of the empire. For the most part, the imperial context of Matthew is not considered at all by feminist readers. This

---

[73]Ibid., 99.

is attested by the lack of suspicion regarding the divergent responses accorded to two Gentiles with faith in Jesus and with a similar request (the Canaanite woman and the Roman centurion).

- Although gender should be one of the major categories of analysis, feminist readers, like male readers, constantly compare the Canaanite woman and the Roman centurion without at all suspecting that gender may be another factor in the divergent responses accorded to them.

- Although feminist readers regard Matthew 15:21–28 as a mission story and compare it with Rahab's story, they remain unsuspicious that the role of women in each case may reflect an ideology of equating women with lands in order to authorize relationships of subjugation and subordination.

- Although mainline feminist biblical discourse has concerned itself with reclaiming women's history in early Christian mission—that is, inclusion—feminist reconstruction of the mission has not been accompanied by a deconstruction of the power relations entailed in the mission passages. For example, while feminists find a link between the Canaanite woman of Matthew and Rahab of the conquest, they still reclaim the mission passages without substantial, if any, deconstruction of the power relations the passage advocates.

- Although white Western biblical feminists have now adopted the new theories of analysis that regard patriarchal oppression as a complex network of such factors as gender, race, class, religion, or culture, on the issue of race, and subsequently culture, it seems there is no acknowledgment that those groups that are usually categorized as belonging to "privileged races" were not born privileged. Rather, these are groups that acquired their identities through constructing themselves as superior to other races in order to validate their colonial projects at some point in their histories or foundation mythologies. (This lack of consciousness is evident in the readings of Matthew 15:21–28, which come to view such construction without problematizing it.)

- Although recent theories have led biblical feminists to abandon categories of a universally oppressive patriarchy and a universally oppressed woman, for these also turned out to be imperialistic impositions of the West on the rest of the world, white middle-class Western biblical feminist readers have not extended this insight to biblical religions. In short, their claims of the mission, without reenvisioning it, continue to assert that biblical religions are universally valid for all cultures, despite the disputation of non-Christian worlds.

- Clearly, the feminist ethical commitment to liberation can be informed by postcolonial theories in both its deconstruction and reconstruction to read for decolonization as well. This would entail familiarization with the various strategies of imperialism and the variegated responses it provokes from the colonized. On applying it to Matthew, it would entail taking the imperial setting of the Matthean text as integral to his or her narrative, problematizing the terms of the mission to the Gentiles, as well as assessing how the Christian mission functioned in different histories.

- Through postcolonial theories, Western biblical feminist readers can become conscious of their social location and their relation to historical and recent empires in order to begin reading for decolonization. This would entail problematizing the role of Western intellectuals and theorizing the geographical location of the West as an imperial center of power and how it has affected and still affects Other worlds through its economic and political systems as well as its cultural texts.

The above sections underline the need to depatriarchalize as well as to decolonize texts before any attempt is made to reclaim them. They show that the patriarchal category of analysis does not necessarily translate into imperial criticism. They progressively highlight some of the factors a decolonizing reading could look out for: the historical perspective of a text with regard to contemporary and ancient empires and its independent imperialistic ideologies. They focus on how Western male and feminist readers have, by and large, bracketed imperialism and, hence, subscribed to it.

These decolonizing stages form an important part of liberation discourse, yet they are deconstructive and are not identical to liberation. The crucial question, therefore, is, How can women and all concerned readers of various social locations read for liberating interdependence, in addition to highlighting imperialist and patriarchal strategies in the text? So far, my reading of Matthew 15:21–28 has struggled with "Rahab" insofar as she is a construction and reconstruction of her subjugators. At this stage, I turn to the voices that represent the "Rahabs" of Mother Mary Magdalene–the doubly colonized subjects who proclaim their own resurrection against imperial and patriarchal death, who tell their own stories in their own voices.

Reading for Liberating Interdependence: AICs Women

Introduction

The approach of African Independent Churches (AICs) women offers a vision of reading for liberating interdependence. Unlike an early feminism that emphasized individuality or autonomy,[74] or a contemporary Western biblical feminism that confines itself to biblical texts as if the latter have no connection with other cultural texts and critique patriarchy,[75] and early Two-Thirds World independence movements, whose nativist approach emphasized the preservation of colonized cultures to the extent that any criticism of their oppressive aspects was not permissible,[76] the approach of AICs movements from the beginning recognized the interdependence and interconnection of cultures, sexes, races, religions, and nations. Through its resistance to perception of life in terms of an exclusive opposition of white and black, Christian salvation and African paganism, men and women, the written and the oral word, AICs movements perceived relationships as interdependent rather than disconnected.

The term *interdependence* is used here, therefore, to describe and to underline the interconnectedness of different histories, economic structures, and political structures as well as the relatedness of cultural texts, races, classes, and genders within specific and global contexts. Imperialist movements championed global interconnectedness, though contemporary forms of the media are maximizing it.[77] The very act of colonizing other nations is an eloquent attestation of the colonizers' need to depend on and to have a relationship with the very people they victimize. The postindependence experience of many Two-Thirds World countries has also rudely shown that "independence" from other nations and cultures, even from those that oppressed them, is neither practical nor the best means for survival. Similarly, while early feminism emphasized autonomy and espoused separatist approaches, feminism now emphasizes the relatedness and interconnectedness of people and things.[78] The interdependence of nations, continents, genders, races, cultures, and political and economic systems, therefore, has always been a given and remains one of the most important aspects of survival. Nonetheless, most interconnections are built on

---

[74]See Rosemarie Tong, *Feminist Thought: A Comprehensive Introduction* (San Francisco: Westview Press, 1989); discussions on various types of feminist thought, in particular liberal feminism, 31–39.

[75]See Ursula King, "World Religions and Christianity," in *Dictionary of Feminist Theologies,* ed. Letty M. Russell and J. Shannon Clarkson (Louisville, Ky.: Westminster John Knox Press, 1996), which points out that, "when looking at contemporary interfaith dialogue from a critical gender perspective, it is evident that feminism is, by and large, a missing dimension in the dialogue...Nor has Christian feminist theology done much work so far on the encounter between Christianity and other religions," 324.

[76]See Chandra T. Mohanty, Ann Russo, Lourdes Torres, eds., "National Liberation and Sexual Politics," in *Third World Women and the Politics of Feminism* (Bloomington: Indiana University Press, 1991), 215–51; and Harlow, *Resistance Literature,* 29, for the conflicts between independence movements and feminist agendas.

[77]See Said, *Culture and Imperialism,* 262–336, on the interconnectedness of the former colonizers to their former victims.

[78]See Leslie Griffin, "Interdependence," in *Dictionary of Feminist Theologies,* ed. Letty M. Russell and J. Shannon Clarkson, 154–55, for a feminist definition of interdependence.

foundations that are both oppressive and exploitative. The term *liberating interdependence* is therefore used here to define the interconnectedness of relationships that recognize and affirm the dignity of all things and people involved. The crucial question, therefore, is, How can we begin to articulate a vision of liberating interdependence? How can we read biblical texts for liberating interdependence? This is where the reading practices of AICs women offer viable strategies.[79]

Acquiring Data

The interpretations of AICs women were collected in the summer of 1994 through administering a questionnaire and recording sermons in selected AICs churches.[80] In approaching the respondents for the interpretations of the passage, I and my research assistants (Tsholofelo Matswe and Keitumetsi Sekhute) always clearly stated: "We have come to learn from you."[81] This assertion was a genuine search, which in part acknowledges my own difference, that is, it recognizes the Western academic interpretive communities that inform my biblical interpretation and estrange me from AICs perspective. It was also an acknowledgment of both my position and their position as suppressed/colonized knowledges as well as an attempt to subvert the dominant Western discourses by bringing in different interpretive communities in the academy. Basically, I was searching for modes of reading that would be subversive to imperialistic and patriarchal domination and offer models of liberating interdependence. I shall now present the reading practices of the AICs women by introducing their reading framework and their interpretations of Matthew 15:21–28. In a conclusion, I will discuss some of the AICs reading strategies that offer a vision of liberating interdependence.

A Semoya Reading Grid

The perspective that I wish to present is one that we encountered several times among our respondents. When we had read the passage aloud to them (most of them had little or no reading skills), we would begin to ask questions designed to solicit their interpretations of Matthew 15:21–28.

---

[79]An earlier version of what follows, from here to the end of the chapter, has been published in an article titled "Readings of *Semoya*: Batswana Women's Interpretations of Matt. 15:21–28," *Semeia* 73 (1996), 111–29.

[80]For a detailed description of the methods used to collect their interpretations see "*Reading with*" *African Overtures, Semeia* 73, ed. Gerald West and Musa Dube (Atlanta: Scholars Press, 1996).

[81]The fact that these women were respected for their communities' leadership tipped the power relations in their favor. Nevertheless, the anticolonial historical beginnings of these churches subjected them to censorship and scorn from both the church and state, for obvious reasons. As a result, my presence as university personnel was not always without impact, for sometimes readers felt obliged to give an interpretation that they thought would be correct and acceptable to me.

Frequently, the respondents defined the boundaries of our discussion by pointing out, *"Kana re bua ka dilo tsa Semoya,"* that is, "Remember, we are discussing issues of the Spirit." As mentioned in chapter 1, *Moya* is a central element among the AICs. It is the Spirit that chooses and empowers women and men to be prophets, faith-healers, church founders, and leaders in the business of restoring and maintaining life. *Semoya* (of the Spirit) was thus a prevalent perspective among the AICs women. *Moya* as God's agent of empowerment and communication with people justified the position of these women. As the conversation with Bishop Virginia Lucas shows (see chapter 2), *Moya* is regarded as an ever-present and new word of God.

The interpretations that follow are drawn from sixteen AICs Botswana women readers, of Old Naledi, Mogoditshane, and Maruapula, most of whom were in leadership positions.[82] The questions are presented in the sequence in which they were asked, and each question serves as a sub-heading for their interpretations.

AICs Women's Readings of Matthew 15:21–28

QUESTIONNAIRE INTERPRETATIONS

"Why do you think Jesus went to Tyre and Sidon? (v. 21)." Eleven readers held that Jesus was following his daily routine of preaching, teaching, and healing. The remaining five held that he was particularly led by *Moya,* the Spirit, to go there in order to meet and heal the daughter of the Canaanite woman. They all assumed that Jesus went to do good. This assumption set the tone for their interpretation of the story.

"Why did Jesus not respond to this woman's request?" Six readers said Jesus was testing the faith of this woman. When we questioned this, the respondents held that the act of testing her faith does not indicate a lack of knowledge on the part of Jesus; they also did not see such an act as unusual in matters of faith. Abraham and Job were cited as examples of people who were tested because they already had faith. These interpreters held that the fact that the Canaanite woman's faith was tested proves that she had great faith (v. 28).

Three other respondents also attributed Jesus' silence to a testing of faith, but added that Jesus was testing the faith of the disciples. In this case, Jesus wanted to see what the disciples would do to help this woman. If this was to test the disciples, they probably failed the test, since we are told that "his disciples came and urged him, saying, 'Send her away for she keeps shouting after us'" (v. 23).

---

[82]I am grateful to the following sixteen women who provided their time and interpretations: Bishop Boitumelo Ngwako, Bishop Virginia Lucas, Bishop Mokgele, Bishop Mmautleyangane, Bishop Mmangwedi, Bishop Mmamadisakwane, Bishop Grace Galetshetse, Mmamosebeletsi Mmadipina, Mmamoruti Christina Kasai, Steward Mmamarumo, Mme Mmakokorwe, Moefangedi Mmatshiping, Mme Mmajarona, Mme Mmasebokolodi, Mmamoruti Mmaletsholo, Mme Catherine Kgwefane.

Three respondents said Jesus knew that this woman would finally receive her request, while two said that Jesus was still praying to God to heal her daughter. One respondent said Jesus was in the habit of remaining silent sometimes, as at his trial and crucifixion. Another one pointed out that Jesus was still debating whether to help this woman or not because she was not his follower.

"Why did Jesus say, 'I am sent only to the lost sheep of the house of Israel' (v. 23), and what did he mean?" The response to this question can be divided into two groups. The first group concentrated on the phrase "I am sent only to the lost sheep." These held that Jesus was responding to the disciples' request that he dismiss this woman (v. 23). Rejecting their view, Jesus was pointing out that, on the contrary, he could not possibly send this woman away because he was sent to people who were lost such as this Canaanite woman.

In most cases, we had to push the respondents to address the specificity of Jesus' statement, that is, the phrase "to the lost sheep of the house of Israel." This was not a disturbing question to most of them. "Israel" was interpreted to mean "those who believe." Several respondents asserted that "the lost sheep of Israel" were lost believers. The Canaanite woman was identified with believers, because she came to Jesus with faith (vv. 21, 28), but she was also "lost" because her daughter was possessed by demons (v. 21).

On the other hand, those who accepted that Jesus was neglecting this woman asserted that Jesus was sent to the "lost sheep of Israel," that is, those without faith; this woman, on the other hand, had great faith (v. 28). Consequently, Jesus thought this woman was wasting his time, because she had all the faith she needed to heal her daughter successfully.

"'Jesus answered the woman and said, "It is not good to take the children's food and throw it to the dogs"'(v. 26) Who are the children and who are the dogs? (a) Israelites; (b) Canaanites; (c) other." To begin with the identity of the children, thirteen out of sixteen held that "children" referred to the Israelites. This interpretation must be understood from their perspective, that is, Israel referred to all those who believe in the God of Israel. On the basis of the woman's faith, three held that "children" also referred to the Canaanites.

Concerning the identity of "dogs," most respondents emphasized that Jesus always spoke *ka ditshwantsho*, that is, "in parables." This emphasis was a warning that the meaning of his words was not always apparent nor to be taken literally. The answers to this question were more varied. Six said the "dogs" were the Canaanites. One said the "dogs" referred to "the lost sheep," that is, the Israelites. In other words, believers who have now lost their faith. Seven of them held that "dogs" could refer either to the Israelites or the Canaanites, but that it generally refers to those who do not have faith. One respondent held that Jesus was challenging this woman to faith because she was not yet one of his believers. Another one said that Jesus was just testing this woman's faith.

"Do you think this woman is among the dogs or the children?" While the previous question focused on the nations, Israel versus Canaan, this question focused on the woman herself. Eight respondents were of the opinion that the Canaanite woman was one of the children on the basis of her faith. The other half was of the opinion that she was among the "dogs" for various reasons. Two of them attributed this label to her nationality, because the Canaanites did not know God's law. The majority said "dogs" referred not to the woman, but to the demonic spirits. The latter held that Jesus was challenging the woman to believe first, and thus to become a child, before she could receive the children's bread.

Bishop Mmangwedi, one of the respondents, gave this saying of Jesus an ironic interpretation; in effect Jesus was agreeing with this woman and saying, "Indeed it is not good to take the children's food and throw it to the dogs. Rather, it must go to those who deserve it, like you!" This reader used the whole ministry of Jesus to substantiate her ironic reading, holding that generally Jesus was ready and willing to heal and restore life. Another respondent held that the distinction between the "dogs" and the "children" should not be overemphasized because both of them designate dependents in the house.

"What does the Canaanite woman mean when she says, 'Yes, Lord yet even the dogs eat the crumbs that fall from their master's table' (v. 27)?" The majority of the respondents held that this woman perceived how Jesus felt that she did not deserve the children's food, either because of her nationality, inadequate faith, servanthood, demonic spirits, or lack of faith in the God of Israel. However, the Canaanite woman was insisting that, regardless of the nature of her inadequacy, she was not incapable of improving, that is, of picking up the crumbs. Therefore, the woman was insisting that nothing could make her a permanently undeserving child, despite her current inadequacy.

One respondent held that this woman was insisting that she too was a child of God, just like the Israelites. This respondent held that through her very word, "even the dogs eat the crumbs," the Canaanite woman became one of the children.

Mmamosebeletsi Mmadipina, a woman who had worked as a domestic servant in South Africa, held that people tend to look down on other races. Mentioning a few local oppressed groups such as the Basarwa and Bakgalagadi, she pointed out that this woman was humbling herself in the face of humiliation. She found a correlation between the dogs/children, crumbs/food of the passage and the South African apartheid system.

For Bishop Mmangwedi, the interpreter who found irony in this story, the words of the Canaanite woman served to underline the words of Jesus.

That is, while Jesus' answer was negative to the disciples who asked for her dismissal, this woman was actually saying, "Yes, I am one of the deserving children, yet even those inferior outsiders—the dogs—deserve something." In other words, the Canaanite woman's response endorsed and surpassed that of Jesus by holding that no one was totally undeserving.

"*What did Jesus mean when he said, 'Woman, great is your faith. Let it be done to you as you desire' (v. 28)?*" Their responses hinged on two aspects: *boitshoko le tumelo*, that is, "perseverance and faith." Jesus' words and the healing of the daughter were perceived as a recognition of the woman's faith and perseverance through all that seemed to hinder her wishes. At this point, the response of Jesus was said to express his appreciation for the sincerity of her faith, which was not shaken by silence, the disciples' requests, or Jesus' statements.

"*Is this story a case of racism between Canaanites and Israelites?*" The answers were yes and no, for different and contradictory reasons. Six of the eleven who affirmed that it was racism did not substantiate their answers. The other five gave various observations. One of them said, "But what is important is that we should overcome racism as it is overcome in the story." One of them said this story served to show us that apartheid was real in the world. While another identified the passage as a case of racism, she also held that the story showed that Jesus had come to do away with it. Two of them identified the discrimination of the passage as pertaining to those with faith and those without, involving good and evil rather than two different races. Two of the five respondents who denied that this was a case of racism did not give any reason for their answer. Three others said the story was about testing the woman's faith to help her understand her own standpoint. Regardless of whether the respondents identified racism in the passage or not, they consistently emphasized that Jesus had come for all people.

SERMON INTERPRETATIONS

It must be noted that in the questionnaire we brought our preset questions and asked respondents to answer back. In this way we were initiators, and we to some extent predetermined our findings. In a sermon setting we were not initiators, but listeners. In this case we wanted to listen to the interpretations as they occurred under normal circumstances, without the intrusion of a researcher. Although I cannot claim that our presence did not affect the mode of interpretations at all, our findings in these visits were indeed significantly different from those of our questionnaire.

Basically, I can sum up our findings by saying that their interpretations were characterized by methods of interpretation rather than the content of interpretation. In other words, the meaning of the passage was intricately woven into the acts of interpretation. In an attempt to present these findings, I will speak of communal interpretation, participatory interpretation through the use of songs, interpretation through dramatized narration, and interpretation through repetition.

To begin with communal interpretation, it must be noted that in most AICs, preaching is not the exclusive right of one individual during a service. Once the text of the day has been read, all are free to stand up and expound on the text in their own understanding. This communal form of interpretation is inclusive and allows the young and old, women and men, to be heard in the church, if they so wish. Here communal interpretation becomes a ritual of bonding, as all members participate.

Communal interpretation is supplemented with participatory interpretation through the use of songs. As the preacher is expounding on the passage, listeners contribute to the interpretation by occasionally interrupting with a song that expounds on the theme of the passage according to the way listeners understand the interpreter. Conversely, the interpreter herself/himself can pause and begin a song that expresses the meaning of the passage. In the case of Matthew 15:21–28, an example of one of the songs that was used in a participatory interpretation is, "*ante Jeso one a mpona ha ke lela jwale*," that is, "Oh, so Jesus was listening to my plea when I pleaded." Such a song underlines the Canaanite woman's plea for help and Jesus' positive response. Its use becomes the listeners' way of participating in the interpretation of the passage.

Most interpretations were largely grounded on the assumption that "a story well told is a story well interpreted." This indigenous method of interpretation capitalizes on recalling, narrating, and dramatizing the story without explicitly defining what it means. Instead, the meaning is articulated by graphically bringing the story to life through a dramatic narration. Those who lacked the gift of dramatic presentation still laid emphasis on the act of recalling and retelling the story almost verbatim. Although it was particularly striking and confusing that in most cases the dramatic retelling was all there was to the interpretive act, we soon realized that the nuances of interpretation were to be read in the interjected songs and the repeated phrases.

Repetition as another mode of interpretation emphasized a particular point or theme. For example, speakers who viewed the seeking of healing as the point of the story would repeat perhaps two or three times the Canaanite woman's request, her insistence, and the guaranteed healing (vv. 22b, 25, 28). Those who found the trial of faith to be the main theme tended to repeat Jesus' silence (v. 24), his discouraging statements (v. 26), the disciples' request (v. 23), and, finally, the triumph of enduring faith (v. 28). This mode of interpretation, as an oral exercise, was accompanied by the use of tone, such as a raised, lowered, or whispering voice to underline whatever point the interpreter wished to highlight.

Although I have highlighted communal and participatory modes of interpretation, we encountered several other churches where the pastor was the only speaker of the day while the rest silently listened. Similarly, while dramatic recalling, retelling, and repetition was quite prevalent, it was by no means the only way of reading. There were several other churches who struggled with the metaphors of the story and tried to explicate them. Some employed other biblical stories to interpret the passage, while others drew examples from everyday life. I have also called these modes of interpretation indigenous, assuming that they arose organically from the culture, but at the end of my research one respondent gave a biblical reason for guarded ways of interpretation by the AICs. She read Revelation 22:18, which says, "I warn everyone who hears the words of the prophecy of this book: if anyone adds to them, God will add to that person the plagues described in this book."

In sum, the questionnaire and sermon findings highlight the difference in methodological approach. The questionnaire reflects my academically informed approach, which is both Western and textual-centric. The sermons, on the other hand, reflect an approach which is both oral and indigenous. Obviously, my Western training has oriented me toward textual-centric interpretations and leaves me less equipped to give an in-depth understanding of oral interpretations. However, it was through combining these two different methods, my training and their expertise, that I perceived myself as "reading with" these AICs women.

Rahab Resurrected: God Never Opened the Bible!

How do the reading strategies of AICs women offer a vision of liberating interdependence? In answering the above question, I shall look at four aspects of their readings: the framework of *Semoya*; the wisdom of a creative integration of different religious traditions; a feminist model of liberation; and healing as an act of political struggle and survival.

To begin with the framework of *Semoya*, what strategies of reading does it offer us? It is important to recall once again that *Moya*, the Spirit, is central to the AICs. It is *Moya* that empowered them to reject the discriminatory leadership of missionary-founded churches and to begin their own churches. From the beginning, *Moya* revealed to them the gospel—the call of justice and its liberating inclusiveness over against the discriminatory tendencies of the colonial and patriarchal church. Consequently, when they rejected the discriminatory colonial church, they took upon themselves the responsibility of interpreting the gospel from a *Semoya* perspective. A *Semoya* framework, therefore, is a mode of reading that resists discrimination and articulates a reading of healing: healing of race and gender relations; of individuals, classes, and nations. It is an interpretative practice that seeks healing of relations by underlining the interconnections of things and people rather than their disconnectedness—and highlighting the need to keep the relationships affirming to all the involved parties.

In keeping with their historical beginnings, that is, the AICs' rejection of a discriminatory gospel and their move to creatively define a gospel of healing, a *Semoya* framework cultivates a space for liberating inclusiveness.

The inclusiveness of a *Semoya* reading is apparent in the respondents' interpretations of "Israel" and "Canaan." Israel has become an all-inclusive category for all those who believe in God. But Canaan too is a rich land of faith, sought by all Israelites. In accordance with their decolonizing inclusive approach, the appreciation of biblical religions does not entail the disappearance or the reduction of other cultures to secondary positions. Rather, their decolonizing *Semoya* readings are a transgression of boundaries that seeks healing by seeing interdependence of cultures rather than emphasizing exclusive oppositions.

Their insistence on reading for the healing of relations and their belief in the inclusiveness of the word of God was brought home to me when one reader explained the relation of Canaanites and Israelites. "Israelites were taken from Egypt, where they were enslaved," said the respondent, "and sent to Canaan, a land that flowed with milk and honey. This Canaanite woman with great faith illustrates for us what it means that their land flowed with milk and honey." This imaginative interpretation highlights the power and will of AICs women to map a vision of liberating interdependence.[83] By asserting that the land of the Canaanites, or the colonized, was rich both materially and spiritually, the reading is a subversive postcolonial interpretation: It decolonizes the imperial strategies that employ the rhetoric of poverty and lack of religious faith among the colonized in order to justify dominating Other nations. By asserting that material and spiritual wealth were the aspects that led Israelites to occupy Canaan, AICs women highlight the interdependence rather than disconnectedness of things and people. Moreover, it is a reading that confronts a story that has been extensively used to justify imperial imposition and apartheid and articulates a reading that seeks healing between different races by refusing to privilege any cultural and racial supremacy.

Second, their approach exhibits the wisdom, the courage, and the creativity of integrating different religious faiths in the service of life and difference. Historically born within imperial times, which proceeded by dispossessing people of their cultural and religious integrity through the promotion of Christianity as the universal religion, the AICs subvert this imperial strategy. They reject the imposition of Christianity as the one and only valid religion and freely cull from both religious cultures whatever wisdom these traditions offer in the enhancement of life and nurturing difference. For today's multicultural and multifaith global village, a mode of reading that allows one to encounter and to acknowledge the strengths

---

[83]See Renita Weems, "Reading Her Way Through the Struggle: African-American Women and the Bible," in *Stony the Road We Trod: African American Biblical Interpretation*, ed. Cain Hope Felder (Minneapolis: Fortress Press, 1991), who notes that the fact that some "factors are suppressed in the reading process says more about the depth of human yearning for freedom than it does about lack of sophistication on part of the readers," 71.

and weakness of our different cultures as well as to respectfully learn cross-culturally, without subscribing to the oppressive aspects, is imperative. These AICs women readers offer just this mode of reading.

One may be asking, What is the aspect drawn from African religious views in this paper? First, the emphasis on healing, its approach, and its function—which I shall further elaborate below—is a thoroughly African religious worldview. Second, I have constantly referred to *Moya* or Spirit, without adding its biblical adjective "Holy."[84] I have maintained this because it is how the AICs women readers generally spoke. The Spirit as the divine agent, which enters and empowers women and men, is quite prevalent in the southern African religious spirituality. In the claims of *Moya*, we therefore encounter a perfect example of the integration of two religious traditions, a fact well-documented by most AICs scholars.[85] This validation of two different traditions is both a model of resistance and healing from imperial cultural forces of imposition, which depend on devaluing difference and imposing one universal standard.[86] Their anti-imperial approach does not subscribe to the artificial cultural dualisms and hierarchies that only serve the interests of domination and the suppression of difference. Rather, it offers a radical transgression of boundaries, for it fearlessly yokes biblical texts with African religious traditions. This creative integration offers a liberating vision for today's multicultural and multifaith global village—it shows how difference can be encountered, nurtured, and critically reappropriated.

Third, the *Semoya* model of reading not only resists imperial forces of imposition and domination but also offers a feminist model of liberation. The AICs women insist that the written word is a tradition of wisdom, which has goodness for all, but they also insist that they are by no means limited to it. They maintain that God's agency is contained in but not limited to the written word. They experience divine communication directly through God's spirit, and they have experienced God's spirit empowering them for human service. As the above words of Virginia Lucas express, when God spoke to her, *God never opened the Bible.* In these words of Lucas

---

[84]See the discussions of G. C. Oosthuizen, *Post-Christianity in Africa,* 119–42, a white man who writes from a colonial perspective, who calls it "the misinterpretation of the Holy Spirit."

[85]See Emmanuel Martey, *African Theology,* 76–78; Ngubane, "Theological Roots of AICs and Their Challenge to Black Theology, 71–90; Sundkler, *Zulu Zion,* 237ff; Oosthuizen, *Post-Christianity in Africa,* 119–42.

[86]Inculturation, indigenization, or Africanization are some of the names that African scholars have adopted to speak of and develop a theology of liberating interdependence. See Martey, "African Theology as Inculturation Theology," in *African Theology,* 63–94; Elizabeth Amoah and Mercy A. Oduyoye, "The Christ for African Women," in *With Passion and Compassion,* ed. Virginia Fabella and Mercy A. Oduyoye, 35–46.

and all the AICs women who hear the word of the Spirit, we encounter and hear the resurrected Rahabs, who refuse to reproduce stories that were written about them; rather, they retell and weave their own stories of healing and empowerment.

Through listening to the word of the Spirit, the AICs women offer a feminist strategy that breaks free from the patriarchal and canonical constraints of biblical traditions. It allows them to claim divine empowerment and leadership despite their gender. Moreover, this feminist model of reading is by no means ungodly or less biblical. It is biblically grounded, since such books as the gospel of John provide for a direct dependence on the Spirit (14:26). It is also godly because it is guided and justified by a consideration of whether the word of the Spirit empowers one with the responsibility to restore and to enhance life through leadership and healing.

Fourth, healing among the AICs women is a ritual language of political resistance and survival. Healing involves all aspects of one's life. For example, healing includes tackling unemployment, breakdown of relationships, bad harvests, lost cows, evil spirits, bodily illness, and misfortune. In short, healing becomes an act of restoring and maintaining God's creation against all forces that inhibit the fulfillment of individuals in society.

Evidently, this use of healing is a political act against structural forces behind unemployment, breakdown of family relationships, poverty, and lack of success. Through their claim that God's spirit empowers them to heal these social ills, AICs join hands with God in a constant protest and struggle against institutional oppression. They offer the promise and the solution. This space of healing becomes their political discourse for confronting social ills, not as helpless beings who are neglected by God, but as those who are in control and capable of changing their social conditions. This confrontation of social ills has undoubtedly made the AICs the biggest and most popular movement, for its members address the political struggles of Africa and offer solutions.

In conclusion, the above readings of AICs women do not offer a vision of liberating interdependence in and of themselves, but as a package of interpretative practices. Their vision lies in their continued history of resisting imperialism and patriarchy; in readings and practices that reject the privileging of biblical texts and religions above other cultural perceptions of reality (a radical transgression of boundaries); in their movements and practices, which have always included men and women in membership and leadership; and in their capacity to read the biblical text (and a substantial amount of resistance to interpretation), while insisting on the authority of hearing the unwritten word of the Spirit. These interpretative practices cultivate that most necessary postcolonial new space of decolonizing and depatriarchalizing, a new space for reading of the word and a hearing of the Spirit for liberating interdependence.

10

A Luta Continua:
The Struggle Continues

The Postcolonial Condition, the Bible, and Women

The twentieth century has been characterized by massive colonizing movements and by decolonizing and anti-patriarchy liberation movements.[1] The planting and uprooting of power and powerlessness is not at all a smooth, sequential plot. Colonizing and imperializing powers, as we now know, have a chameleonlike capacity for persistence. Decolonization and liberation are, therefore, not a given, nor a finished business. Similarly, many feminist victories have been won, but patriarchy and its institutions have not fully yielded to women's demands. To be in the struggle for justice and liberation is, therefore, to be in *a luta continua,* the struggle that always continues. Nonetheless, the most outstanding phenomenon of the last half of the twentieth century is the struggle for justice and liberation. Oppressed groups of various backgrounds no longer accept their oppression. Blacks, women, homosexuals, Two-Thirds World masses, Jews, children, the poor, or just about every minority and oppressed group, demand justice and liberation. They ask what and who denies them liberation, thereby suggesting that their oppression is also intimately connected to someone other than themselves. They ask how their oppression is executed, that is, which methods and means in social structures are used to maintain their domination. In this way, they probe the interconnection of their

---

[1]See Fernando F. Segovia, "And They Began to Speak in Other Tongues: Competing Modes of Discourse in Contemporary Biblical Criticism," in *Reading from This Place,* vol. 1, 3.

realities, speaking against oppressive and exploitative groups and institutions, and seeking liberating interdependence.

The quest of this book owes its birth to some of these major liberation currents of the twentieth century, particularly the Two-Thirds World postcolonial and feminist liberation movements. While feminism defines women's movements of various backgrounds and practices that are committed to the liberation of women, the postcolonial condition defines the panorama of modern imperialism, beginning with the process of colonialism, the struggle for political independence, the attainment of independence, and the emergence of the neocolonial/globalization era. As a Two-Thirds World postcolonial feminist subject, living under the shadow of past colonialism(s), protracted independence victories, current globalization and the postfeminist era, I can truly say, in Nelson Mandela's words, that "the struggle is my life."[2] This is not because I wish to be in *a luta continua*, but because I find myself in this social location. Nonetheless, in this book I sincerely sought to say to my readers: "My freedom and yours cannot be separated,"[3] thereby acknowledging the interconnection and interdependence of males and females, Two-Thirds World and One-Third World economic/political systems, black and white races, Christian and non-Christian cultures, the past and the present, and so on. In other words, I have sought to invite conversations and negotiations for better relations and for a better world of liberating interdependence. For me, therefore, the postcolonial condition describes the persistence of imperializing powers, but most importantly, as Homi Bhabha tells us, it points "to the beyond,"[4] to the alternative of justice and liberating interdependence—an alternative we can indeed choose.

My voice in this book speaks with and adds to the Two-Thirds World postcolonial and feminist liberation movements. I thus build on two of their insights. First, that the Bible is the most influential book in the West, and it is also patriarchal. Second, that modern Western imperialism was effected not only through military power but also through the use of an ideology of Western cultural texts, including the Bible. For me and for other Two-Thirds World subjects, the Bible is, therefore, not only patriarchal but also imperialistic. To occupy this social location is to inhabit a position of collision between the two liberation movements. For while early white feminists largely ignored imperialism and thus participated in and maintained the oppression of the colonized subjects, the Two-Thirds World liberation movements, articulated mostly by men, ignored women's issues, insisting that imperialism was the major oppression. This position situated most Two-Thirds World postcolonial women in the crossfire, with friends

---

[2]Nelson Mandela, *Long Walk to Freedom: The Autobiography of Nelson Mandela* (New York: Little, Brown, 1994), 123.

[3]Ibid., 456.

[4]Bhabha, *Location of Culture*, 4.

and enemies in both camps. This is the position that I occupy. Standing in this crossfire, the questions I sought to address were: How can I, and all those who seek liberation and justice, read the Bible in the postcolonial era without subscribing to its patriarchal and imperialistic oppression? How can we address each form of oppression with the seriousness that it deserves in our search for liberation and justice? Put differently, What demands does the postcolonial condition lay on a feminist reader of cultural texts, in this case, the Bible?

Recommendations and Suggestions

Although I have summarized my findings, recommendations, and suggestions at various points in the book, nevertheless, my approach to the whole problem proposes and constitutes a number of viable postcolonial feminist strategies of reading. Some of these can be outlined as follows:

1. Reading contemporary oral stories, critical writers of the formerly colonized nations, and the writings of the colonial heroes of modern centuries to highlight an intimate connection between the Bible, its readers, its institutions, and modern imperialism (see chapter 1).

2. Reading Western critical feminist scholars to highlight that their liberation discourse remains implicated within the imperialistic agendas of their countries, thereby indicating that patriarchal critique does not necessarily translate into anti-imperial discourse (see chapters 2, 4, and 9).

3. Reading non-Western and non-Christian biblical and theological feminist works to indicate that their decolonizing discourse insists on differences, which include acknowledging the presence and viability of other religions and decolonizing exclusive Christian claims (see chapter 2).

4. Decolonizing the Western biblical academy and proposing a model of liberating interdependence by introducing AICs women readers to subvert the promotion of Western readings as the universal standard for interpretations of the Bible and to propose a new postcolonial feminist space and reading strategies that can acknowledge the text and override it at the same time (see chapters 2 and 9).

5. Reading sacred and secular texts, ancient and contemporary texts, and imperializing and decolonizing texts, side by side, to highlight:

    (a) The ways in which they propound imperializing or decolonizing ideology;

(b) their use of gender in the discourse of subordination and domination;

(c) that in the postcolonial era literary practitioners can be categorized into decolonizing, collaborating, or imperializing communities of reader-writers; and

(d) that women are usually patriarchally oppressed beings, but some women are also imperial oppressors of Other women (see chapter 5).

6. Proposing a type-scene of land possession to highlight:

(a) the relationship between certain literary-rhetorical forms, intertextuality, and the reproduction or the rejection of some patriarchal and imperial ideologies of oppression; and

(b) the use of gender in the articulation of both patriarchal and imperial relationships of subordination and domination (see chapters 4 and 8).

7. Reading mission narratives with the understanding that they are the key biblical texts that authorize international travel and relations in order to interrogate the power relations they advance (see chapter 8).

8. Reading white Western male and female academic interpretations for decolonization to highlight:

(a) that their literary practices maintain the imperialistic agendas of their countries;

(b) that white middle-class feminist discourse has remained imperialistic; and

(c) that feminist readers should not only be resisting readers but also decolonizing readers, if meaningful coalitions are to be established in the postcolonial era between international women's liberation movements (see chapter 9).

9. Reading the cross-cultural AICs women's biblical interpretations to emphasize that in the postcolonial era literary practitioners must read beyond decolonization for liberating interdependence. From their interpretations a *Semoya* reading strategy and a new feminist space was proposed. This is the approach that was captured in the assertion that God need not open the Bible to speak and to be heard (see chapter 3).

In addition, two other aspects of this book also constitute viable postcolonial feminist strategies of reading: Rahab's reading prism and the criteria I tabulated and used to establish whether a text is imperializing or anti-imperial. First, because mainline biblical study is largely textual, these questions can assist postcolonial readers to read against imperial and patriarchal forms of oppression:

(a) Does this text have a clear stance against the political imperialism of its time?

(b) Does this text encourage travel to distant and inhabited lands and how does it justify itself?

(c) How does this text construct difference: Is there dialogue and liberating interdependence or is there condemnation of all that is foreign?

(d) Does this text employ gender and divine representations to construct relationships of subordination and domination?

Further, I proposed Rahab's reading prism as a helpful model for a decolonizing and antipatriarchal reading, precisely because the story of Rahab embodies both patriarchal and imperial literary forms of representation. Rahab illustrates that empire-building constitutes four Gs: God, gold, glory, and gender. Feminist readings indicate that depatriarchalizing readings do not necessarily translate into anti-imperializing readings. In this way, theorizing the story of Rahab as a woman who embodies two intertwined forms of oppression is a useful reading strategy in the postcolonial era for two reasons: It helps feminist readers to resist both forms of oppression; and it highlights that, while women are patriarchally colonized, some women are doubly colonized. Rahab's reading prism thus keeps in view that different social locations in the postcolonial era make some women imperial oppressors of the Other women. Theorizing Rahab's story as a reading strategy, therefore, offers a model that takes seriously both patriarchal and imperial oppression of the past and present and thus provides an understanding that can advance strategic coalitions between international feminist movements in the postcolonial era as well as begin to articulate relationships of liberating interdependence between genders, races, ethnicities, continents, cultures, nations, and the environment.

Select Bibliography

Achebe, Chinua. *Hopes and Impediments: Selected Essays.* New York: Doubleday, 1989.

Alter, Robert. *The Art of Biblical Narrative.* New York: Basic Books, 1981.

Amadiume, Ifi. *Male Daughters, Female Husbands: Gender and Sex in an African Society.* Atlantic Highlands, N. J.: Zed Books, 1987.

Anderson, Janice Capel. "Matthew: Gender and Reading." *Semeia* 28 (1983): 3–27.

Anderson, Janice Capel, and Stephen D. Moore, eds. *Mark and Method: New Approaches in Biblical Studies.* Minneapolis: Fortress Press, 1992.

Ashcroft, Bill, Gareth Griffiths, and Helen Tiffin, eds. *The Empire Writes Back: Theory and Practice in Post-colonial Literatures.* New York: Routledge, 1989.

——, eds. *The Post-colonial Studies Reader.* New York: Routledge, 1995.

Auerbach, Eric. *Mimesis: The Representation of Reality in Western Literature.* Princeton, N. J.: Princeton University Press, 1946.

Bach, Alice, ed. *The Pleasure of Her Text: Feminist Readings of Biblical and Historical Texts.* Philadelphia: Trinity Press International, 1990.

Banana, Canaan. "The Case for a New Bible." In *"Re-writing" the Bible: The Real Issues.* Ed. J. L. Cox, I. Mukomyora, and F. J. Vestrelen. Gweru: Mambo Books, 1993.

Bhabha, Homi, ed. *Nation and Narration.* New York: Routledge, 1990.

——. *The Location of Culture.* New York: Routledge, 1994.

Bible and Culture Collective, The. *The Postmodern Bible.* New Haven, Conn.: Yale University Press, 1995.

Blackham, H. J. *The Future of Our Past: From Ancient Greece to Global Village.* Amherst, N.Y.: Prometheus Books, 1996.

Blaut, J. M. *The Colonizer's Model of the World: Geographical Diffusionism and Eurocentric History.* New York: Guilford Press, 1993.

Blunt, Alison. *Travel, Gender, and Imperialism: Mary Kingsley and West Africa.* New York: Guilford Press, 1994.

——, and Gillian Rose, eds. *Writing Women and Space: Colonial and Postcolonial Geographies.* New York: Guilford Press, 1994.

Boehmer, Elleke. *Colonial and Post-colonial Literature.* Oxford: Oxford University Press, 1995.

Boring, Eugene. "Matthew," 87–505. In *The New Interpreter's Bible.* Vol. 8. Nashville: Abingdon Press, 1995.

Brown, Raymond E. *The Gospel and Epistles of John.* Minneapolis: Liturgical Press, 1988.

Brueggemann, Walter. *The Land.* Philadelphia: Fortress Press, 1977.

——. "Exodus," 675–982. In *The New Interpreter's Bible.* Vol. 1. Nashville: Abingdon Press, 1994.

Buckingham, Thomas. *Moses and Aaron.* New London: T. Green, 1729.

Cohen, Shaye J. D. *From the Maccabees to the Mishnah.* Philadelphia: Westminster Press, 1987.

Conrad, Joseph. *Heart of Darkness.* New York: Bantam Classic Books, 1981. (First published in 1902.)

Daneel, Inus. *Quest for Belonging.* Gweru: Mambo Press, 1987.

Dangarembgwa, Tsitsi. *Nervous Conditions, A Novel.* Seattle: Seal Press, 1988.

Darby, Phillip. *Three Faces of Imperialism: British and American Approaches to Asia and Africa, 1870–1970.* New Haven, Conn.: Yale University Press, 1987.

Davies, Carol. *Ngambika: Studies in African Literature.* Trenton, N.J.: Africa World Press, 1986.

Day, Peggy L., ed. *Gender and Difference in Ancient Israel.* Minneapolis: Fortress Press, 1989.

Dickson, Kwesi. *Uncompleted Mission: Christianity and Exclusivism.* Maryknoll, N.Y.: Orbis Books, 1991.

Donaldson, Laura. *Decolonizing Feminisms: Race, Gender, and Empire Building.* Chapel Hill: University of North Carolina Press, 1992.

——, ed. *Postcolonialism and Scriptural Reading. Semeia* 75. Atlanta: Scholars Press, 1996.

Dube, Musa W. "Consuming the Colonial Cultural Bomb: Translating *Badimo* into Demons in the Setswana Bible (Matt. 8:28–34; 15:22; 10:8)" *Journal for the Study of the New Testament* 73 (1999): 33–59.

——. "Reading for Decolonization (John 4:1–42)." *Semeia* 75 (1996).

——. "Toward a Postcolonial Feminist Interpretation of the Bible." *Semeia* 78 (1997).

Dube Shomanah, Musa W. "Post-colonial Biblical Interpretations." Pp. 299–303 in John H. Hayes, ed., *Dictionary of Biblical Interpretation* (Nashville: Abingdon Press, 1999).

Eagleton, Terry. *Literary Theory: An Introduction.* Minneapolis: University of Minnesota Press, 1983.

Edwards, Richard A. *Matthew's Story of Jesus.* Philadelphia: Fortress Press, 1985.

Fabella, Virginia, and Mercy A. Oduyoye, eds. *With Passion and Compassion: Third World Women Doing Theology.* Maryknoll, N.Y.: Orbis Books, 1990.

Fanon, Frantz. *The Wretched of the Earth.* Translated by Constance Farrington. Harmondsworth, England: Penguin, 1967.

——. *Black Skins, White Masks.* London: Pluto Press, 1986.

Fatum, Lone. "Women, Symbolic Universe and Structures of Silence: Challenges and Possiblilities in Androcentric Texts," *Studia Theologia* 43 (1989): 61–80.

Felder, Cain Hope. *Troubling the Biblical Waters: Race, Class, and Family.* Maryknoll, N.Y.: Orbis Books, 1989.

Fewell, Danna Nolan, and David Gunn. *Gender, Power, and Promise: The Subject of the Bible's First Story.* Nashville: Abingdon Press, 1993.

Frye, Northrop. *The Great Code: The Bible and Literature.* New York: Harcourt Brace Jovanovich, 1982.

Fuchs, Esther. "Structure and Patriarchal Functions in the Biblical Betrothal Type-Scene: Some Preliminary Notes" *Journal of Feminist Studies in Religion* 3, no. 1: (Spring 1987): 7–11.

Funk, Robert W. *New Gospel Parallels,* vols. 1 and 2. Sonoma, Calif.: Polebridge, 1990.

Garland, David E. *Reading Matthew: A Literary and Theological Commentary on the First Gospel.* New York: Crossroad, 1993.

Garnsey, Peter, and Richard Saller. *The Roman Empire: Economy, Society and Culture.* Berkeley: University of California Press, 1987.

Guardiola-Saenz, Leticia. "Breaking Bread Together: A Mexican-American Reading of Matthew 15:21–28." Paper presented at Society of Biblical Literature meeting in Philadelphia, 1995.

Hale, Edward E. *The Desert and the Promised Land.* Boston: C. C. P. Moody, 1863.

Harlow, Barbara. *Resistance Literature.* New York: Methuen, 1987.

Holmes, Timothy. *Journey to Livingstone: An Exploration of an Imperial Myth.* Edinburgh: Canongate Press, 1993.

Horsley, Richard A. *Jesus and the Spiral of Violence: Popular Jewish Resistance in Roman Palestine.* Minneapolis: Fortress Press, 1993.

——. *Sociology and the Jesus Movement.* New York: Crossroad, 1989.

Kalu, Anthonia C. "Those Left in the Rain: African Literary Theory and Re-invention of African Woman." *African Studies Review* 37, no. 3 (September 1994).

King, Ursula, ed. *Feminist Theology from the Third World: A Reader.* Maryknoll, N.Y.: Orbis Books, 1994.

Kingsbury, Jack D. *Matthew as Story.* Philadelphia: Fortress Press, 1986.

Kinyatti, Maina wa, ed. *Thunder from the Mountains: Poems and Songs from Mau Mau.* Trenton, N.J.: Africa World Press, 1990.

Knight, Wilson G. R., trans. *The Aeneid.* London: Penguin Books, 1956.

Kwame, Appiah A. *In My Father's House: Africa in the Philosophy of Culture.* New York: Oxford University Press, 1992.

Kwok Pui-lan. *Discovering the Bible in the Non-Biblical World.* Maryknoll, N.Y.: Orbis Books, 1995.

Lawson, Alan, and Chris Tiffin, eds. *De-scribing Empire: Post-colonialism and Textuality.* New York: Routledge, 1994.

Levine, Amy-Jill. *"Go Nowhere Among the Gentiles": (Matt. 10:5b).* In *The Social and Ethnic Dimensions of Matthean Salvation History.* Vol. 1. New York: E. Mellen Press, 1988.

Livingstone, David. *Missionary Travels and Researches in South Africa: Illustrated.* Philadelphia: J. W. Bradly, 1858.

——. *Narrative on an Expedition to the Zambezi and its Tributaries, and of the Discovery of the Lakes Shirwa and Nyassa, with Map and Illustrations.* New York: Harper & Brothers, 1866.

Lorde, Audre. *Sister Outsider: Essays and Speeches.* Freedom, Calif.: Crossing Press, 1984.

Luz, Ulrich. *Matthew in History: Interpretation, Influence, and Effects.* Minneapolis: Fortress Press, 1994.

Malina, Bruce J., and Jerome H. Neyrey. *Calling Jesus Names: The Social Value of Labels in Matthew.* Sonoma, Calif.: Poleridge, 1988.

Mandela, Nelson. *Long Walk to Freedom: The Autobiography of Nelson Mandela.* New York: Little, Brown, 1994.

Martey, Emmanuel. *African Theology: Inculturation and Liberation.* Maryknoll, N.Y.: Orbis Books, 1993.

Maunier, Rene. *The Sociology of Colonies: An Introduction to the Study of Race Contact.* Vol. 1. London: Routledge, 1949.

Mazrui, Ali. *Cultural Forces in World Politics.* London: James Curry, 1990.

Meeks, Wayne. *The First Urban Christians: The Social World of the Apostle Paul.* New Haven, Conn.: Yale University Press, 1983.

——. "The Man from Heaven in Johannine Sectarianism." *Journal of Biblical Literature* 91 (1972): 44–72.

Mohanty, Chandra T., Ann Russo, and Lourdes Torres, eds. *Third World Women and the Politics of Feminism.* Bloomington: Indiana University Press, 1991.

Moore, Stephen D. *Poststructuralism and the New Testament.* Minneapolis: Fortress Press, 1994.

Morgan, R., ed. *Sisterhood is Global: The International Women's Anthology.* New York: Doubleday, 1984.

Morrison, Toni. *Playing in the Dark: Whiteness and the Literary Imagination.* New York: Vintage Books, 1993.

Mosala, Itumeleng. *Biblical Hermeneutics and Black Theology in South Africa.* Grand Rapids, Mich.: Eerdmans, 1989.

——."Race, Class, and Gender as Hermeneutical Factors in the African Independent Churches' Appropriation of the Bible." In *"Reading With": An Exploration of the Interface Between Critical and Ordinary Readings of the Bible. Semeia* 73 (1996): 43–57.

——, and Buti Tlhagale, eds. *The Unquestionable Right to be Free: Black Theology from South Africa.* Maryknoll, N.Y.: Orbis Books, 1986.

Mudimbe, V. Y. *The Idea of Africa.* London: James Curry, 1994.

——. *The Invention of Africa: Gnosis, Philosophy and the Order of Knowledge.* Indianapolis: Indiana University Press, 1988.

Muzorewa, Ngwinyai. *The Origins and Development of African Theology.* Maryknoll, N. Y.: Orbis Books, 1985.

Ngubane, John A. "Theological Roots of the African Independent Churches and their Challenge to Black Theology." In *The Unquestionable Right to be Free*. Ed. Itumeleng Mosala and Buti Thagale. Maryknoll, N. Y.: Orbis Books, 1986.

Ngugi wa Thiongo. *Decolonizing the Mind: The Politics of Language in African Literature*. London: James Curry, 1986.

——. *Moving the Center: The Struggle for Cultural Freedoms*. London: James Curry, 1993.

Oduyoye, Mercy. *Hearing and Knowing: Theological Reflections on Christianity in Africa*. Maryknoll, N. Y.: Orbis Books, 1986.

——, and Musimbe Knyoro, eds. *The Will to Arise: Women, Tradition and the Church in Africa*. Maryknoll, N. Y.: Orbis Books, 1992.

Oosthuizen, G. C. *Post-Christianity in Africa: A Theological and Anthropological Study*. London: C. Hurst, 1968.

Orwell, George. "Shooting an Elephant." In *Major Modern Essayists*. Ed. Gilbert H. Muller and Alan F. Crooks. Englewood Cliffs, N.J.: Prentice Hall, 1994.

Overman, Andrew J. *Matthew's Gospel and Formative Judaism: The Social World of Matthean Community*. Minneapolis: Fortress Press, 1990.

——. *Church and Community in Crisis: The Gospel According to Matthew*. Valley Forge, Penn.: Trinity Press International, 1996.

Patte, Daniel. *The Gospel According to Matthew: A Structural Commentary on Matthew's Faith*. Philadelphia: Fortress Press, 1987.

Pobee, John, and Barbel Von Wartenberg-Potter. *New Eyes for Reading: Biblical and Theological Reflections from the Third World*. Geneva: WCC Publications, 1986.

Pratt, Mary Louise. *Imperial Eyes: Travel Writing and Transculturation*. New York: Routledge, 1992.

Quint, David. *Epic and Empire*. Princeton, N.J.: Princeton University Press, 1993.

Ruether, Rosemary. *Sexism and God Talk: Towards A Feminist Theology*. Boston: Beacon Press, 1983.

Russell, Letty, ed. *Feminist Interpretation of the Bible*. Philadelphia: Westminster Press, 1985.

——, and J. Shannon Clarkson. *Dictionary of Feminist Theologies*. Louisville, Ky.: Westminster John Knox Press, 1996.

Said, Edward. *Culture and Imperialism*. New York: Alfred A. Knopf, 1993.

——. *Orientalism*. New York: Vintage Books, 1978.

——. *Representations of the Intellectual*. New York: Pantheon Books, 1994.

——. *The World, the Text, and the Critic*. Cambridge: Harvard University Press, 1983.

Sakenfeld, Katharine Doob, and Sharon Ringe, eds. *Reading the Bible as Women: Perspectives from Africa, Asia and Latin America*. Semeia 78. Atlanta: Scholars Press, 1997.

Saldarini, Anthony J. *Matthew's Christian-Jewish Community*. Chicago: Chicago University Press, 1994.

Sarna, Nahum M. "Exodus, Book of." In *The Anchor Bible Dictionary.* Vol 2. Ed. David Noel Freedman. New York: Doubleday, 1992.

Schaberg, Jane. *The Illegitimacy of Jesus: A Feminist Theological Interpretation of the Infancy Narratives.* San Francisco: Harper and Row, 1987.

Schneiders, Sandra. *The Revelatory Text: Interpreting the New Testament as Sacred Scripture.* San Francisco: HarperCollins, 1991.

Schüssler Fiorenza, Elisabeth. *But She Said: Feminist Practices of Biblical Interpretation.* Boston: Beacon Press, 1992.

——. *In Memory of Her: A Feminist Theological Reconstruction of Christian Origins.* New York: Crossroad, 1992.

——, ed. *Searching the Scriptures: A Feminist Introduction.* Vol. 1. New York: Crossroad, 1993.

——, ed. *Searching the Scriptures: A Feminist Commentary.* Vol. 2. New York: Crossroad, 1993.

Segovia, Fernando F., and Mary Ann Tolbert. *Reading from This Place:Social Location and Biblical Interpretation in the United States.* Vol. 1. Minneapolis: Fortress Press, 1995.

——. *Reading from This Place: Social Location and Biblical Interpretation in the Global Scene.* Vol. 2. Minneapolis: Fortress Press, 1995.

Segovia, Fernando F., ed. *"What is John?": Readers and Readings of the Fourth Gospel.* Atlanta: Scholars Press, 1996.

Setel, Drorah O'Donnel. "Exodus," 26–35. In *The Women's Bible Commentary.* Ed. Carol A. Newsom and Sharon H. Ringe. Louisville, Ky.: Westminster/John Knox Press, 1992.

Snyder, Louis L., ed. *The Imperialism Reader: Documents and Readings on Modern Expansion.* New York: Van Nostrand, 1962.

Stambaugh, John, and David L. Balch. *The New Testament in Its Social Environment.* Philadelphia: Westminster Press, 1986.

Stanton, Graham N. *A Gospel for a New People: Studies in Matthew.* Louisville, Ky.: Westminster/John Knox Press, 1992.

Stephanson, Anders. *Manifest Destiny: American Expansion and the Empire of Right.* New York: Hill and Wang, 1995.

Strobel, Margaret. *European Women and the Second British Empire.* Indianapolis: Indiana University Press, 1991.

Sugirtharajah, R. S. ed. *Voices from the Margin: Interpreting the Bible in the Third World.* Maryknoll, N.Y.: Orbis Books, 1991.

Sundkler, Bengt. *Zulu Zion and Some Swazi Zionists.* Oxford: Oxford University Press, 1976.

Swanson, Tod. "To Prepare a Place: Johannine Christianity and the Collapse of Ethnic Space." *Journal of the American Academy of Religion* 62, no. 2 (Summer 1994): 241–63.

Szymanski, Albert. *The Logic of Imperialism.* New York: Praeger, 1981.

Talbert, Charles H. *Reading John: A Literary and Theological Commentary on the Gospel of John and the Johannine Epistle.* New York: Crossroad, 1994.

Taussig, Michael T. *Shamanism, Colonialism and the Wild Man: A Study in Terror and Healing.* Chicago: University of Chicago Press, 1987.

Thomas, Norman E., ed. *Classic Texts in Mission and World Christianity.* Maryknoll, N.Y.: Orbis Books, 1995.

Tong, Rosemarie. *Feminist Thought: A Comprehensive Introduction.* San Francisco: Westview Press, 1989.

Torontle, Mositi. *The Victims.* Gaborone: Botsalo Books, 1993.

Wainwright, Elaine. *Towards a Feminist Critical Reading of the Gospel According to Matthew.* Berlin: De Gruyter, 1991.

Weems, Renita. "Reading Her Way Through the Struggle: African American Women and the Bible." In *Stony the Road We Trod: African American Biblical Interpretation.* Ed. Cain Hope Felder. Minneapolis: Fortress Press, 1991.

West, Gerald and Musa W. Dube. *"Reading With" African Overtures. Semeia* 73. Atlanta: Scholars Press, 1996.

White, Jonathan, ed. *Recasting the World: Writing After Colonialism.* Baltimore: Johns Hopkins University Press, 1993.

Williams, Patrick, and Laura Chrisman, eds. *Colonial Discourse and Postcolonial Theory: A Reader.* New York: Columbia University Press, 1994.

Scripture Index

Author Index

Subject Index